A timely, creatively imagined and wide-ranging collection that not only demonstrates the exclusionary consequences of narrow, normative models of development but also how their transgression and transformation remains an urgent political project that goes beyond mere inclusion to the emancipation of all.

Erica Burman, *Professor of Education,*
University of Manchester, UK

Different Childhoods presents fresh thinking on the implications of entrenched developmental thinking that constructs a narrow range of particular childhoods as normative and all others as 'non-normative' transgressions. In the best possible way, this collection of essays constitutes a transgressive text that deserves to be widely read. Together they show why theory matters for everyday policies and practices dealing with children and childhood.

Ann Phoenix, *Professor at the Institute of Education,*
University College London, UK

DIFFERENT CHILDHOODS

Different Childhoods: Non/Normative Development and Transgressive Trajectories opens up new avenues for exploring children's development as contextual, provisional and locally produced, rather than a unitary, universal and consistent process.

This edited collection frames a critical exploration of the trajectory against which children are seen to be 'different' within three key themes: deconstructing 'developmental tasks', locating development and the limits of childhood. Examining the particular kinds of 'transgressive' development, contributors discuss instances of 'difference' including migration, work, assumptions of vulnerability, trans childhoods, friendships and involvement in crime. Including both empirical and theoretical discussions, the book builds on existing debates as part of the interrogation of 'different childhoods'.

This book provides essential reading for students wishing to explore notions of development while also being of interest to both academics and practitioners working across a broad area of disciplines such as developmental psychology, sociology, childhood studies and critical criminology.

Lindsay O'Dell is a Senior Lecturer in the Faculty of Health and Social Care at the Open University, UK. Her research interests focus on children, young people and families who are in some way 'different', including neurological difference, working children, young carers and language brokers.

Charlotte Brownlow is an Associate Professor in the School of Psychology and Counselling at the University of Southern Queensland, Australia. Her research interests focus on understandings of diversity and difference and the impacts that these have on the crafting of individual identities, particularly for individuals identifying as being on the autism spectrum.

Hanna Bertilsdotter-Rosqvist is an Associate Professor in Sociology. She holds a position as Senior Lecturer at the Department of Social Work, Umeå University, Sweden. Her research interests include autism politics and identity constructions among adults with autism. Other areas of interest are homonormativity, representations of bisexuality and intersecting notions of age, space and sexuality.

DIFFERENT CHILDHOODS

Non/normative development and transgressive trajectories

Edited by Lindsay O'Dell, Charlotte Brownlow and Hanna Bertilsdotter-Rosqvist

Routledge
Taylor & Francis Group

LONDON AND NEW YORK

First published 2018
by Routledge
2 Park Square, Milton Park, Abingdon, Oxon OX14 4RN

and by Routledge
711 Third Avenue, New York, NY 10017

Routledge is an imprint of the Taylor & Francis Group, an informa business

British Library Cataloguing in Publication Data
A catalogue record for this book is available from the British Library

Library of Congress Cataloging in Publication Data
Names: O'Dell, Lindsay, editor. | Brownlow, Charlotte, 1974- editor. | Bertilsdotter-Rosqvist, Hanna, 1976- editor.
Title: Different childhoods: non/normative development and transgressive trajectories / edited by Lindsay O'Dell, Charlotte Brownlow and Hanna Bertilsdotter-Rosqvist.
Description: New York: Routledge, 2018.
Identifiers: LCCN 2017007778| ISBN 9781138654037 (hbk: alk. paper) | ISBN 9781138654044 (pbk: alk. paper) | ISBN 9781315623467 (ebk)
Subjects: LCSH: Children–Research. | Child development–Research.
Classification: LCC HQ767.85 .D54 2018 | DDC 305.231–dc23
LC record available at https://lccn.loc.gov/2017007778

ISBN: 978-1-138-65403-7 (hbk)
ISBN: 978-1-138-65404-4 (pbk)
ISBN: 978-1-315-62346-7 (ebk)

Typeset in Bembo
by Deanta Global Publishing Services, Chennai, India
Printed and bound by CPI Group (UK) Ltd, Croydon, CR0 4YY

CONTENTS

ACKNOWLEDGEMENTS

The editors would like to thank Erica Burman, Tony Cline, Sarah Crafter and Andy Rixon for their helpful feedback, as well as Jan du Preez for his contributions to the development of the book.

We would also like to thank our friends and families for their support and the extended Psychology of Women community.

AUTHOR BIOGRAPHIES

Joanne Alexander is a Researcher based in the Institute of Health and Wellbeing at the University of Northampton. Joanne is also a doctoral candidate, exploring the intergenerational transmission of family violence.

Hanna Bertilsdotter-Rosqvist is an Associate Professor in Sociology and currently a Senior Lecturer at the Department of Social Work, Umeå University, Sweden. Her recent research is around autism, identity politics, and sexual, gendered and age normativity.

Charlotte Brownlow is an Associate Professor in the School of Psychology and Counselling at the University of Southern Queensland, Australia. Her research interests focus on understandings of diversity and difference and the impacts that constructions of these have on the crafting of individual identities, particularly for individuals identifying as being on the autism spectrum.

Jane Callaghan is a Professor of Psychology at the University of Northampton, where she leads the MSc in Child and Adolescent Mental Health. Her research interests include gender, family life, mental health and experiences of violence, and her recent work includes a specific focus on children's experiences of domestic violence.

Tony Cline is a member of the Educational Psychology Group at University College London and contributes to its Professional Doctorate for experienced Educational Psychologists. He initially worked in inner-city and suburban areas around London as a teacher in primary and secondary schools and as an educational psychologist and educational psychology tutor. He then spent eight years as Principal Educational Psychologist for the Inner London Education Authority. Subsequently, he moved into higher education, where he led professional training in Educational Psychology at University College London and headed the Department of Psychology and the Centre for Education Studies at the University of Luton (and its successor, the University of Bedfordshire) before returning to University College London to take up his present post in September 2004. His publications have covered a wide range of subjects, including child language brokering, the education of bilingual children, psychological assessment, dyslexia and selective mutism. He is co-author of the textbook *Special Educational Needs, Inclusion and Diversity*.

Sarah Crafter is a Senior Research Officer in the Thomas Coram Research Unit at University College London, Institute of Education. She has a Ph.D. in Cultural Psychology and Human Development and her theoretical and conceptual interests are grounded in sociocultural theory, transitions, migration, critical or contested ideas of 'normative' development and cultural identity development. Her broad interests are in the constructions or representations of childhood in culturally diverse settings.

Guida de Abreu is a Professor in Cultural Psychology at Oxford Brookes University. She earned a Ph.D. from the University of Cambridge. Her research interests focus on the impact of sociocultural contexts on learning and identity development. Her research explores young people's experiences of key aspects of their lives, such as the relationship between home and school mathematics, being an immigrant or minority student, acting as a language broker, acting as a young carer, and living with a chronic illness. This work includes the perspectives of teachers and parents.

Brid Featherstone is a Professor of Social Work at the University of Huddersfield and was Co-Investigator on the Open University/Action for Children research study *Beyond male role models: Gender identities and work with young men* (ESRC Grant No: ES/K005863/1). She has a long-standing interest in researching gender issues and particularly in exploring how social work and social care services engage fathers. She has recently written (with Anna Gupta) on the issues for black fathers in the child protection system. Her book with Sue White and Kate Morris, *Reimagining Child Protection: Towards Humane Social Work*, has been highly influential in challenging the current child protection system and she is very involved in rethinking practice approaches to domestic abuse.

Lisa Fellin holds a Ph.D. in Clinical Psychology and is a systemic family therapist. She is currently the Research Director of the Professional Doctorate in Counselling Psychology at the University of East London, UK. She teaches, researches and publishes in the area of systemic and family therapy, critical perspectives on mental health and domestic violence.

Amanda Holt, Ph.D., is a Reader in Criminology in the Department of Social Sciences, University of Roehampton, London, UK. Her research interests broadly address issues concerning families, identity, violence and harm. She has been actively researching with children, parents and families for over a decade and is the author of over 20 peer-reviewed articles, chapters and books. Amanda applies a multidisciplinary approach to her research and analysis, drawing on critical psychology, sociology, social policy and sociolegal perspectives.

Katherine Johnson is a Reader in Psychology in the School of Applied Social Science, and leads the Transforming Sexuality and Gender research cluster at the University of Brighton, UK. Her research focuses on issues of social justice in LGBT lives, particularly related to mental health and health inequalities. She has published on topics such as transgender embodiment, LGBT mental health, sexuality, shame and suicidal distress, global mental health and neo-colonialism, feminist and queer theory, and qualitative research methods. In her research she has used a range of qualitative approaches, including discourse analysis, memory work, photography and creative-arts-based visual methods and participatory-action research. Her major publications include *Community Psychology and the Socio-Economics of Mental Distress: International Perspectives* (Palgrave, 2012) and *Sexuality: A Psychosocial Manifesto* (Polity, 2015). Her current projects include the Marie Curie-funded ACCESSCare project to improve end-of-life healthcare practice for LGBT people and writing a book based on her research with a transgender youth group called 'Trans Youth: What matters?'

Stanford Taonatose Mahati is a Postdoctoral Fellow at the African Centre for Migration & Society, University of the Witwatersrand. A ZEIT-Stiftung Ebelin and Gerd Bucerius "Settling into Motion" alumni, he earned his Ph.D. at the University of the Witwatersrand, Johannesburg. He is interested in the sociology and social anthropology of childhood, child migration, transnational migrant families, child work, children's sexualities, sociology of health, qualitative research methods, and designing, monitoring and evaluating interventions targeting vulnerable children and their households. His current research is funded by the Wellcome Trust and the Wits University School of Governance's Life in the City Project, and is part of the Migration & Health Project (maHp). He is critically examining the various shades and impacts of masculinities and femininities and what these mean for migrant children and gender relations in Johannesburg, a city characterised by poverty and violence, amongst other challenges.

Lindsay O'Dell is a Feminist Critical Developmental Psychologist in the Faculty of Wellbeing, Education and Language Studies at the Open University, UK. Her work focuses on children, young people and families who are in some way 'different', including autism, ADHD, young carers and language brokers. Lindsay is an active member of the Psychology of Women Section of the British Psychological Society and co-editor of the journal *Children & Society*.

Ingrid Palmary is Professor and Director of the African Centre for Migration & Society at the University of the Witwatersrand (Wits). She joined Wits in 2005 after completing her Ph.D. (psychology) at Manchester Metropolitan University, UK. Prior to this she worked at the Centre for the Study of Violence and Reconciliation as a Senior Researcher. Her research has been in the field of gender, violence and displacement. She has published in numerous international journals and is the author of *Gender, Sexuality and Migration in South Africa: Governing Morality* (Palgrave) and co-editor of *Healing and Change in the City of Gold* (Springer), *Gender and Migration: Feminist Interventions* (Zed Press) and *Handbook of International Feminisms: Perspectives on Psychology, Women, Culture and Rights* (Springer).

Martin Robb is a Senior Lecturer in the Faculty of Wellbeing, Education and Languages at the Open University, UK, and was Principal Investigator on the Open University/Action for Children research study *Beyond male role models: Gender identities and work with young men* (ESRC Grant No: ES/K005863/1). His research has focused mainly on issues of gender and care, and has included studies of men working in childcare and fathering identities. Before joining the Open University, he worked on community education projects with ex-offenders and other disadvantaged groups. He is the author of a book on men, masculinities and the care of children, to be published by Routledge in 2017.

Sandy Ruxton is an Independent Policy Advisor and Researcher, specialising in gender (especially men and masculinities), children and families, and poverty and social exclusion. He was Consultant to the Open University/Action for Children research study *Beyond male role models: Gender identities and work with young men* (ESRC Grant No: ES/K005863/1). He has held various policy-related posts in the UK voluntary sector, and has undertaken projects for a wide range of organisations, including the EU Presidency, European Commission, Oxfam, Save the Children, and the European Women's Lobby. Recent commissions include working for the British Council in Egypt on engaging men in tackling violence against women, and developing a White Ribbon Campaign for the European Institute for Gender Equality. A trained teacher, he has worked with boys and young men in schools, in the community and in prisons. He is an Ambassador for the White Ribbon Campaign UK, a member of the steering group of the NGO alliance MenEngage Europe and an Honorary Research Fellow at the University of Liverpool.

Georgena Ryder is currently completing a Ph.D. in Clinical Psychology at the University of Southern Queensland, Australia. She is interested in understandings of difference, particularly for those with a label of autism, in both her research and clinical practice. Her current research explores the educational choices made by families who have a member on the autism spectrum.

Michael R.M. Ward, Ph.D., was a Research Assistant on the Open University/ Action for Children research study *Beyond male role models: Gender identities and work with young men* (ESRC Grant No: ES/K005863/1). His work centres on the performance of working-class masculinities within and beyond educational institutions. He is the author of *From Labouring to Learning, Working-class Masculinities, Education and De-industrialization* (Palgrave MacMillan) and the editor of *Gender Identity and Research Relationships*, which is volume 14 in the Studies in Qualitative Methods book series (forthcoming Emerald). He has taught sociology at both further and higher education institutions to students of all ages and is a tutor at the Lifelong Learning Centre at Cardiff University and an Associate Lecturer at the Open University, UK. Mike is also co-convenor of the BSA Education Study Group and editorial board member for *Sociological Research Online* and the *Journal of Boyhood Studies*.

Maxine Woolhouse is a Senior Lecturer in Psychology at Leeds Beckett University (UK). Her research interests and current teaching lie in the areas of critical, feminist and discursive approaches to gender, sexuality, social class and health. In particular, Maxine's research focuses on critical understandings of mothering, 'mother blame' and family foodwork, and the discursive intersections of gender, social class and 'obesity'.

1

INTRODUCING NORMATIVE AND DIFFERENT CHILDHOODS, DEVELOPMENTAL TRAJECTORY AND TRANSGRESSION

Lindsay O'Dell, Charlotte Brownlow and Hanna Bertilsdotter-Rosqvist

Introduction

At the time of writing this chapter, the first of the children from the 'Jungle' in Calais, France (a supposedly temporary camp for refugees), have been permitted by the British government to join their families in Britain. The reporting, particularly in the right-wing press, has been concerned with the supposed age of these children. Concerns have been expressed that instead of saving *children* (a notion linked back, sometimes explicitly, to a romanticised representation of British sentiment and actions regarding kindertransport during the late 1930s), the British public are being duped, as these are not children. The images of young, vulnerable children are in sharp contrast to the young men who have (finally) arrived in the United Kingdom.

Particular images of childhood have been brought into play in discussions about the children arriving from the 'Jungle' in which assumptions about age, vulnerability, ethnicity and, arguably, gender are evident. Whilst children are seen to be vulnerable and in need of protection, the children in question are not seen as deserving or in need of such services. 'Difference' in this instance has an obviously political and moral frame, with the underlying message that if these are indeed children, they are not the kind of children 'we' were expecting.

It is a difficult but important time to be considering 'different childhoods' and to be challenging ideas about 'development'. In the British context, but also more widely in Europe and around the world, ideas about development position children as either deserving or undeserving of help and protection, and naturalise particular ways of developing through time. Burman (2008a) and others point to the cultural production of developmental psychology within the United States, United Kingdom and more generally the global north, and its importation in other places. To continue with our example, the concept of age as a mechanism for determining actions taken on behalf of children/adults has been clearly and powerfully invoked in media concern about refugees from the 'Jungle' and elsewhere (for example, in policy/practice with unaccompanied child migrants in Caritas Sweden, n.d.). Whilst there is no reliable medical test to determine age (Burman, 2016), the use of mechanisms such as dental testing are being called for in public commentary to determine whether the person is *in actual fact* a child. The status of 'child' thus affords protection and refuge that is not afforded to adults.

Whilst it is possible (and we argue, essential) to talk about deconstructing development, developmental discourse exerts a powerful influence. Concepts of age, development and the differential status of children are very much in evidence with a contrast drawn between 'real' children and 'others', and between adults and children. The notion of normative development is core to developmental psychology as a discipline as well as everyday knowledge and understandings of children. The aim of this collection is to consider the impact of developmental psychology and developmentalist discourse more broadly and to discuss how ideas about normative development position children who stand outside of these developmental norms (for a wide range of reasons) as 'different' and transgressive in some way.

Normative development?

As evident in the example discussed in the previous section, normative development, and normative childhoods, are easily recognisable in their transgression. In their imagining, developmental psychology and other 'psy' disciplines articulate development in particular ways. Rose (1989) argued that this applies not only to psychology but also to related disciplines which draw on psychological knowledge in their practice, such as therapists and school nurses. Our intention is not to simplify developmental psychology into a singular entity; we recognise that there are many different approaches, methodologies and theories within the discipline. However, we draw on a variety of critical resources to argue that the view of development as a (largely) universal, progressive accumulation of skills and ability through time is a discursive production.

Theorists such as Rose (1985) and Vandenburg (1993) have drawn our attention to the concept of 'development' as an assumed progression through time as a product of a specific cultural/historical moment that has become naturalised and taken for granted as an enduring fact. The notion of development as progressive arose at a time when Judeo Christian theology viewed humans' movement through time as progressive, and also at a time in the global north that saw the advent of evolutionary thinking (Vandenberg, 1993). The concept of time from this perspective assumes linearity, with a move towards a specific end point, rather than movement through time as a cyclical or degenerative process. The concept of a movement through time applies to both humans as a species and to individual children specifically.

Constructing development in this way enables individual children to be measured and benchmarked against norms derived from measurements of populations of children, setting up normative practices of evaluation in order to monitor (and if necessary intervene) to ensure 'appropriate' development (Rose, 1989). Developmental psychology became the mechanism by which children's development through time is understood, normalised and taken to be 'natural'; it seems obvious that children grow to adulthood (Rose, 1989). Hence, development is naturalised, with children's development coming to be seen as a biological process of incremental steps and advances in abilities and proficiency through time (Morss, 1990).

The move from theology to science, and in particular developmental science, positioned psy disciplines as not just charting or observing development but also making judgements about what is 'right and good' (Vandenberg, 1993). The proposition of a developmental trajectory sets up an automatic link between the past, present and future as something that is obvious and natural. Invoking 'natural' or biological explanations of development serves to construct 'appropriate' and 'inappropriate' developmental activities and, hence, normative and transgressive developments. Cultural priorities (of the global north) are woven through ideas about development, such as the desired outcomes of development, rationality and independence, and being able to literally (and metaphorically) stand on your own two feet (Burman, 2008b, 2016; Walkerdine, 1993).

Rose (1989), drawing on Foucault, argued that 'normative' childhood is understood through deviation, through making visible those who stand outside of the norm and are in need of intervention and correction. Children who stand outside of normative expectations of the developing child are seen as different and often pathological (Walkerdine, 1993).

Themes and structure of the book

Contributors to this book have taken as their starting point the view that development is partial, contextual and relational. The chapters offer a discussion about difference and transgression through a series of empirical, conceptual and literature-based exemplars. In framing this edited collection, we have used the concept of 'transgression' purposively, drawing on its meaning as 'violating a formal rule and/or moral principle, crossing a boundary of acceptable conduct' (Blackwell Sociology reference, n.d) to illustrate the sense of evaluation and judgement made when assuming difference. The production of (a particular kind of) childhood is embedded within particular systems of meaning, largely produced within the global north. Hence, the use of the concept of transgression makes visible the 'norm', enables us to challenge the view of the norm as neutral, natural and enduring, and highlights the moral dimension and risks of being 'different'.

In this book we, along with the other contributing authors, explore what is meant by normative childhoods and how children who transgress this constructed notion are understood and positioned. Across the collection, the authors address the ways in which normative ideas about childhood impact on understandings of particular kinds of children and set up assumptions about the norms against which 'others' are judged. The theoretical frame of the book overall draws on a conceptualisation of childhood and child development as an intersectional and shifting set of identities, attributes and representations, invoked in diverse ways. Authors engage with 'difference' as a multifaceted construction to examine how difference is articulated and assumed within specific developmental issues and topics. The chapters draw on a range of dimensions of difference, including how difference is manifested through geographical location; economic differentiation and identification through social class; embodied differences such as gender and disability; and through a developmental lens, which demarcates activities as congruent within a particular developmental age or as transgressive.

The topics covered in this edited collection should not be seen as either a 'compendium of deviations' (as was a fear of one of the reviewers of our book proposal) or as illustrative cases of alternative developments, which would buttress naturalised assumptions about how children move through time by illustrating 'deviations' or special cases. The exemplars provided are a few of the many ways of configuring 'different' childhoods. We, and many others, assume that the notion of the 'normal child' is in itself a 'cultural invention' (Kessen, 1979). What is core to the examples selected for this collection is the opportunity to consider the locatedness of development through specific instances of children's lives. The chapters seek to understand and theorise these instances in ways that attend to the local, contingent and partial knowledges about contexts of development and movements through time.

The collection is organised around three core themes: deconstructing developmental tasks, locating difference and the limits of childhood. The themes are informed by, and aim to complement, the themes of Burman's framing of her book *Deconstructing Developmental Psychology*. In her book, Burman explores how developmental descriptions and methods produce particular kinds of children and how "normative descriptions provided by developmental psychologists slip into naturalised prescriptions" (Burman, 2016, p. 4). She also questions a lack of focus on context and the abstraction of the child from their environment, and centres on the roles of mothers in particular, but also fathers, and assumptions about appropriate mothering.

The first section of this book, *deconstructing developmental tasks*, explores aspects of normative development and subjects these to scrutiny. The production of both the 'normative' and by implication the 'non-normative child' is assumed and regulated through tools, such as developmental checklists that describe developmental tasks relevant to the age of individual children. Theorists such as Burman (2016) and Walkerdine (1993) have argued that developmental descriptions are not neutral but actively *produce* particular kinds of subjects, where descriptions provide not only the language but also the practices through which children are produced as subjects of concern, intervention and study. Understandings of normal development become enshrined in everyday practices such as the 'red book', which in the United Kingdom is a record of a child's development given to all parents/carers of newborn children (Personal Child Health Record, Royal College of

Paediatricians, 2009, in Goodley et al., 2016). The 'red book' enables practitioners to record measurements of growth (such as the height and weight of the child). Developmental tasks are recorded as milestones charting progression through time, such as when the child began to crawl, first words, and so on.

Developmental tasks articulated and assumed within developmental psychological descriptions are the activities children must negotiate and master as part of normative development. The examples that are discussed in this collection are focused on the development of 'appropriate' sociality and gender. In Chapter 2, Georgena Ryder and Charlotte Brownlow examine how developmental understandings assume that children's engagement in hobbies and interests is evidence of an appropriate developmental trajectory. However, when a child has a label of autism, such interests and hobbies take on a special function, and therefore require the scrutiny of psy-professionals to ensure that such interests are within a normative range or trigger the need for intervention and correction. In Chapter 3, Katherine Johnson draws on the experiences of transgendered children in making sense of their own and others' experiences of gender. In the final chapter of the first section, Hanna Bertilsdotter-Rosqvist and Charlotte Brownlow examine assumptions about how girls develop friendships and assumptions about what are appropriate friendship roles as portrayed by girls' magazines published in Australia, Sweden and the United Kingdom.

The second section of the edited collection focuses on the *locatedness of development* within broad geopolitical and societal spaces. Burman (2008b, p8) asked of developmental psychology, "why is it that gender should function as the key axis of difference (…) whereas, for example, notions of classed or racialised/ethnic positions do not". Her view, and also our position in this book, is that an intersectional analysis is required to interrogate the many axes of difference that produce shifting positions of privilege and otherness.

The chapters in the second section of the book locate development in relation to social class, gender, geography and ideas about nation. In Chapter 5, Maxine Woolhouse examines issues of social class in relation to 'foodwork', and the intersections of class and gender in the ability to demonstrate 'successful mothering' in the raising of healthy children. Issues of gender and parenting are also explored in Chapter 6, in which Martin Robb, Brid Featherstone, Sandy Ruxton and Michael R.M. Ward examine the expectation that male role models are important for boys' development. They argue that this assumption oversimplifies experience, boys' development and understandings more broadly of the role of gender in working with children. In Chapter 7, Jane Callaghan, Joanne Alexander and Lisa Fellin explore how assumptions about a child's agency and perceived vulnerability set up particular understandings and practices with children who have experienced domestic violence.

The final section of the book addresses the *limits of childhood*, examining the constructed distinction between adulthood and childhood. As discussed earlier, critical social science, including critical developmental psychology, have subjected the dominant understanding of development as a move between childhood and adulthood to scrutiny. The constructed categories of 'adult' and 'child' are both seen as illusory, but also as evident in everyday representations and policies concerning children's lives. The assumptions about childhood are most clearly seen in reactions to those children who transgress notions about 'appropriate' childhood activities. The chapters in this section examine the limits of childhood in relation to engagement in the 'adult' world of work and in criminal activity. In the first chapter in this section, Stanford Taonatose Mahati and Ingrid Palmary explore how migrant children in Southern Africa are positioned within understandings of the nation state and individual development. In Chapter 9, Lindsay O'Dell, Sarah Crafter, Guida de Abreu and Tony Cline examine how constructions of normative development position children in relation to appropriate engagement with work and the ways in which child workers transgress assumptions about childhood. In the final chapter, Amanda Holt explores research and media debates that frame understandings of children who kill to discuss the limits of childhood and how children who have committed murder move between constructions of a damaged child and a culpable adult.

In the concluding chapter of the book, we draw together issues from the specific exemplars offered in the central chapters to reflect on the three interrelated themes that have structured the collection. These provide the basis for an exploration of analytical tools with which to refine and extend knowledge about non-normative development, 'different' or alternative childhoods and the notion of transgression from normative trajectories.

References

Blackwell (n. d.). Encyclopedia of Sociology Online. Available at http://www.sociology-encyclopedia.com/public/LOGIN?sessionid=18eb7de60a001839ad4018a972a9e4d8&authstatuscode=400.

Burman, E. (2008a). *Developments: Child, Image, Nation*. London, New York: Routledge.

Burman, E. (2008b). *Deconstructing Developmental Psychology* (2nd Edition). London: Routledge.

Burman, E. (2016). *Deconstructing Developmental Psychology* (3rd Edition). London: Routledge.

Caritas Sweden (n.d). Age assessment and legal representation of unaccompanied children. Available online at www.assylumineurope.org (accessed 24 November 2016).

Goodley, D., Runswick-Cole, K. & Liddiard, K. (2016). The DisHuman Child. *Discourse: Studies in the cultural politics of education*, 37(5), 770–784.

Kessen, W. (1979). The American child and other cultural inventions. *American Psychologist*, 34(10), 815–820.

Morss, J. R. (1990). *The Biologising of Childhood: Developmental Psychology and the Darwinian Myth*. Hove: Lawrence Erlbaum Associates.

Rose, N. (1985). *The Psychological Complex: Psychology, Politics and Society in England 1869–1939*. London: Routledge.

Rose, N. (1989). *Governing the Soul*. London: Routledge.

Vandenburg, B. (1993). Developmental Psychology, God and the Good. *Theory & Psychology*, 3(2), 191–205.

Walkerdine, V. (1993). Beyond Developmentalism? *Theory & Psychology*, 3(4), 451–469.

PART I

Deconstructing 'developmental tasks'

2

EXPLORING LEISURE, HOBBIES AND SPECIAL INTERESTS

The constructive role of special interests for children with ASD

Georgena Ryder and Charlotte Brownlow

The word autism, first used in the early 1900s by Swiss psychiatrist Eugen Bleuler (1911), came from the Greek word 'autos' (the self) and was then independently adopted by Kanner (1943) and Asperger (1944) to describe child patients who were seemingly disinterested in the outside world. Several decades after Kanner and Asperger, Wing and Gould (1979) presented the 'triad of impairments', comprised of 'deficits' in social interaction (e.g. the ability to make friends), social communication (e.g. the ability to use age-appropriate language) and social imagination (e.g. the capacity for diverse movements and interests). This triad was adopted by the American Psychiatric Association (APA) when creating their third and fourth editions of the *Diagnostic and Statistical Manual of Mental Disorders*. Later, due to a strong correlation between the social and communication components, the APA elected to combine the two in the DSM's fifth edition (DSM-5, 2013), thus creating a dyad. This new conceptualisation places a firm focus on issues related to communication and behaviours, and interests that might be considered restricted or repetitive. The core childhood tasks of developing appropriate social interaction and appropriate interests and hobbies are therefore central to the current diagnostic criteria for Autism Spectrum Disorder (ASD). This chapter seeks to explore understandings of special interests, the constructed boundaries between 'appropriate' and 'inappropriate' interests, and whether the way children engage in their interests is viewed as acceptable or otherwise.

A strong focus on 'deficits' and 'impairments' has specific impacts – most often negative – both on the way that individuals with autism view themselves (i.e. their self-identity), and on the way that an identity is constructed for them by others. An alternative perspective that is becoming increasingly taken up by researchers, educators and advocates challenges such a medical model, instead drawing on a discourse of neurodiversity. The neurodiversity paradigm puts forth a 'difference' (not deficit) position, and through this lens the tendencies that one is born with are not seen to be the only factors predicting or stopping success (Mooney, 2011; see also Armstrong, 2010 for more on the development of neurodiversity and its applications). Pollak (2009) notes that with the number of neurodiverse students entering university, there is no better time to be discussing the difference of people's brains (see also Taylor & Colvin, 2013), and Grandin and Panek (2013) argue that the focus should be on what is "right" with the autistic mind and not what is "wrong" with it (p. 56). Of course it remains essential to recognise that the challenges faced by individuals with ASD are very real, and that some characteristics are unquestionably unhelpful and/or upsetting. However, we would argue that societal norms and expectations place unnecessary pressure on neurodiverse groups who may or may not wish to engage in such a socially rule-bound 'world'. Neurodiverse individuals are therefore seen to transgress the boundaries of what can be considered 'normal' child development through their reluctance to engage in neurotypical (non-autistic) activities, and therefore pose a counterpoint to the construction of normative childhoods.

The purpose of this chapter is not only to discuss ASD from the position of difference and societal inclusion, but to draw on one core aspect of the diagnosis of ASD – special interests. Diagnostically speaking, special interests are the "highly restricted, fixated interests that are abnormal in intensity or focus" that fall within the "restricted, repetitive patterns of behaviour, interests, or activities" criteria of the DSM (APA, 2013, p. 50). Special interests were mentioned early on by Kanner (1943) as interests that some autistic children devote all time and energy to, and Asperger also commented on several narrow and isolated interest areas, including the natural sciences, poisons, numbers and machinery. Special interests have also been termed circumscribed, perseverative or restricted interests, or even 'obsessions' (see Baron-Cohen & Wheelwright, 1999). Special interests shall be used here as the term is considered to promote a strengths-based approach and is commonly used by those with ASD (Winter-Messiers, 2007).

Despite estimates that around 90 per cent of those on the autism spectrum develop special interests (Attwood, 2003; see also Klin, Danovitch, Merz & Volkmar, 2007), much about them remains unknown and they receive less attention than social/communication criteria (Richler, Huerta, Bishop & Lord, 2010). We are even unsure as to how to separate them from 'the norm', with Anthony et al. (2013) commenting that "there is insufficient empirical evidence documenting the boundary between a typical interest and a CI (circumscribed interest)" (p. 2). Much of the taken-for-granted knowledge surrounding special interests is that they will be different to the interests of neurologically typical (NT, non-autistic) children. Interestingly, the literature indicates that the number of interests pursued is the same in both groups, in contrast to prevailing assumptions (Turner-Brown, Lam, Holtzclaw, Dichter & Bodfish, 2011; see also Anthony et al., 2013; Attwood, 2003). Thus, special interests are not actually more 'restricted' than everyday neurotypical interests (despite what the DSM-5 would tell us). Additionally, special interest topics are really very broad and not all are related to facts, objects and science as has been argued in the literature (see, for example, Anthony et al., 2013;

Asperger, 1944; Baron-Cohen & Wheelwright, 1999; Kanner, 1943; Turner-Brown et al., 2011). Caldwell-Harris and Jordan (2014), for example, found those with ASD to actually have interests in more categories than the NT group, indicating a high level of diversity. Whether in the ASD or NT population, boys are twice as likely to develop intense interests than girls (DeLoache, Simcock & Macari, 2007), although it may be the case that such interests are expressed differently in girls due to societal expectations. Also, though interests are very individualistic, a significant overlap in video gaming has been found between NT males and males with ASD (Anthony et al., 2013). These findings are in stark contrast to the pathologising narrative for special interests that is typically associated with ASD.

Hobbies, interests and extracurricular activities are widely promoted as positive in youth development (Peck, Roeser, Zarrett & Eccles, 2008), and are mostly governed by parental rules, expectations and individualistic/collectivistic culture (Newman et al., 2007). However, one of the distinctive features of special interests for individuals with ASD is that they are almost always discovered or developed by the child and not the parent (Attwood, 2003). As previously indicated, those with ASD are often interested in and collect the same things as their same-aged peers (Attwood, 2003; Bancroft, Batten, Lambert & Madders, 2012; Marchewka & Sułkowska, 2008) – for example superheroes – but unusual interests are not uncommon. It is in the teenage years that special interests are most likely to mirror the interests of typical peers (Attwood, 2003), however these may be accelerated. An example is one male with ASD who liked football and trained eight times a week (Bancroft, Batten, Lambert & Madders, 2012), showing determination that is prized in most cultures, but which could equally be positioned as excessive when placed within the context of ASD.

Finally, whilst special interests are renowned for taking too much time, a specific amount has not been documented, further contributing to the 'grey area' in the production of the division between a 'hobby' and a 'special interest'. Here the border between these concepts moves based on the context (i.e. ASD or NT) that they are placed within. For example, a significant amount of time (one hour, thirty-seven minutes on average per day, excluding school hours) is spent on extracurricular activities by Australian adolescents overall (Short et al., 2013), and yet this is in no way positioned as problematic.

Central to this 'autistic special interest versus NT interest' argument is the question of whether neurotypical children experience interests to the same level of intensity as children with ASD. The literature indicates that quite often it is found to be the case that NT children experience comparable intense levels of interests. For example, after surveying 177 parents, DeLoache, Simcock and Macari (2007) found that almost one-third of young children have "extremely intense interests" (p. 1579) that emerge, on average, at 18 months of age. Further, challenging perceptions that most NT interests are quite 'normal' in content, the researchers found interests to range from 'highly stereotypical' (e.g. vehicles, dolls and dinosaurs) to 'wholly idiosyncratic' (such as pouring liquids, U.S. presidents, and brooms, brushes and mops; pp. 1582–1583). They also found that whilst parents mostly viewed such interests positively and actively supported them, a number were seen as disruptive and required limit-setting. Another study that highlighted not only the pursuits of the ASD population but also the fascinations developed by people generally was conducted by Caldwell-Harris and Jordan (2014) using young adults. The findings point towards an unclear differentiation between societally endorsed 'hobbies and interests' and 'problem special interests'. For example:

> Since I was a child, I have loved organizing and planning. Sometimes I spend a whole day [...] clean[ing] my room. Especially, my closet has to be in some order.
>
> *(NT female, p. 103)*

> I like to write things down in my yearly organizer, if I have any plans. Only when cleaning my room, I sometimes like to arrange objects in a certain order.
>
> *(ASD female, p. 103)*

So we can see that the boundary between 'special interests' and 'typical interests' is blurred. Whilst special interests might (sometimes) be different to the interests of NTs in intensity and content, it seems that the real distinction between the two is made within the context of ASD. When viewed in conjunction with other diagnostic markers (i.e. communication/social 'impairments' or other repetitive physical or cognitive behaviours), intense interests are not appropriate, yet in everyday life, enjoyment of and knowledge about something is seen as acceptable, even commendable (and hobbies/extracurricular activities are widely promoted as positive in development). Clinically, special interests are viewed as additional social liabilities for those with ASD (Volker, 2012), interfering with other activities and being "predictive of lower social and communicative adaptive behaviour later in life" (Klin et al., 2007, p. 89). Some may argue that special interests need to be managed or limited because the longer such 'obsessions' continue the harder they are to reduce (Brereton, 2009). However, this again raises the question of the patrolling of the borders between interests and special interests and the perceived social legitimacy of these.

Given the uncertainty within the literature regarding the impact of special interests, but the central role adopted by special interests with respect to the diagnosis of ASD, we sought to more fully understand the role of special interests from the perspectives of mothers of children on the spectrum. By focusing on mothers we could access the impacts of special interests on individual children and the family as a whole. We could also investigate how one might determine that a hobby has moved away from a typical developmental task of 'healthy' childhood to become a clinically relevant special interest. Moreover, these mothers were able to share in-depth accounts about children across a broad age range, from as young as five. That said, we acknowledge the importance of a range of voices, particularly those of individuals on the spectrum, and their experiential accounts of special interests are certainly an important area for further research if we want to fully understand this topic (some studies do already exist, such as those detailed earlier in this chapter). In this exploratory project, however, we limited responses to the voices of parents.

Parents have positions of insight, often becoming advocates and experts for their children after diagnosis (see, for example, Leite, 2013; Mulligan, MacCulloch, Good & Nicholas, 2012). Mothers were specifically targeted given that they are still the primary carers in most families (see, for example, Hosking & Western, 2008). The focus on mothers also potentially enables a linked narrative to be explored, that of the "good mother", something that is picked up in the chapter by Maxine Woolhouse in this collection. However, with respect to ASD specifically, despite the knowledge and experience that parents, and specifically mothers may have, little is known about parental attitudes towards special interests.

Research approach

Following research ethics approval from a university Human Research Ethics Committee, we interviewed four mothers of children with a diagnosis of ASD, drawing on a semi-structured interview technique. Our research sample captured the experiences of parents whose children spanned early childhood through to early adulthood. These are summarised in Table 1.

Susan[1] spoke about her son Simon (5 years) and his evolving interests, which saw a shift from a commonly reported interest in the group of Thomas the Tank Engine to superheroes and Lego. Susan also spoke about her other son, Konrad (7 years), whose interests had also evolved from those earlier ones, and which now focused on IT-related games and superheroes.

TABLE 1 Past and Present Interests Engaged in by the Children of the Four Women Interviewed

Participant and Child (incl. age)	Child's Past Interests	Child's Present Interests
Adalyn and Sebastian (12)	Thomas the Tank Engine, death, Spiderman, gaming	Yu-Gi-Oh! cards and Pokémon cards, dancing
Zoe and Niamh (24)	Teddy bears and dolls, colouring, diary-writing, lullaby music at night	Books/magazines, CDs, iPad (esp. Facebook and YouTube), iPod, photo albums, hair ties, cooking, craft
Susan and Konrad (7)	Thomas the Tank Engine, Fireman Sam, World War II tanks, The Wiggles	iPad/computers/IT-related games, Masters (hardware store), Star Wars, rocks/gems, Superhero Squad, Spiderman
Susan and Simon (5)	Thomas the Tank Engine, Elmo	Lego and other small figurines, Star Wars, Superhero Squad
Claire and Jake (17)	Sesame Street, tombstones/ cemeteries, The Wiggles, the weather	Dr Who, politics, Indian cooking

Adalyn spoke about her son Sebastian (12 years), who had earlier interests in Thomas the Tank Engine and death, but had since changed focus to Pokémon, Yu-Gi-Oh! cards and dancing. Claire spoke about Jake (17 years) who had a diverse range of interests from tombstones/cemeteries and Sesame Street when he was younger, to Dr Who and politics in more recent times. Finally, Zoe spoke about Niamh's interests (24 years), which shifted from teddy bears when younger to iPads, magazines and cooking in more recent times. From these brief descriptions it can already be noted that the interests of these individuals are not static or fixed in a traditional sense, nor in the majority of cases significantly different from those of NT children, with all of the parents reporting a developmental change in interests linked with chronological age that we would expect of NT children. The transgressions from normative development would seem unclear without the context of the label of ASD.

The interviews were transcribed verbatim and analysed using techniques of thematic analysis informed by Braun and Clarke (2006). From our analysis of the interviews we identified two core themes that specifically related to special interests: parental involvement in special interests and parental perceptions of the value of special interests. Both of these themes will be presented in the following sections.

Theme 1: Parental involvement in special interests

All four women reported being involved in their child/children's special interests to some extent, and that in most cases special interests were discovered by the child. A common pattern was also identified in that the extent of parental involvement lessened as the children aged. The women all reported contributing time and money to the development of special interests. This is particularly evident in Adalyn's case, who reported: "I would have close to probably five thousand dollars' worth of Thomas gear". Further, Adalyn and her mother painted and decorated an entire toilet-room to make it Thomas the Tank Engine-themed, and her sister had laminated Sebastian's Yu-Gi-Oh! cards because he was worried about the edges turning up:

> ...we probably use all our resources...to keep him happy...in that interest and activity.

Similarly, Claire described how she had bought Jake a weathervane when he was interested in the climate, and a movie camera when he wanted to make Dr Who films. In addition to financial commitment, much time and effort had also been given by, for example, Claire's husband, Mike, when he built a full-sized tandoor oven in the garage to support Jake's interest in Indian cooking. What is interesting to note is that in their reflections on special interests, none of the mothers explicitly stated that they believed that their children's interests were unusual or departed from the expected norm in any way. Further, while the mothers here could be construed as 'unusually invested' in their child's well-being, it could be argued that parents of NT children also encourage and promote the interests of their children in similar ways.

With respect to the introduction of specific topics of interest, in line with Attwood (2003), the women considered the children themselves to have instigated most interests. Two exceptions were: Susan purchasing an iPad for Konrad and Niamh's school being the encouraging force behind her interest in keeping a diary. Otherwise the mothers commented that the children had "gravitated" towards (Susan), or "hone[d] in" on (Claire) certain things. Sebastian found a dancing pamphlet in the mailbox and gave it to Adalyn, Susan's boys were drawn to certain TV characters, and Jake's love of Dr Who most likely stemmed from his family. Some interests were adopted based on current popularity, such as Sebastian's Yu-Gi-Oh! cards, and the mothers had "no idea" (Claire) where others, such as Jake's tombstone fascination, came from. However, the women reported that the special interests selected by their children were not necessarily to the exclusion of all other interests or activities, which is a position commonly assumed. The children were able to participate in other pursuits, as directed by others. For example, Adalyn started Sebastian playing softball to develop "leadership and team skills"; Jake's school had mandatory work experience; and Niamh often went bowling or shopping with her carer.

A typical pattern did emerge with respect to parental involvement over time and for Zoe and Claire, whose children are now young adults, there was a noticeable lessening in their involvement in their child's special interest. This reduction in parental involvement echoes typical developmental expectations of increasing child autonomy and parental support for this through the gradual withdrawal of involvement over time. Claire noted that she still supported Jake's Dr Who interest (buying him Dr Who-related Christmas presents and being around to take him to a Dr Who-themed music concert) but also that she did not really know what type of Dr Who-related activities Jake now engaged in, the computer being something he "guards". Zoe reported that her involvement in some of Niamh's interests had been "handed ...over" to "carers [who] are like her friends". For Zoe, certain special interests, like craft and cooking, brought the pair together, being part of their "special time", but Zoe said that her involvement does not often extend beyond this.

All of these descriptions could potentially be given about a NT child's interests, but the clinical focus on special interests as a diagnostic indicator for ASD places a specific lens over interpretations. For this group of women, special interests were something that their individual child identified for themselves, were diverse in nature, and did not necessarily preclude involvement with other parentally encouraged activities such as team sports. The central role that special interests play in diagnosing ASD therefore seems to be a little more flexible in the experiences of these women, with a diverse range of interests being engaged in that developmentally shift over time.

Theme 2: Parental perceptions of the value of special interests

Three main areas emerged regarding the mothers' attitudes towards special interests: embracing and encouragement; moderation, redirection and removal; and distinctions between hobbies and special interests. Despite some mixed responses, the overwhelming feeling was that interests should be encouraged. Susan positioned special interests as positive and said that whilst those that were not 'peer-appropriate' could be difficult – such as Konrad's past interest in World War II tanks – she would always encourage talk about them at home.

Like Susan, Adalyn reported that Sebastian's interests have "mostly…been positive" and encouraged other parents to:

> …utilise it for all it's worth…the best time to communicate [*with*] your child is when you're involved in their interest.

Zoe echoed Adalyn's sentiments, reporting that she would tell parents to "try and build the positive things around [*the interest/s*]". Adalyn and Zoe believed that through their special interests their children had grown in wisdom, patience, maturity and skill, and that their interests had "matured" with them (Adalyn).

However, a small number of special interests were considered to be unacceptable. This clearly established boundaries as to what were considered appropriate and inappropriate interests, and therefore some special interests were encouraged and supported and others were not. For example, Adalyn advised:

> If [*an interest*] is positive embrace it, if it's negative police it, step on it…you're the parent. If you're not comfortable with the fixation, deviate it in a different direction.

The 'negative' special interests mentioned were Sebastian playing shooting-themed video games, Jake's focus on tombstones which became unacceptable when "he put [*other children's*] names on the tombstones", and Jake's interest in politics which was "a source of angst for him". The women reported that these types of special interests should be prevented or "discourage[d]" (Claire).

Crucially, three women also referred to negative *behaviours*:

> The only things ASD-wise…definitely not [*okay*] are…the…truly OCD [*obsessive compulsive disorder*] behaviours…picking…that sort of stuff.
>
> (Susan)

> The obsessive-compulsive things which cause [Niamh] distress like the tidying-up things [*should be*] nip[*ped*] in the bud.
>
> (Zoe)

> Smearing faeces all over the bathroom wall…wasn't acceptable…in a two-year-old…and it certainly wouldn't be in a seventeen-year-old.
>
> (Claire)

Restricted interests are a separate DSM-5 item to repetitive behaviours, but perhaps a tendency to lump *interests* with obsessive-compulsive or unacceptable *behaviours* has negatively influenced the perception of special interests, and the constructive role that they may play for an individual. As many of the women contributing to this study expressed, special interests do not need to be constructed as negative, and can form a positive role in creating relationships through creating a shared focus for attention and interaction.

When asked about what distinguished the children's interests from typical hobbies, Adalyn reported that Sebastian was "more serious" when playing Yu-Gi-Oh! cards, and Zoe said that hobbies "come and go" whereas Niamh "still [*has some interests*] dragging along". She compared Niamh to her son who would be consumed by an interest and then never touch it again. Claire agreed with this distinction:

> people grow out of [*hobbies*]...or might come back to them, or might continue to grow with them...but with Jake's [*it is*] a final sort of thing.

Susan's experience was also similar:

> they probably transition...in and out of interests less frequently...they tend to...know a lot more...and they're more likely to have...the whole range... [*it*] is quite all-encompassing.

Whilst this capacity to maintain special interests longer than others can be viewed negatively, it could be advantageous, especially as special interests may indicate natural abilities, which if harnessed could promote positive outcomes for individuals (Attwood, 2003; Jordan & Caldwell-Harris, 2012).

From the mothers' perspectives, it was the 'intensity' rather than the 'focus' that distinguished special interests from hobbies. This, however, does need to be considered within the context of what is thought to be a socially appropriate interest and activity. Adalyn commented that Sebastian spent many hours focused only on Thomas the Tank Engine but now his card games, whilst still a daily occurrence, mainly happen at school. Susan reported that Simon would spend around two hours each day playing Lego, and he would spend more time if it were not for the home routine – to the extent that "you have to remind him to eat and go to the toilet".

Interestingly, simply being perceived as 'abnormal' in some way (APA, 2013) was not reason enough for the mothers to discourage the special interests; if they were not harmful or inappropriate then they were encouraged, and even used positively as learning tools, an aid to socialisation and a mechanism through which their children could express themselves. For example, despite the DSM-5 in its social communication criteria stating that those with ASD may show "reduced sharing of interests, emotions, or affect" (2013, p. 50), the mothers reported that their children do share their special interests with others, and that special interests had the ability to improve social understanding and generate manageable interpersonal connections. It may therefore be that special interests have a role in facilitating an alternative type of sociality that does not necessarily have to follow 'NT social rules' but can be adapted to include 'ASD social rules'. For example, Adalyn described how Sebastian's interest in Yu-Gi-Oh! cards helped him develop unexpected friendships:

> ...[*if a*] child didn't really want to be friends with him, they are friends now through this interest.

Zoe described how Niamh's iPad gave her a "feeling of connection" and Jake, Claire reported, would not receive mail if it were not for his Dr Who fan club membership, and had "even been to some of their meetings...by himself".

Zoe commented that when she and Niamh do craft activities together, Niamh is able to develop "self-esteem" and "be the leader":

> her chest puffs out...I love it...because it gives us an avenue [*of*]...communicating at her...interest".

Finally, Adalyn, Susan and Zoe reported that special interests had helped their children to make sense of people. Both Adalyn and Susan referred to Thomas the Tank Engine and a sense of constancy:

> Asperger's children...find our faces...off the charts because they are constantly changing... 'oh what's the situation, oh what should I be doing?'...He loved Thomas 'cause he always knew what every...Thomas friend felt...he knew Cranky Crane was always cranky...because that's the face he had...he was very clever...because he put himself in an environment where he knew what everyone felt.
>
> *(Adalyn)*

> ...they loved Thomas...and [*were*] really interested in the faces on them...lots of people with autism...find it difficult to think and look at people's faces at the same time...they're not static and they're not predictable. So I wonder if like with the trains...it is much more static and... there's no body language... it's just that one thing they're trying to interpret.
>
> *(Susan)*

Research by the National Autistic Society in the United Kingdom found that "57 per cent of children on the autism spectrum associate with Thomas before any other children's character" (2002, p. 2) and that their relationship with him extended two years beyond the average. While this may indicate that there is a chronologically appropriate age at which interest in Thomas moves on, it does raise some interesting points concerning the utilisation of characters like Thomas in order to better make sense of the often NT-dominated social context in which these children live. Challenges in the understandings of people were raised by several of the women contributing to the study. For example, Zoe reported that whilst Niamh "loves" and is "obsessed" with books and magazines, she used to find pictures of people "distressing":

> ...she can't read facial signs and...she always wanted to black out the faces... I think they then disturbed her...or gave her anxiety...Later on she started doing things like she'd circle the eyes and then she'd blacken the teeth...it was almost like 'well these are eyes'...'this is teeth'.

The women were therefore proposing that the children were using their special interests to learn about feelings in a safe and manageable environment, one that can follow ASD rules rather than be dominated by NT social rules. The role that special interests may play in social facilitation was something embraced by all of the parents interviewed.

In addition to the perceived benefits in the management of social situations, all of the mothers reported that special interests had a key role to play in enhancing learning. Zoe and Susan, for example, noted that iPads and iPhones had helped their children to communicate:

> ...[*Niamh's*] articulation blows me away...the vocabulary [*and*] ideas that she puts into her texts...I've got to give her intelligence more credit...because she doesn't express it verbally.
>
> *(Zoe)*

> Konrad uses his iPad every day at school...he has dysgraphia like many autistic children [*so he uses*] his keyboard with the iPad...that really reduces his frustration...they just collect the work samples from that.
>
> *(Susan)*

The experiences of Zoe and Susan reflect research that uses iPods, iPads and other mobile devices to help those with ASD in navigating their surroundings (Robinson, 2013). Capitalising on their children's interest in such technologies was also enabling and supporting them within their formal education. Aside from technology, many other special interests could be utilised in the school setting, and resulted in various academic accomplishments. For example, Claire reported that Jake "doesn't like reading...[*but will*] read Dr Who magazines". Susan was the firmest believer in the potential of special interests:

> [*Konrad is*] doing persuasive writing at school...I said 'if you make the topic about Pirate 101 [*an online game*] he's gonna be in'...[*if*] it's not really about the topic then for the love of God just let him write about what he's interested in.
> ...if I wanted to teach them a concept I would always use their interests... it was the only way...to engage them at all...When we count we count

Lego guys...he learnt colours by The Wiggles characters...and counting we'd use 'well you know Percy's the number six and...Thomas is the number one - what's six add one?'...we always used...their interest areas to motivate them...to learn.

In addition to specific educational uses, special interests were also used for broader learning concepts, such as self-help skills. Adalyn, for example, discussed the use of Thomas the Tank Engine in toilet-training:

[*Thomas*] was a good learning tool...for behaviours and things...we used Thomas for toileting...we painted my...mum's toilet...we had a bell...he could ring when he went to the toilet...and he'd pick out what carriage he wanted and...if [*he*] did this many wees or this many poos [*he'd get it*].

Susan incorporated Star Wars when teaching her boys appropriate behaviour:

...[*we use interests*] in lots of ways, even with behaviour like we've always talked about using 'the force'...'there's a disturbance in the force [*Star Wars reference*]'

Lastly, Claire and Zoe mentioned their children's interests in the context of employment. Claire reported how the school was seeking work experience for Jake at a restaurant due to his love of cooking. Similarly, Zoe described how Niamh, who attends an art school for people with disabilities, could utilise her interest in craft and art further:

I'd like to see Niamh...producing and selling the art, which is supposed to be the progression...she has potential...They say 'while Niamh is extremely slow at her artwork she is very meticulous and very focused'.

All four mothers also mentioned that at least one of their child's special interests brought some kind of calmness, relaxation, comfort or security.

For example, Susan reported the soothing effects of Simon's Lego:

He loves the little guys and this re-enacting...even as a one-year-old with the trains...it would be an exact re-enactment of a show. The same language and...what have you...I think it is calming.

Similarly, Claire described Dr Who as being "a source...of relaxation" for Jake, reporting that "it supports an emotional need" and that "he feels safe...doing Dr Who stuff". Another emotive example was given by Susan who would tell her boys to "use [their] Jedi mind powers [*a Star Wars reference*]" in order to overcome challenging situations such as blood tests. We argue then that these interests play a significant role for individuals with ASD, and might potentially be a way to self-regulate and re-energise after a stressful day of interactions with others in complex NT environments such as school (see also Attwood, 2003).

There is a popular conception that those with ASD are 'literal' or 'concrete thinkers' who experience difficulties expressing themselves (Hobson, 2012). However, the interviews called this assumption into question as the women presented a connection between special interests and imagination/creativity. For example, Adalyn painted a vivid picture when describing Sebastian's expression through dancing:

> ...I've never seen him happier...he can move like he wants to move...it's amazing...to see a child that...looks sometimes so clumsy and awkward...[*be*] so fluent on the dance floor.

She also felt that Yu-Gi-Oh! cards represented more than just a game:

> ...he's been able to express himself...Because the cards, at a fantasy level, are...strong and powerful...[*I*] wonder...when he's playing that card does he feel...at his best,...his strongest...not confused or frustrated?...He's throwing [*that card*] down and he... knows his- its capabilities... its powers...perhaps that gives him a sense of self.

Zoe reported that Niamh's diary-writing had given her a better understanding of her daughter:

> [*it is*] a window into what's going on in...[*Niamh's*] mind...that she cannot express verbally.

Star Wars was a source of play and imagination for Konrad and Simon who "love dressing up in their costumes" and "play[*ing*] games where Max [*father*] is a Gundark [*a Star Wars villain*] and [*Susan is*] a princess in distress". Finally, in terms of imagination and aspiration, Claire described Dr Who as having made Jake "think bolder about...his life", with him saying that he now wants to be an actor.

While the dominant construction of autistic special interests is one that draws on negative representations, the narrative provided by the mothers contributing to this research calls this into question, often positioning them as tools of enablement. Such alternative perspectives further open up possibilities for understanding the diverse functions of special interests – many of which are often not included in NT-dominated conversations.

Final reflections

Whilst the interests reported in our study may not all fit within the DSM-5's 'restricted interests' criteria, they were included because they entered into the participants' lives and were greatly important to their children. The fact that it is difficult to distinguish between what fits the criteria of 'restricted interest' (contributing to an ASD diagnosis) and what would be called a 'hobby' draws attention to how difficult it is to determine what is 'abnormal' with respect to an individual's interests. This is further confused by the position that typically developing children should engage in hobbies and follow interests as this demonstrates 'appropriate' development and may further facilitate growth in cognition and socialisation. We would argue that for the participants contributing to this research, their children's interests did facilitate cognitive growth and enabled manageable social interactions with others (many other studies have also found special interests to be vastly important to young people with ASD, and have even incorporated them into therapeutic or skill-building programs; see, for example, Koegel, R., Kim, Koegel, L. & Schwartzman, 2013; Moree & Davis, 2010; Tavernor, Barron, Rodgers & McConachie, 2013; Winter-Messiers, 2007). The place that special interests adopt in the construction of an individual once a label of autistic has been given is clear. The lens with which to view that individual's behaviour takes a particular form, positioning what could be considered as hobbies for NTs as special interests for individuals on the autism spectrum. From our discussions with these mothers, it would seem that the key point in the decision as to whether an interest is 'restricted' or 'normal' largely rests in the interpretation of the interest in light of a label of autism.

An alternative construction of autism was largely reflected in the women's discussions, one that incorporated an appreciation of difference rather than deficit, echoing the perspective of neurodiversity. The women all spoke of the pressures to 'fit in' with a neurotypical worldview and the challenges that this posed for them and their children. While one reaction to this could be to reject the dominant position, the lack of empowerment made this challenging for some. Therefore, in order for ASD to be considered a *difference* rather than a *deficit*, a shift in taken-for-granted understandings about particular behaviours, such as special interests, needs to be accommodated more broadly.

Note

1   All names used are pseudonyms.

References

American Psychiatric Association. (2013). *Diagnostic and Statistical Manual of Mental Disorders* (5th edition). Arlington, VA: American Psychiatric Association.

Anthony, L., Kenworthy, L., Yerys, B. E., Jankowski, K. F., James, J. D., Harms, M. B. & Wallace, G. L. (2013). Interests in high-functioning autism are more intense, interfering, and idiosyncratic than those in neurotypical development. *Development & Psychopathology*, 25(3), 643–652. doi:10.1017/S0954579413000072.

Armstrong, T. (2010). *Neurodiversity: Discovering the extraordinary gifts of autism, ADHD, dyslexia, and other brain differences*. Cambridge, MA: Da Capo Press.

Asperger, H. (1944). 'Autistic psychopathy' in childhood (Frith, U. Trans.). In U. Frith (Ed.) (1991), *Autism and Asperger Syndrome* (pp. 37–92).

Attwood, T. (2003). Understanding and managing circumscribed interests. In M. Prior (Ed.), *Learning and behaviour problems in Asperger Syndrome* (pp. 126–147). New York: The Guilford Press.

Bancroft, K., Batten, A., Lambert, S. & Madders, T. (2012). *The way we are: Autism in 2012*. Available at http://www.autism.org.uk/get-involved/50th-birthday/survey-report.aspx.

Baron-Cohen, S. & Wheelwright, S. (1999). 'Obsessions' in children with autism or Asperger syndrome: Content analysis in terms of core domains of cognition. *The British Journal of Psychiatry*, 175, 484–490. doi:10.1192/bjp.175.5.484.

Bleuler, E. (1911). Dementia Praecox oder Gruppe der Schizophrenien. In G. Van Aschaffenburg (Ed.), *Handbuch der Psychiatrie* (pp. 1–420). Leipzig: Duticke.

Braun, V. & Clarke, V. (2006). Using thematic analysis in psychology. *Qualitative Research in Psychology*, 3(2), 77–101. doi:10.1191/1478088706qp063oa.

Brereton, A. V. (2009). *Part one: Managing special interests in young children with autism* [Fact sheet]. Available at www.med.monash.edu.au/spppm/research/devpsych/actnow.

Caldwell-Harris, C. L. & Jordan, C. J. (2014). Systemizing and special interests: Characterizing the continuum from neurotypical to autism spectrum disorder. *Learning and Individual Differences*, 29, 98–105. doi:10.1016/j.lindif.2013.10.005.

DeLoache, J. S., Simcock, G. & Macari, S. (2007). Planes, trains, automobiles–and tea sets: Extremely intense interests in very young children. *Developmental Psychology*, 43(6), 1579–1586. doi:10.1037/0012-1649.43.6.1579.

Grandin, T. & Panek, R. (2013). What's Right with the Autistic Mind. *Time*, 182(15), 56.

Hobson, R. (2012). Autism, Literal Language and Concrete Thinking: Some Developmental Considerations. *Metaphor & Symbol*, 27(1), 4–21. doi:10.1080/10926488.2012.638814.

Hosking, A. & Western, M. (2008). The effects of non-standard employment on work-family conflict. *Journal Of Sociology*, 44(1), 5–27. doi:10.1177/1440783307085803.

Jordan, C. J. & Caldwell-Harris, C. L. (2012). Understanding differences in neurotypical and autism spectrum special interests through internet forums. *Intellectual and Developmental Disabilities*, 50(5), 391–402. doi:10.1352/1934-9556-50.5.391.

Kanner, L. (1943). Autistic disturbances of affective contact. *Nervous Child*, 2, 217–250. Available at http://simonsfoundation.s3.amazonaws.com/share/071207-leo-kanner-autistic-affective-contact.pdf.

Klin, A., Danovitch, J. H., Merz, A. B. & Volkmar, F. R. (2007). Circumscribed interests in higher functioning individuals with Autism Spectrum Disorders: An exploratory study. *Research & Practice for Persons with Severe Disabilities*, 32(2), 89–100.

Koegel, R., Kim, S., Koegel, L. & Schwartzman, B. (2013). Improving socialization for high school students with ASD by using their preferred interests. *Journal of Autism and Developmental Disorders*, 43(9), 2121–2134. doi:10.1007/s10803-013-1765-3.

Leite, K. (April 2 2013). My son shines in the dark. *The Australian*. Available at www.theaustralian.com.au.

Marchewka, A. & Sułkowska, B. (2008). Wpływ szkół: Specjalnej, integracyjnej i publicznej na rozwój zainteresowań i wykorzystanie czasu wolnego uczniów. [The influence of special needs school, integrated school and ordinary school for development of after school hobbies and for consumption of pupils' leisure time.]. *Medycyna Sportowa*, 24(5), 330–336.

Mooney, J. (July 21, 2011). Neurodiversity: A compass to a changing world [Video File]. Available at www.youtube.com/watch?v=srWWMVKG56M.

Moree, B. N. & Davis III, T. E. (2010). Cognitive-behavioral therapy for anxiety in children diagnosed with autism spectrum disorders: Modification trends. *Research in Autism Spectrum Disorders*, 4(3), 346–354. doi:10.1016/j.rasd.2009.10.015.

Mulligan, J., MacCulloch, R., Good, B. & Nicholas, D. B. (2012). Transparency, hope, and empowerment: A model for partnering with parents of a child with Autism Spectrum Disorder at diagnosis and beyond. *Social Work in Mental Health*, 10(4), 311–330. doi:10.1080/15332985.2012.664487.

National Autistic Society. (2002). *Do children with autism have a special relationship with Thomas the Tank Engine and if so, why?* Available at www.nas.org.uk/nas/jsp/polopoly.jsp?d=368&a=2683&view=print.

Newman, J., Bidjerano, T., Özdoğru, A., Chin-Cheng, K., Özköse-Bıyık, Ç. & Johnson, J. J. (2007). What do they usually do after school? *Journal of Early Adolescence*, 27(4), 431–456. doi: 10.1177/0272431607302937.

Peck, S. C., Roeser, R. W., Zarrett, N. & Eccles, J. S. (2008). Exploring the roles of extracurricular activity quantity and quality in the educational resilience of vulnerable adolescents: Variable- and pattern-centered approaches. *Journal of Social Issues*, 64(1), 135–156. doi:10.1111/j.1540-4560.2008.00552.x.

Pollak, D. (2009). *Neurodiversity in Higher Education: Positive Responses to Specific Learning Differences*. Chichester, UK: Wiley-Blackwell.

Richler, J., Huerta, M., Bishop, S. L. & Lord, C. (2010). Developmental trajectories of restricted and repetitive behaviors and interests in children with autism spectrum disorders. *Development and Psychopathology*, 22(1), 55–69. doi:10.1017/S0954579409990265.

Robinson, B. (2013). The i-Pad Research Initiative: The Impact of i-Pads as Engagement Tools for Children with Asperger's Disorder. *McNair Scholars Research Journal*, 6(1), 125–136. Available at http://commons.emich.edu/mcnair/vol6/iss1/11.

Short, M., Gradisar, M., Lack, L., Wright, H., Dewald, J., Wolfson, A. & Carskadon, M. (2013). A cross-cultural comparison of sleep duration between U.S. and Australian adolescents: The effect of school start time, parent-set bedtimes, and extracurricular load. *Health Education & Behavior*, 40(3), 323–330. doi:10.1177/1090198112451266.

Tavernor, L., Barron, E., Rodgers, J. & McConachie, H. (2013). Finding out what matters: Validity of quality of life measurement in young people with ASD. *Child: Care, Health and Development*, 39(4), 592–601. doi:10.1111/j.1365-2214.2012.01377.x.

Taylor, C. M. & Colvin, K. L. (2013). Universal Design: A Tool to Help College Students with Asperger's Syndrome Engage on Campus. *About Campus*, 18(3), 9–15. doi:10.1002/abc.21118.

Turner-Brown, L. M., Lam, K. L., Holtzclaw, T. N., Dichter, G. S., & Bodfish, J. W. (2011). Phenomenology and measurement of circumscribed interests in autism spectrum disorders. *Autism: The International Journal of Research & Practice*, 15(4), 437–456. doi:10.1177/1362361310386507.

Volker, M. A. (2012). Introduction to the special issue: High functioning Autism Spectrum Disorders in the schools. *Psychology in the Schools*, 49(10), 911–916. doi:10.1002/pits.21653.

Wing, L. & Gould, J. (1979). Severe impairments of social interaction and associated abnormalities in children: Epidemiology and classification. *Journal of Autism and Developmental Disorders*, 9(1), 11–29.

Winter-Messiers, M. A. (2007). From tarantulas to toilet brushes: Understanding the special interest areas of children and youth with Asperger syndrome. *Remedial and Special Education*, 28(3), 140–152. doi:10.1177/07419325070280030301.

3

BEYOND BOY AND GIRL

Gender variance in childhood and adolescence

Katherine Johnson

Achieving a stable recognition of one self as either a boy or girl is seen as a key developmental marker in childhood. Psychological theories, from psychoanalysis to cognitive neuroscience, have sought to identify the processes by which this occurs and are implicated in wider public discourse that sees gender uncertainty as the result of some breakdown or rupture in 'normal' development. Yet, everyday terms such as 'gender identity' and 'gender role' are relatively recent psychological concepts. They emerged in the mid- to late-twentieth century as psychologists sought to identify explanatory factors and development pathways for their clinical observations of non-normative practices that came to be labelled as intersexuality, homosexuality and transsexuality. Ensuring a taxonomy that was distinct for these was central to early research in the field of transsexualism (Benjamin, 1966). Without a sound etiological basis, significant debate ensued about the status of cross-gender identification as a form of psychopathology or an unusual, but non-pathological, developmental anomaly worthy of medical intervention (see Johnson 2007a). These debates have heightened in recent years as the focus has shifted to diagnosing and managing gender uncertainty in childhood. Critics always acknowledge the distress that trans people face, yet the clinical practices involved in diagnosis and treatment have been subject to careful analysis from those working within queer perspectives, raising issues about pathologisation and autonomy, and questioning the types of gender and sexuality norms that are presupposed and how they limit gender diverse subjectivities (e.g. Butler, 2004; Roen, 2011; Stryker, 1994).

In this chapter, I draw on these critiques to examine the impact of psychological theory and practice through a 'queer lens'. The aim is to reflect on how the knowledge and treatment protocols for gender variance shape and produce normative expectations for gender in childhood and the impact this has on those whose experience does not fit neatly within these norms. In the opening section I introduce the principles of a queer approach, demonstrating the value of the concept 'queer' for critical developmental psychology perspectives and illustrating how gender identity disorder in childhood (GIDC) has emerged as a category of concern for queer studies. The contribution of psychological knowledge and practice to contemporary understandings of gender variance in childhood is then organised into three themes, which are read with attention to the norms they support and their implication for gender different childhoods. The first theme outlines development theories of gender identity, in particular the work of John Money and the legacy his opus has in competing explanations for how gender identity develops. The second theme explores contemporary debates about diagnosis and treatment, and the role of managing gender uncertainty in childhood. The final theme examines a more recent trajectory that seeks to understand the impact of minority stress on young trans people, with a focus on mental health and social inequality. All of these themes represent important endeavours underpinned by an impetus to understand and relieve bodily distress. They also tell us about the complex positions open to gender variant children and adolescents who must negotiate normative expectations of gender in childhood and dominant narratives and scripts for what it means to be trans. The conclusion pulls these observations together and argues for the development of more spaces where gender variance can be explored and celebrated. It also promotes the importance of listening to the complexity and variation of trans youth voices as they shape their own understandings of what it means to be different and how they find ways to live inside and out of dominant gender norms.

Gender development through a queer lens

Reading psychological studies through a 'queer lens' offers the potential to reinvigorate and reframe debates by unsettling fixed notions of identities and unpicking normative assumptions (Johnson, 2015). Queer approaches are of radical importance to developmental psychology, unsettling core assumptions such as temporal notions of development as linear or a stage-like process, as well as critiquing figurative portrayals of the child as 'innocent' (Bond Stockton, 2004) or 'the future' (Edelman, 2004). There is particular purchase for queer readings in developmental accounts of gender identity given that their analytic power emerged against a backdrop of feminist debates about the relationship between gender and sexuality in the 1980s. Even today, within psychology, Judith Butler, and more specifically her text *Gender Trouble* (1990), is a frequently cited source when referring to 'queer theory' or a 'queer approach'. There are of course other versions of Butler that we could draw on (see Segal, 2008), but central to her thesis on troubling gender were the concepts of 'gender performativity' and the 'heterosexual matrix'. The first drew attention to how a core gender identity appears stable, but only through the repetition of acts, gestures and desires that produce the illusion of an internal essence. For Butler, there is nothing natural about gender, rather it is a process of becoming. The second concept demonstrated the way that normative expectations about the relationship between bodies and genders (e.g. male/masculine and female/feminine) both regulate and construct normative expectations of sexuality (e.g. heterosexuality). These principles underpin a queer imperative to question all norms and to understand their impact on conduct, subjectivity and desire, especially when thinking about the relationship between gender and sexuality.

This anti-normative stance was also apparent in the work of Eve Kosofsky Sedgwick, another key theorist in early queer studies. Sedgwick drew explicit attention to the role of psychology in maintaining normative assumptions about the relationship between gender and sexuality. For example, following the removal of homosexuality from the *Diagnostic and Statistical Manual* by the APA in 1973, she was an early identifier of the shift in psychological practices of pathologisation from sexuality to gender variance. Sedgwick (1991) set out these concerns in the provocatively titled essay 'How to bring your kids up gay: The war on effeminate boys', arguing, as I have summarised previously (Johnson, 2015, p. 99), that

> ...although homosexuality had been depathologized in terms of 'an atypical sexual object-choice' it had now been 'yoked to the new pathologization of an 'atypical gender identification' (p. 159). This move was signalled by the inclusion of a new diagnosis, 'Gender identity disorder of childhood', which for Sedgwick 'renaturaliz(es) gender' (p. 159), by problematizing and pathologizing gender expressions in childhood that do not follow normative pathways.

Central to Sedgwick's concern at this time was 'gay development', particularly for the 'sissy boy', the boy who did not conform to gendered expectations in childhood and the fear this instilled in parents, teachers and the social world, that this non-normative gender performance was a predictor of adult homosexuality. Psychological research, with its search for the ontological origins of homosexuality, has long contributed to the popular assumption that there might have been another developmental outcome, one more desirable that 'growing up gay' (Johnson, 2015). Yet, as legislative transformations have challenged inequalities in the field of sexuality, the 'gender identity in childhood paradigm' (Hegarty, 2009) has over the last 30 years been increasingly strengthened and entrenched in recent editions of the DSM (APA, 2013), with some researchers continuing to investigate predictive patterns between gender uncertainty in childhood and adult sexuality, and increasingly adult gender identity (e.g. Drummond et al., 2008).

A focus on ascertaining whether gender variance in childhood leads to either a homosexual or trans identity in adulthood inevitably brings criticism that the imperative here is to intervene to ensure that this is avoided. Sedgwick's point was that research that seeks to explain non-normative behaviour is always underpinned by a desire to eradicate it, and for her, increased attention to GIDC emerged as a way of identifying and treating early indicators of homosexuality. However, the increased focus of GIDC in research has also contributed to changing the social landscape in terms of familiarity with transgender as a legitimate category of gender variance, such that the link between GIDC and adult sexuality has loosened.

We may have reached what has been widely cited in the media as a 'transgender tipping point'. This is further implicated in the number of people seeking support for cross-gender identifications in childhood. For instance, in the United Kingdom, NHS Gender Identity Services are experiencing unprecedented numbers of referrals (Lyons, 2016). The number of referrals to the only specialist gender identity service for children and adolescents, run by the Tavistock and Portman NHS Trust, has risen year-on-year since 2007/8, increasing from 50 to 1419 in 2015/16, with a dramatic 100 per cent increase in the last 12 months. To date, from these referrals, approximately 40 per cent of young people go on to undergo physical treatments (Carmichael, 2016). Less is known about the long-term outcomes for the 60 per cent who do not receive a diagnosis that leads to hormonal interventions, although many will form non-normative gender and/or sexuality desires and identification, identities that might include queer, non-binary trans, genderqueer or gender fluid, which have emerged in recent times to name a personal experience of not fitting within binary norms of gender expression and sexual desire.

The upward trajectory in referrals and a 10-month waiting list leads to questions of why as well as how access to services might be improved. It could be an indicator that trans subjectivities are far more widespread than previously thought and that greater knowledge amongst both the general public and general practitioners is allowing more people to access appropriate treatment. It could indicate that gender variance is being overly referred to 'experts' as there is little space for young people to explore their identities and desires outside of a binary gender system. These theories are speculative, but what we can be sure of is that the current normative conditions of gender identities and their expectations for 'being boy' or 'being girl' are constraining, uncomfortable and distressing for many.

Developing gender identity theories: A controversial science

The term gender identity is now so entrenched in everyday life that it is difficult to imagine a time before it entered popular parlance. Tracing the historical emergence of the term, it might be attributed to feminist perspectives that sought to use 'gender' to document the constructed nature of a social role that was distinct from inherent biological differences better accounted for as 'sex' (e.g. de Beauvoir, 1953; Oakley, 1972). Yet, feminist perspectives on sexual difference and the social construction of gender emerged in parallel to the field of sexology that had been developing in the early twentieth century. Sexology is the scientific and clinical study of sex and sexuality and was central to what Foucault described as a "new persecution of the peripheral sexualities" that entailed the study of "perversions and a new specification of individuals" (Foucault, 1990, pp. 42–3). Central to this field have been studies of patients deemed sexually ambiguous, often classified as intersex or transsexual. This history can be traced in Magnus Hirschfield's invocation of the term 'travestite' and Freud's psychosexual developmental accounts of personality, but it is John Money who is frequently afforded the most prominent role in reconfiguring understandings of sex differences and cementing the concept of gender identity within the popular psyche (e.g. Butler, 2004; Downing, Morland & Sullivan, 2015; Fausto-Sterling, 2012).

John Money came to prominence in the 1950s via his research on intersexuality, homosexuality and transsexualism where he distinguished gender identity/role (G-I/R) from the biological properties of sex. His opus spread over 50 years and in recent times he has re-emerged as a figure worthy of critical attention by those working in queer, historical and cultural perspectives, exemplified by the text *Fuckology* (Downing, Morland & Sullivan, 2015). Central to Money's thesis was the notion that gender identity/role was a developmental process and that, over time, we develop a 'gendermap' (Money, 1995) in a stage-like and sequential fashion. Like Freud, Money saw a relationship between the development of gender and sexuality, such that the "developmental process of gendermapping that affects an individual's sense of self as male, female, both, or neither, simultaneously codes one's 'love map as masculine, feminine, or bisexual'" (Sullivan, 2015a p. 135). Similar to Freud's account of sexuality, Money also emphasised a period of flexibility or 'plasticity' in early development with "one road with a series of forks where each of us turns in either the male or the female direction" (Money & Tucker, 1975 p. 6). He argued that this window would be most flexible up to age two and would be firmly closed by age four. Despite this, Sullivan (2015b p. 21) argues that some interpretations of Money's complex and extensive oeuvre often emphasise the role of brain plasticity in early life, such that he can be misconceived as a "quintessential social constructionist". This overlooks his commitment to sex dimorphism and frequent references to biological determinants in the augmentation of gender development and sexual orientation. Other cultural theorists (e.g. Germon, 2009) draw attention to the potential value in his theory for its 'biosocial' focus, and its interactional account of culture and biology, cells, environment and experience.

While Money's oeuvre is wide-ranging, he is best known for the controversial case of Joan/John and the story of David Reimer (Colapinto, 2001). David Reimer was born Bruce, the identical twin of Brian, in Canada in 1965. At eight months old, both twins underwent a routine circumcision operation to alleviate phimosis, a condition that causes soreness due to the narrowing of the foreskin. An accident occurred with the electrical equipment and Bruce's foreskin was burnt. The injury was so profound that he was left with irreparable damage to his penis, a situation that was interpreted at the time as one which "destined Bruce to a life away from society" because of his inability to ever achieve "normal heterosexual relations" (Morland, 2015 p. 71). Ten months later, with this prognosis in mind, Bruce's parents were watching a current affairs programme where John Money was discussing his pioneering work at John Hopkins University. This involved innovations in sex change surgery that were also being applied to intersex babies in order to 'fix' biological anomalies that had left them with indeterminate genitals, genitals that Money described as "unfinished" (Colapinto, 2001 p. 22). Following the show, Bruce's parents saw an opportunity to help him achieve a more 'normal life' and arranged an appointment with Money to discuss what might be possible for Bruce. Morland argues that "Money's message in the February 1967 television program, which prompted the Reimers to write and request an appointment, was that completed genitals of either sex could confer on an 'unfinished' infant a flourishing life" (2015, p. 74). This assumption was based on a confidence in his theory of gender plasticity in early childhood, such that he "put to the audience his view that a child with atypical genitalia could be raised successfully in either sex, provided that appropriate surgical techniques were employed" (2015, p. 74).

Bruce was renamed Brenda and underwent surgery to feminise her genitalia. Money's proposition was that Brenda would be susceptible to education and socialisation and would develop an identity as a girl in line with her genitals. Brenda attended annual check-ups with Money until 1974, and from 1972, Money began to publish accounts of the case, arguing that it supported his gender theory and had been a therapeutic success. But, as Colapinto (2001) and Morland (2015) have documented, from the 1980s, the success story began to unravel as scepticism about Brenda's adjustment to the female role emerged (e.g. Diamond, 1982). Milton Diamond was a lifelong critic of Money's gender theory on the basis that he saw the window of plasticity as much longer. He argued that no irreversible changes should be made to the genital configuration of intersex babies as biological substrates would influence how identities settle, contra to Money's conviction that if intervention happened early enough, gender identity could align with either sex. In the 1990s, Diamond made contact with Brenda, who was now called David, who was shocked to hear how his case had been widely published and used to support early treatments of the intersexed. David's story was not one of 'completion', rather one of masculine interests in childhood, resistance to embracing the new gender identity prior to being told about the operation, refusal to attend meetings at John Hopkins, eventual reassignment to his male identity in his mid-teens, and marriage to his female partner and adoption of her children in his mid-twenties (Diamond & Sigmundson, 1997).

The impact of Money's work has been wide-reaching. At the time it was taken up by those favouring social explanations for gender development across the social sciences and humanities. Feminist biologist Anne Fausto-Sterling (2012, p. 44) states that "John Money's downfall ushered in an almost complete swing of the nature-nurture pendulum. Claims of biological determinism of gender identity formation ascended while the idea that socialization contributed importantly to gender identity formation became subject to ridicule". This is an overstatement. One controversial case could never determine an either/or argument, but there has been continued investment in pursuing biological explanations for the development of transgender identities (e.g. Boston University Medical Center, 2015). Despite this, both socialisation and biological discourses continue to function in shaping wider social norms of gender evidenced in everyday talk, such as 'boys will be boys', or emphasising the role of socialisation and education in raising gender neutral or a-schematic children. The field remains open to competing theories and there is no generally accepted scientific evidence for a biological explanation for either gender identity or sexual orientation, even if certain biological markers exhibit more or less influence (Gooren, 2006).

Viewing this controversial science through a queer lens enables us to ask what norms these polarised explanations support and the impact they might have for living a different childhood. Undoubtedly, the science of gender development is based on a two-sex model with an emphasis on understanding variations from this as 'problems of development' worthy of interventions that support the alignment of gender identities with the binary sex model. Socialisation accounts open up the possibility that a cross-gender identification might have been different, that normal development might have been disrupted. Notions of brain plasticity imply that an identity might not yet be settled, that it could be open to change. The emphasis on openness is helpful to those who want to question tightly regulated gender norms and provide space for greater exploration and expression of gender variance. But they raise problems for those who want to see interventions made available to children and adolescents at younger ages. In contrast, biological discourses lean towards notions of certainty, of being born that way. Biology can be powerful in closing down accusations of pathology: to be based in biology can be considered 'natural', even if not of the norm. The risk of a biological discourse is that in seeking to find the determinants, there is always a desire to iron out these anomalies, a desire to 'fix', and a desire to maintain the norm.

Towards gender certainty: Diagnosis and clinical management of GIDC

The developmental theories that emerged to explain how a discrepancy between biological sex and sense of gender self might occur (e.g. Green & Money, 1969) were crucial in legitimising a treatment pathway that operated on the body, rather than the mind. But, in order to access interventions to reshape their body, the trans person has to first be referred by a psychiatrist and/or psychologist. Clinical practices involved in diagnosis and treatment have been subject to critical analysis from those working within postmodern perspectives, raising issues about pathologisation, autonomy, and the types of gender and sexuality norms that are presupposed and how these might regulate a binary gender system (e.g. Bartlett et al., 2000; Butler, 2004; Roen, 2011; Stryker, 1994). In this section, I examine how GIDC emerged as a diagnostic category and the role that 'gender certainty' plays in diagnosis and practice, before reflecting on the implication this has for gender different childhoods.

Even though clinicians had been debating diagnosis and intervention practices for gender variance since the 1950s (e.g. Benjamin, 1953; Fisk, 1973), 'transsexualism' first appeared as a diagnostic category in DSM III in 1980. Some argued that the term transsexualism presupposed the treatment path within the diagnosis, so it was subsequently replaced with a cross reference to gender dysphoria in 1987, and was replaced by gender identity disorders (GIDs) with specific distinctions drawn between children, adolescents and adults in 1994 and 2000 (APA, 1994/2000). A GID is defined as "a strong and persistent cross-gender identification" combined with "evidence of persistent discomfort about one's assigned sex or the sense of appropriateness in the role of that sex" (APA, 2000 p. 576). In DSM-5 (APA, 2013), GIDs were replaced with gender dysphoria, orientating discussions around relieving bodily distress, but maintaining an emphasis on persistent discomfort and cross-gender identification in childhood.

The status of the diagnosis has been highly contentious since its inclusion with concerns raised about its validity and suitability, as well as the social norms it pre-supposes (e.g. Bartlett et al., 2000; Wilson et al., 2002). In a comprehensive review of the emergence of GIDC, Bryant (2006, p. 24) illustrates that critiques "have been central in shaping both the diagnosis and the evaluation and treatment prac-tices associated with it". For example, he cites that one important intervention prior to the 1980 reiteration came from feminist mental health practitioners and members of the APA Committee on Women who raised questions about the dis-tinct social value attached to boys and girls. Noting that all the research and clinical evidence to date had been based on clinical cases of natal boys, there were deep concerns about the generalisation of GID to childhood more broadly, especially without acknowledging that "in a civilization in which adult males, by and large, have more status, privilege and power than adult females, it is natural that percep-tive little girls would identify somewhat with males" (letter cited by Bryant, 2006 p. 32). Under such a social distinction, there was a risk that natal females may well become diagnosed when expressing cross-gender behaviours and identifications that could be considered a reasonable response to the different social values placed upon men, women, boys and girls.

Queer readings illustrate the norms GIDC presumes and suggest how these might shape the subsequent desires and conduct of young people. In *Undoing Gender*, Judith Butler (2004) applied her deconstructive technique to question the ongoing inclusion of any gender identity disorder as a category of diagnosis within the DSM. Her reasoning was that diagnosis has been argued as either a pathologis-ing practice that should end, or as a crucial step for transautonomy by support-ing trans people to access appropriate healthcare interventions that would enable their transition. But, she asks, does diagnosis really offer the "support" individuals require "to exercise self-determination with respect to gender" (p. 76). Rather, she continues, there are a number of troubling assumptions underpinning the practice of diagnosis that undermine transautonomy:

> It subscribes to forms of psychological assessment, which assumes that the diagnosed person is affected by forces he or she does not understand. It assumes that there is a delusion or dysphoria in such people. It assumes that certain gender norms have not been properly embodied, and that an error and a failure have taken place. It makes assumptions about fathers and moth-ers, and what normal family life is, and should have been. It assumes the language of correction, adaptation, and normalisation. It seeks to uphold the gender norms of the world as it is currently constituted and tends to patholo-gise any effort to produce gender in ways that fail to conform to existing norms (or, fails to conform to a certain dominant fantasy of what existing

norms actually are). It is a diagnosis that has been given to people against their will, and it is a diagnosis that has effectively broken the will of many people, especially queer and trans youth.

(Butler, 2004 p. 77)

In a similar fashion to Sedgwick, Butler's critique also alludes to a broader concern that the clinical classification GIDC has become an indirect way of diagnosing homosexuality as a gender identity problem after the removal of homosexuality from the DSM in 1973 and 'ego dystonic homosexuality' in 1987. This thesis has itself received criticisms for being cisgendered (a term applied to those whose birth sex and gender align) or 'cisnormative' (Ansara & Hegarty, 2011), because queer theorists primarily see GIDC in terms of pathologising sexuality, rather than as evidence of trans subjectivity. For instance, Bryant (2008, p. 60) has argued that those who argue against GIDC on the basis of homophobia are valuing "gayness…over and above other forms of queerness, especially transsexual and transgender forms". While this may be the case for some authors, I do not think this is Butler's position here. Rather, Butler is trying to do two things. First, she is drawing attention to the role of diagnosis in either opening up or closing down opportunities related to autonomy and self-expression. Second, in line with her theory of gender as a process of becoming, she is questioning the way the act of diagnosis seeks to establish gender as a "relatively permanent phenomenon" (Butler, 2004 p. 81). This idea is particularly pertinent to concerns about contemporary clinical practice and the role of certainty, both in terms of gender certainty and clinical certainty (Bertilsdotter-Rosqvist et al., 2014; Roen, 2011), but also alludes to debates about brain plasticity in theories of gender identity development that emerged in the twentieth century.

In clinical practice, GIDC have increasingly been orientated around discussions of when children and adolescents should be offered puberty blockers, and more controversially cross-sex hormones. For some, the interval between ages 10–13 is seen as crucial in terms of whether gender dysphoria will 'persist' or 'desist' (Shumer & Spack, 2013; Steensma et al., 2011) and there is no consistent agreement on the "best age of initiating treatment" (Nicholson & McGuinness, 2014 p. 29). Despite the continued search for biological etiological determinants, the practitioner field maintains an allegiance to understanding gender diversity developmentally, even if models vary in their commitment to the concept of identity stability and the timing of early intervention. Here debates are underpinned by a concern for what might be best for the young person, specifically when cross-sex hormones should be made available. This concern is embedded in apprehensions about whether the young person might later 'change their mind', as well as unknowns about the long-term impact of hormones on their physical and psychological well-being and development. While support for psychological benefits of early intervention has grown over the last 20 years, the age at which interventions are offered has dropped from 16–18 years to 12–16 years in some countries (Cohen-Kettenis et al., 2008). This puts more emphasis on a need for 'certainty' in clinical decision making as well as the certainty of parents and young people that this is the right trajectory for them. Yet, as clinical psychologist Bernadette Wren (2014 p. 271) notes, this emerges as a troubling tension for those working clinically with trans youth, where empirical evidence and theoretical sensitivities suggest "a view of sex and gender categories as undecided and fragmented", while clinical experience working with adolescents and their families suggests a "need for many for a coherent and settled sense of self".

Katrina Roen (2011), who suggests a queer deconstructive engagement with the language of the clinical management of gender variant youth, also tells us about the potential pathways and possibilities for non-normative gender subjectivity that are either made available or closed down. She argues that "psychomedical intervention in early puberty can be used to buy time for reflection, to ensure that gender variant youth are offered psycho-social support to survive their teens in various states of uncertainty, gender fluidity or gender transition" and that psychologists should "seize opportunities to engage in discursive and clinical practices that enable gender variant subjects to prosper" (pp. 64–65). The idea that puberty blockers offer a 'pause' or some relief from both bodily distress and the drive towards gender certainty is an interesting one as it unsettles the temporal assumptions of developmental psychology and the broader theory of gender identity development as a process of becoming. In my research with transmen and women (Johnson, 2007b, p. 67), I illustrated that transgender embodiment was the result of an interaction between biological processes and cultural practices and involved an ongoing process of both becoming and unbecoming. This was to argue that a sense of one's gender's place in the world can be inherent to that individual, but if that involves a cross-gender identification, the ability to be that gender is not. Instead, it requires hormonal and surgical intervention alongside learning and unlearning the "culturally located practices that define sexual difference in adulthood" (Johnson, 2007b p. 67). The idea that hormonal interventions offer a 'pause' for reflection is because hormone blockers offer the young person a pause in the physical processes of becoming related to puberty. How this offers relief from entrenchment in other sociocultural norms, scripts and expectations for the gender and age they are perceived to be is less clear. If their psychic identifications are cross-gender, then they will continue to observe, learn and position themselves within the cultural norms of that gender, potentially resulting in a non-binary embodiment that unsettles normative understandings of male and female. This is not necessarily problematic, and may in fact be beneficial, fitting with expressions of some young people who identify as non-binary trans. It does, however, open them up to experiences of stigma and potential violence, which are frequently directed at those who do not conform to gender norms and because the first step in transition presupposes that the pause is a waiting game until they are old enough to start cross-sex hormones.

In contrast, those who receive cross-sex hormones are facilitated physically along the journey of gender becoming and unbecoming. If we set aside broader political concerns about how this maintains a binary gender system, the interaction between biology and cultural practices through late adolescence enables these young trans people to meet some of the same developmental indicators that mark out all young peoples' transition to adulthood, in becoming men and women. There are perceived additional benefits of beginning hormonal interventions early, particularly for natal boys, as testosterone marks the body in irreversible ways that are difficult to countenance in later life transitions, affecting the ability of transwomen to 'pass' (Johnson, 2007a). This pathway is therefore frequently judged as the most preferable by parent advocacy groups and many young people, but as Roen (2011, p. 66) notes, it is also the pathway most "modelled on a heteronormative success story", and access to it might be limited to those deemed most likely to flourish. So, while seeing the benefit that puberty blockers might offer, she cautions against their use to "reinforce norms, or compel gender variant youth to aspire to norms" as normativity can be considered "a trap: both for those it includes and those it excludes" (p. 66).

Reviewing practices of diagnosis and clinical management brings focus to the role of the contemporary clinic in shaping norms of transgender development within shifting societal norms. Concerns for gender certainty reflect debates about the role of autonomy and inevitably feed into normative scripts of trans subjectivity where gender variant people feel compelled to repeat the story of persistent cross-gender identification and bodily distress they know will lead to diagnosis. With such focus on the issue of 'certainty', it closes down the opportunity for young people to discuss a range of ways of experiencing gender variance for fear that their future pathway to treatment will be blocked. Yet, some at the forefront of clinical practice also question the dominance of the 'gender certainty' discourse and the way it closes down a genuinely therapeutic relationship with their clients. As Wren (2014, p. 289) summarises:

> The work of clinicians should not be deemed a matter of coming up with an increasingly 'accurate' description of variant gender identity and then working out how best to manage it... The decision to recommend physical treatment for young people is [then] a genuinely shared but imperfect decision, involving the client, family, other professionals in the context of a wider cultural world, in which the meaning of trans is constantly shaped and re-shaped, but which rests on no foundation of truth. The therapist is not burdened with needing to be right or certain, but to offer a reflexive and thoughtful space to help clients explore the architecture and borders of their gendered world view.

From diagnosis to stigma and minority stress

The third theme within recent literature on GIDC is the growing concern for the developmental issues faced by trans youth. As Bryant (2006) has suggested, in getting caught up in debates about the inclusion or elimination of the diagnostic category, and focusing criticism on GIDC as a backdoor attempt to control against homosexuality as an adult sexual outcome, "critics have missed an opportunity to rethink mental health support for gender-variant children in terms of general psychological health instead of narrow psychosexual outcomes" (p. 24). In contrast, he suggests shifting discourse away from gender variant children and youth as the problem, to instead consider how to help "children and their families cope with [the] stigma instead of trying to change gender-variant behaviour itself" (p. 36). In this final section I outline some of the key issues trans youth face and illustrate how research that focuses more broadly on the impact of stigma also sets up narrative pathways for trans youth identity and experience.

A recent Lancet series highlighted the marginalised status of trans people and the ill consequences this has on health. Stigma is cited as a primary cause of discrimination, verbal and physical abuse, poor educational outcomes, unemployment and poverty, and a lack of social support (Winter et al., 2016) and within the literature on trans youth is often couched as 'minority stress' (Meyer, 2003). This research sets out to demonstrate that being part of a minority group results in particular 'stressors' that the young person is unable to cope with (e.g. bullying, social exclusion) and that the family is not a good source of support as they do not share the minority identity. In this vein, a US study identified that 35 per cent of participants who expressed their gender identity or gender non-conformity between age 5 and 18 were victim to physical violence and 78 per cent experienced harassment (Grant et al., 2011). Others illustrate how trans youth are at risk of substance abuse, HIV/ AIDS, dropping out of or leaving school before completing their education, poor family support and running away from home (e.g. Singh et al., 2014). A number of national surveys in the United States, Canada and the United Kingdom have also established that there is a high risk of suicidal distress amongst transgender people (Grant et al., 2011; Haas et al., 2014; Bauer & Scheim, 2015; McNeil et al., 2012) and in studies of LGBT youth indicate that issues of suicidal distress and self-harm are amplified amongst those who identify as trans and non-binary (e.g. McDermott et al., 2016). Identifying unmet needs is crucial for ensuring appropriate healthcare services are made available to gender variant youth. Yet, the current focus in research is on identifying developmental 'risks', a strategy that carries its own risk for creating specific narrative pathways where to be non-normative is only defined in terms of distress. For example, in a handbook to support the parents of trans teenagers, the authors warn that "adolescence is a dangerous time" (Brill & Kenney, 2016 p. 144) before presenting numerous statistics about poor mental health and suicidal distress. This is a well-meaning resource that sets out to sensitise parents and other professions to the issues that trans youth are likely to be facing. While we must not negate this distress, it is also important to reflect on what the dominance of the 'at risk of suicide' label might do for conduct if there are no alternative stories about queer lives. We need to be careful about establishing norms of experience that only allude to distress and tragedy. This can be done through research and public anthologies that offer more complex accounts of trans youth's experiences and showcase their own strategies for building resilience. For example, Singh et al. (2014) illustrate the importance of trans youth being able to define and theorise their own gender as well as connect to trans-affirming communities. In my own research with trans youth, they have illustrated how challenging dominant norms of gender and gaining a sense of belonging with other gender variant peers is as important to them as improving access to gender identity services. Engaging directly with the accounts of trans youth reveals that there are multiple ways of being trans – including, for some, ways that resist the dominance of negative feelings about their bodies. For example, a young trans man in the anthology *Trans Teens Speak Out* states:

> I was never a person who said, 'I hate my body.' I just wanted it to fit more with what I felt inside. (Jessy, p. 3) When I first started my transition, I wanted it to be complete, from one side to the other. But now I'm embracing my in-between-ness. I'm embracing this whole mix that I have inside myself. And I'm happy. So forget the category. Just talk to me. Get to know me.
>
> *(Jessy cited in Kukin, 2014, p. 29)*

Gender variance in childhood: Changing the debate

Parallels in research trajectories that can be traced between sexuality and gender variance might offer future indicators for the status of gender variance in childhood. After the removal of 'homosexuality' from the DSM in 1973, psychological research on LGB minorities began to shift from attempting to find the etiological basis for sexual variation to attempting to model developmental pathways to 'coming out'. Here, a new focus on positive support for identity construction was underpinned by a growing consensus that the impact of growing up 'different' was detrimental for mental and physical health, when that difference was subject to stigma and discrimination. This type of transformation is now beginning to take place in relation to gender variance through three strands. Firstly, there is growing support for the depathologization of gender variance amongst the World Professional Association for Transgender Health (WPATH), particularly as this applies to the diagnosis of GIDC (Winter et al., 2016). Secondly, the inclusion of transgender under the LGBT umbrella brings a greater focus to the impact of stigma on trans youth, and there has been an extension of research into the type of support that is necessary for them and their families. Thirdly, in a field dominated by the perspectives of clinicians and parents, there is an emerging focus on trans youth's voice in accounts of gender variance. What I have demonstrated in this chapter is that all of these trajectories contribute to shaping gender norms and expectations that regulate the conduct, desires and subjectivities of children and adolescents. What is lacking though in deconstructive analyses of diagnostic and clinical practice is the voice of gender youth. Working with and exploring the gender subjectivities of young people offers the chance to unsettle and diversify normative expectations of gender and transgender in an ever-shifting cultural landscape. This crucial development has the potential to enrich available narrative pathways, challenge the dominance of accounts that only pinpoint high levels of distress and the need for early interventions to shore up gender certainty, and tell us much more about what matters to trans youth.

References

American Psychiatric Association. (1994/2000). *Diagnostic and Statistical Manual of Mental Disorders: DSM-iv* (4th Edition).

American Psychiatric Association. (2013). *Diagnostic and Statistical Manual of Mental Disorders: DSM-5.* (5th Edition).

Ansara, Y. G. & Hegarty, P. (2011). Cisgenderism in psychology: Pathologising and misgendering children from 1999 to 2008. *Psychology & Sexuality*, 3(2), 137–160.

Bartlett, N. H., Vasey, P. L. & Bukowski, W. M. (2000). Is gender identity disorder in children a mental disorder? *Sex Roles*, 43(11–12), 753–785.

Bauer, G. R. & Scheim, A. I. (2015). Transgender people in Ontario, Canada: Statistics from the Trans PULSE Project to inform Human Rights Policy. Available at http://transpulse project.ca/wp-content/uploads/2015/06/Trans-PULSE-Statistics-Relevant-for-Human-Rights-Policy-June-2015.pdf. (Accessed 25 January 2017).

de Beavoir, S., (1953). *The Second Sex*. Trans. HM Parshley. London: Jonathan Cape.

Benjamin, H. (1953). Transvestism and Transsexualism. *International Journal of Sexology*, 7, 12–14.

Benjamin, H. (1966). *The Transsexual Phenomenon*. Julian Press: New York.

Bertilsdotter-Rosqvist, H., Nordlund, L. & Kaiser, N. (2014). Developing an authentic sex: Deconstructing developmental–psychological discourses of transgenderism in a clinical setting, *Feminism & Psychology*, 24(1), 20–36.

Bond Stockton, K. B. (2004). Growing sideways, or versions of the queer child: The ghost, the homosexual, the Freudian, the innocent, and the interval of animal. In S. Bruhm & N. Hurley (Eds.), *Curiouser: On the queerness of children* (pp. 277–315). Minneapolis: University of Minnesota Press.

Boston University Medical Center. (February 13 2015). Transgender: Evidence on the biological nature of gender identity. *ScienceDaily*. Available at www.sciencedaily.com/releases/2015/02/150213112317.htm. (Accessed November 28 2016).

Brill, S. & Kenney, K. (2016). *The Transgender Teen: A Handbook for Parents and Professionals Supporting Transgender and Non-binary Teens*. New Jersey, USA: Cleis Press.

Bryant, K. (2006). Making Gender Identity Disorder of Childhood: Historical Lessons for Contemporary Debates. *Sexuality Research & Social Policy*, 3(3), 23–39.

Bryant, K. (2008). In Defense of Gay Children? 'Progay' Homophobia and the Production of Homonormativity. *Sexualities*, 11(4), 455–475.

Butler, J. (1990). *Gender trouble: Feminism and the subversion of gender*. London: Routledge.

Butler, J. (2004). *Undoing gender*. London: Routledge.

Carmichael, P. (June 15 2016). Key Issues for Health Services – Access to Treatment, Patient Pathways & Understanding Care, Westminster Social Policy Forum Seminar: Policy priorities for transgender equality.

Cohen-Kettenis, P. T., Delemarre-van de Waal, H. A. & Gooren, L. J. G. (2008). The treatment of adolescent transsexuals: Changing insights. *The Journal of Sexual Medicine*, 5(8), 1892–1897.

Colapinto, J. (2001). *As nature made Him: The Boy who was raised as a girl*. New York: Harper.

Diamond, M. (1982). Sexual identity, monozygotic twins reared in discordant sex roles and a BBC follow-up. *Archives of Sexual Behavior* (11), 181–186.

Diamond, M. & Sigmundson, K. (1997). Sex reassignment at birth: Long-term review and clinical implications. *Archives of Pediatric and Adolescent Medicine*, 151, 298–304.

Downing, L., Morland, I. & Sullivan, N. (2015). *Fuckology: Critical Essays on John Money's Diagnostic Concepts*. London, Chicago: University of Chicago Press.

Drummond, K. D., Bradley, S. J., Peterson-Badali, M. & Zucker, K. J. (2008). A follow-up study of girls with gender identity disorder. *Developmental Psychology*, 44(1), 34.

Edelman, L. (2004). *No Future: Queer Theory and the Death Drive*. London: Duke University Press.

Fausto-Sterling, A. (2012). *Sex/gender: Biology in a social world*. London: Routledge.

Fisk, N. (1973). Gender dysphoria syndrome. In D. Laub & P. Gandy (Eds.), *Proceedings of the Second Interdisciplinary Symposium on Gender Dysphoria Syndrome*. (pp. 7–14) Palo Alto: Stanford University Press.

Foucault, M. (1990). *The History of Sexuality: An Introduction, Volume I*. Trans. Robert Hurley. New York: Vintage.

Germon, J. E. (2009). *Gender: A Geneology of an Idea*. London, New York: Palgrave MacMillan.

Gooren, L. (2006). The biology of human psychosexual differentiation. *Hormones & Behavior*, 50(4), 589–601.

Grant, J. M., Mottet, L. A., Tanis, J., Harrison, J., Herman, J. L. & Keisling, M. (2011). *Injustice at every turn: A report of the National Transgender Discrimination Survey*. Washington, DC: National Center for Transgender Equality and National Gay and Lesbian Task Force.

Green, R. & J. Money (Eds.) (1969). *Transsexualism and Sex Reassignment*. Baltimore: John Hopkins University Press.

Haas, A. P., Rogers, P.L. & Herman, J. L. (2014). Suicide attempts amongst transgender and gender non-conforming adults. Findings of the National Transgender Discrimination Survey. Available at http://williamsinstitute.law.ucla.edu/wp-content/uploads/AFSP-Williams-Suicide-Report-Final.pdf (Accessed 25 January 2017).

Hegarty, P. (2009). Toward an LGBT-informed paradigm for children who break gender norms: Comment on Drummond et al. (2008) and Rieger et al. (2008). *Developmental Psychology*, 45, 895–900.

Johnson, K. (2007a). 'Transsexualism: Diagnostic dilemmas, transgender politics and the future of transgender care'. In V. Clarke & E. Peel (Eds.) *Out in Psychology: Lesbian, Gay, Bisexual and Trans Perspectives*. West Sussex: Wiley Press.

Johnson, K. (2007b). Changing sex, changing self: Transitions in embodied subjectivity, *Men and Masculinities*, 10(1), 54–70.

Johnson, K. (2015). *Sexuality: A Psychosocial Manifesto*. Cambridge: Polity Press.

Kuklin, S. (2016). *Beyond Magenta: Transgender Teens Speak Out*. London: Walker Books Ltd.

Lyons, K. (10 July 2016). Gender identity clinic services under strain as referral rates soar. *The Guardian*. Available at https://www.theguardian.com/society/2016/jul/10/transgender-clinic-waiting-times-patient-numbers-soar-gender-identity-services (Accessed September 9 2016).

McDermott, E., Hughes, E. & Rawlings, V. (2016). Queer futures: Understanding lesbian, gay, bisexual and trans (LGBT) adolescents' suicide, self-harm and help-seeking behavior. Available at www.queerfutures.co.uk/wp-content/uploads/2016/06/Queer-Futures-Final-Report.pdf (Accessed November 22 2016).

McNeil, J., Bailey, L., Ellis, S., Morton, J. & Regan, M. (2012) Trans mental health and emotional wellbeing survey 2012. Available at www.gires.org.uk/assets/Medpro-Assets/trans_mh_study.pdf (Accessed 25 January 2017).

Meyer, I. H. (2003). Prejudice, social stress, and mental health in lesbian, gay, and bisexual populations: Conceptual issues and research evidence. *Psychological Bulletin*, 129(5), 674–697.

Money, J. (1995). *Gendermaps: Social Constructionism, Feminism, and Sexosophical History*. New York: Continuum.

Money, J. & Tucker, P. (1975). *Sexual Signatures: On Being a Man or a Woman*. Boston: Little Brown.

Morland, I. (2015). Gender, Genitals, and the Meaning of Being Human. In L. Downing, I. Morland & N. Sullivan, *Fuckology: Critical Essays on John Money's Diagnostic Concepts.* Chicago, London: University of Chicago Press.

Nicholson & McGuinness (2014). Gender dysphoria and children. *Journal of Psychosocial Nursing and Mental Health Services*, 52(8), 27–30.

Oakley, A. (1972). *Sex, Gender and Society.* Aldershot: Arena.

Roen, K. (2011). The discursive and clinical production of trans youth: Gender variant youth who seek puberty suppression. *Psychology & Sexuality*, 2(1), 58–68.

Sedgwick, E. K. (1991). How to bring your kids up gay. *Social Text*, (29), 18–27.

Segal, L. (2008). After Judith Butler: Identities, who needs them? *Subjectivity*, 25(1), 381–394.

Shumer, D. E. & Spack, N. P. (2013). Current management of gender identity disorder in childhood and adolescence: Guidelines, barriers and areas of controversy. *Current Opinion in Endocrinology, Diabetes and Obesity*, 20(1), 69–73.

Singh, A., Meng, S. E. & Hansen, A. (2014). "I am my own gender": Resilience strategies of trans youth. *Journal of Counselling & Development*, (92), 208–218.

Steensma, T. D., Biemond, R., de Boer, F. & Cohen-Kettenis, P. T. (2011). Desisting and persisting gender dysphoria after childhood: A qualitative follow-up study. *Clinical Child Psychology and Psychiatry*, 16(4), 499–516.

Stryker, S. (1994). My words to Victor Frankenstein above the village of Chamounix: Performing transgender rage. *GLQ: A Journal of Lesbian and Gay Studies*, 1, 237–254.

Sullivan, N. (2015a). Reorientating Transsexualism: From Brain Organization to Phenomenology. In L. Downing, I. Morland & N. Sullivan, *Fuckology: Critical Essays on John Money's Diagnostic Concepts.* Chicago & London: University of Chicago Press.

Sullivan, N. (2015b). The Matter of Gender. In L. Downing, I. Morland & N. Sullivan, *Fuckology: Critical Essays on John Money's Diagnostic Concepts.* Chicago & London: University of Chicago Press.

Wilson, I., Griffin, C. & Wren, B. (2002). The validity of the diagnosis of gender identity disorder (child and adolescent criteria). *Clinical Child Psychology & Psychiatry*, 7 (3), 335–351.

Winter, S., Diamond, M., Green, J., Karasic, D., Reed, T., Whittle, S. & Wylie, K. (2016). Transgender people: Health at the margins of society. *The Lancet*, 388 (10042), 390–400.

Wren, B. (2014). Thinking postmodern and practising in the enlightenment: Managing uncertainty in the treatment of children and adolescents. *Feminism & Psychology*, 24(2), 271–291.

4

BECOMING A POPULAR GIRL

Exploring constructions of friendships in teen magazines

Hanna Bertilsdotter-Rosqvist and Charlotte Brownlow

The development of relationships is a taken-for-granted aspect of childhood that signals 'appropriate' developmental and emotional maturity. Some relationships, such as friendship, have been extensively theorised within psychology, and a clear set of linear developmental stages have been established which signal the 'normal' development of this social skill. This development can be considered to be gendered, aimed at producing adults expressing sociality in typically gendered ways. This chapter seeks to interrogate meanings of friendship and the successful sociality of pre-teen and early teenage girls. In navigating complex social abilities, girls are provided with a plethora of advice, from friends, parents and a diverse range of media sources. This chapter will draw on narratives of friendship and sociable girls in magazines popular amongst pre-teen and teen girls to explore the content and borders of being a normatively gendered sociable girl.

Tween is a commonly used consumer-media label for girls aged anywhere between 9 and 14 years (MacDonald, 2014). In this chapter, we will explore non/normative sociality in magazines popular amongst tween girls in three national contexts (Australia, Sweden and the United Kingdom), with a particular focus on friendships and relationships with peers. Previous research on girls' magazines has mostly explored issues of heterosexuality and heterosexual romance, including the regulation of inappropriate desires, and the role of magazines in the socialisation of individuals into female heterosexuality (see, for example, Jackson, 2005). In addition, previous work has examined the heteronormative appearance culture and its association with body image disturbances, sociocultural pressures to be thin and body (dis)satisfaction among girls (van Den Berg et al., 2007). Such work also includes the combined influence of media and (girl) peer factors on body dissatisfaction (Clark & Tiggemann, 2006). In focusing on non/normative sociality, we seek to interrogate the repertoires of popularity evident within tween popular culture as portrayed in magazines in the production of the troubled and untroubled girls and girlhoods.

Introducing notions of girls' friendships in research

Friendships are argued to provide a context for the development of social (and relationship) skills (Glick & Rose, 2011), and learning to be friends is proposed to be part of socialisation into adulthood (Ahn, 2011). Establishing oneself as a desirable peer companion while avoiding behaviours deemed problematic is represented as a fundamental challenge of a teenager's social development (Allen et al., 2014). Within the friendship literature there are several ideals of what characterises a 'good' friendship, and we will focus our discussions here specifically on what makes a good *female* friendship. We have themed these as ideals of a homely location of friendship, ideals of gendered similarity, ideals of time invested in a particular friendship and ideals of emotional intimacy.

Researchers within geographies of friendship have stressed the association between children's and young people's geographies and the (re)production of social ordering (see for example Bunnell et al., 2012). Multi-context friendships (e.g. school and non-school) are associated with more stability than single-context friendships (e.g. school only or non-school only; Chan & Poulin, 2007). In addition to the demonstration of friendship across several contexts, the specific location of girls' friendships is considered crucial, and is associated with girls' need for "safe spaces" (Moller & Allen, 2000). For girls, friendship comprises something that takes place in the girls own, female-only, local social world (MacDonald, 2014), in the close neighbourhood (Blazek, 2011), or, even more preferably, at home (Keener et al., 2013). Within these local, female-only homely spaces, girls' friendship practices include both the negotiation and resistance of different competing discourses of femininity (Martz, 2014).

The second ideal concerns girls' gendered similarities, including the homosocial preference for same-sex friendships and friends gendered in particular ways (Mehta & Strough, 2010). We argue that this stresses girls' preferences for same-sex friends due to their perceived gender similarities or sex-typed behaviours (Zucker et al., 1995), such as feminine expressive traits, a cooperative activity orientation and communicative responsiveness (Mehta & Strough, 2010), as well as lovingness, graciousness and attractiveness (Kyratzis, 1999). Girls in same-sex friendships are also represented as similar through having complimentary conversation styles and behaviours (Kyratzis, 1999; Leung, 2009; Pichler, 2005). Such talk serves several purposes ranging from maintaining and managing friendships to (re)negotiating identities (including enacting hierarchical forms of social organisation within the circle of female friends). Cross-sex behaviours are associated with more negative peer-affiliative preferences (Zucker et al., 1995), and are considered as putting girls at psychological and social risk (Mrug et al., 2011). Cross-sex friendships are also associated with unhomely locations outside of school and outside of the girls' homes, an imbalance in giving/receiving support as well as age differences, which has led Poulin and Pedersen (2007) to suggest that cross-sex friendships may place some girls on a "problematic developmental trajectory". The ideal of gendered similarity includes expectance of becoming more similar through time, and can be linked to the influence of friendship, including the establishment and maintenance of friendship group norms that have been particularly noted in girls' friendships (Gaughan, 2006).

The third ideal that we would like to highlight concerns the balance of time invested in friendships (Lam et al., 2014). Such a time balance reflects not only the need to invest appropriate amounts of time with friends, but also has future developmental implications within heterosexual relationships for girls in their early teens, having the expectation of being negotiated in such a way that it does not interfere with the business of 'doing friendship' with girlfriends (Morris & Fuller, 1999). The competition for individual time and the tensions that this might pose to friendships is something that shifts, in terms of allocation expectations, with chronological age. Several studies have explored the troubling of friendships in terms of spending too little time with peers and investing too much in other relationships, such as preferring or spending more time with family. Spending more time with family is represented as normal in younger children (up to 12 years old) (Zeijl et al., 2000). However, in the early teens, girls in particular are expected to have a definite preference for spending time with a single close friend rather than their family (Zeijl et al., 2000). Similarly, spending too much time on romantic relationships in the early teens, including spending too much time with friends talking about romantic relationships, is represented as a dilemma for girls and a problematic influence on their friendships and friendship quality (Thomas, 2012). Thomas further argues that when one friend has a romantic partner, negative effects on friendships can result. For example, one member of the friendship group having a romantic partner can lead to higher conflict-rivalry and co-rumination, resulting in friendships that are characterised as being lower in intimacy.

Time invested in the friendship is connected to the fourth ideal that we would like to highlight – the ideal of emotional intimacy in girls' friendships. This is connected with assumptions of stability and commitment, dyadic relationships and disclosure and reciprocity among girls, including age- and gender-appropriate emotional development. Emotional abilities among girls are associated with (positive) peer friendship nominations (Mestre et al., 2006), in particular female peer friendships (Rowsell et al., 2014) and social adjustment (Leppanen & Hietanen, 2001). Emotionally intimate friendships in girlhood are represented by Fagan (2006) as a way that girls may mature into women, arguing for the importance of exploring sisterhood and the effect of female friendships on the lives of girls and women. In line with the ideals of high and stable intimacy, there is a clear expectation within the literature for girls and women to have a single best friend, with this expectation evident from the early teens (David-Barrett et al., 2015). The ideal of intimacy requires more intensity in friendships, (Baiocco et al., 2011). It includes expectations of friend support (Salomon & Strobel, 1997) as well as the buffering nature of friendship among a diverse range of social and psychological problems (Oliva et al., 2014). It requires more closeness and assertiveness (Bank, 1994), reciprocity and disclosure (Bauminger et al., 2008), and trustworthiness (Rotenberg et al., 2008). The development of both disclosure and trustworthiness is associated with both developmental age and gender – where girls are assumed to develop abilities of both disclosure and trustworthiness earlier than boys (Merten, 1999; Rotenberg et al., 2008). These friendship ideals must be both embraced and negotiated by girls in their developing relationships in order for them to be considered popular girls.

In order to explore a variety of representations of girl popularity within tween magazines, we sampled magazines aimed at tween girls from three geographical contexts: Australia, Sweden and the United Kingdom. The particular focus for the analysis was to explore non/normative sociality in girls' magazines, centring on friendships with peers. In doing so, the taken-for-granted developmental task of establishing a mutual friendship with peers will be examined.

The data

We selected each magazine from each country based on three factors: it has a large readership base; the publication is currently in press; and is popular with 'tween' girls. This led to a final sample of seven magazines. All samples of the Swedish magazines (*Glitter, Frida* and *Julia*) were published in June 2015, the Australian magazines (*Total Girl, Girl Power*) were published in June/July 2015 and the British magazines (*Top of the Pops [TOTP], Shout*) were published in February/March 2016, so all can be considered a current reflection of tween magazine content.

In approaching the analysis, we were looking particularly for examples of markers of 'good friendships', including things to do with friends such as sleepovers, markers of positive friendship feelings, such as love/emotional intimacy, and markers of disruptions of 'good friendships', such as jealousy/betrayal. Our approach to analysis was guided by the framework for thematic analysis suggested by Braun and Clarke (2006).

Findings

Markers of 'good friendships'

Markers of good friendships took many forms within the magazines, each requiring particular roles to be taken on by the girls. Such roles required the girls to excel in particular skills, which in turn helped to facilitate 'good friendships'. Three roles visible in the magazines will be considered here: *the hostess, the social fun girl* and *the BFF*. Common to all these roles is the importance of being an active and happy girl who takes social initiative with self-confidence.

The hostess: Caring sociality

In line with the ideal of friendship support, the hostess role reflects the need for girls to facilitate a good time for them and their friends and generally 'look after' their friends' needs as an expression of a *caring sociality*. One particular activity that was considered central in all of the magazines was that of sleepovers and the need to be a good hostess when organising one with good friends. Indeed, *Total Girl* magazine dedicated a whole issue to a 'sleepover special', which contained several hints and tips concerning what makes a successful sleepover, ranging from the provision of the correct food, to interesting entertainment. For example, in *Total Girl's* sleepover special, detailed advice was given in the form of a list concerning how to be prepared for the perfect sleepover in order to make it a success amongst friends.

The list provided for ensuring a successful sleepover then covered a range of foods, such as popcorn and pizza, gendered activities, such as manicures, and sleepover games to ensure that the guests remain entertained.

The magazines reinforced the importance of having fun at sleepovers by asking contributors to swap their best sleepover memory, thereby reinforcing the need for a hostess to be effective in facilitating a successful sleepover. A successful sleepover was therefore something characterised by positive stories that could be re-told after the event. However, the magazines did acknowledge that this role could be stressful for girls and therefore offered advice as to how to ensure a sleepover success and the consequent creation of good sleepover memories for friends.

To be a good hostess, however, sometimes requires help from others, and the successful hostess therefore needs the support of 'good' parents who can and will facilitate the girl in being a 'good' hostess. In the organising of social events, the girl is also required to be able to bake tasty and healthy snacks for her friends. For example:

> Fix breakfast luxury! [....] Coconut and blueberry pancakes. These deliciously good pancakes are perfect to invite friends to! No one will be able to guess that they are actually healthy!
>
> *(Julia, p. 53)*

Additionally, the creation of a space to both seek and receive advice and support was highlighted as a core part of the role of the caring 'hostess':

> You are a good listener and have a lot of good advice on the stock, so it is to you your buddies will go right now to solve their problems. Wow, talk about that you're a good friend.
>
> *(Glitter, horoscope of the month for Scorpio, p. 56)*

In addition to being the perfect host and having seemingly endless energy to organise social activities, the girl is also required to enjoy and have unlimited energy for attending such activities. It is the role of the socially outgoing girl that we will consider next.

The social fun girl: Fun sociality

The role of the social fun girl is closely tied to that of the hostess and requires the girl to be happy, open to and actively seeking particular kinds of excitement and adventure (such as parties and new friendships), and socially outgoing so as to thrive in such social situations. In other words, the girl must take on the role of the social fun girl and engage in *fun sociality*. Spending time with your friends is considered to be the 'best time ever' and something that young girls should strive for and prioritise over all else.

The importance of being the social fun girl who loves excitement is also reinforced in advertisements and in horoscope sections that run throughout the magazines. For example:

> This month is all about your friends. You hang out with each other all the time, your family can barely catch a glimpse of you, giggle. It becomes mega-fun, it is not a quiet moment!
>
> *(Glitter, horoscope of the month for Virgo, p. 56)*

> Friends – summer holidays lazy days – you love every minute and it shows! The friends flock to you because you will always find fun things to do and be in great spirits.
>
> *(Julia, horoscope of the month for Aquarius, p. 64)*

However, as well as being a social and popular girl in a group and enjoying social activities and excitement, such as sleepovers, through both the attendance and organisation of events, there is also a clear message that a girl needs to also have and be a best friend. It is to the role of the 'BFF' that our analysis will now turn.

The BFF: Intimate sociality

In addition to being a popular girl, it is also necessary to be and have a 'best friend forever' or BFF. Having a BFF fulfils an important role of a friend, that of sharing intimacies and secrets and doing things together as a couple, demonstrating *intimate sociality*. In the narratives of BFFs, all the ideals of friendship as explored in the research overview are present, making it a particular 'ideal' or essential form of an ideal friendship. It is taking place at and is producing a safe exclusive room for oneself, which requires the investment of time and emotion. It is marked by homosociality (nonsexual attractions held by men or women for members of their own sex [Lipman-Blumen, 1976] and friendship support). While such intimacies can be shared within the larger friendship group through playing games at sleepovers such as 'truth or dare' (see for example *Total Girl*, June pp. 60–61), the bond between *best* friends is characterised as something special, which incorporates the fun sociality but is something beyond this that only two people can experience:

> We say… What makes a best mate? Someone who regularly makes you laugh so much you almost pee yourself, of course!
>
> *(Top of the Pops, p. 15)*

When the secret signal of major distress is displayed Coco drops everything to help her best friend. You should make sure you're always there for your friends when they need you.

(Girl Power, p. 45)

You and your BFF are hungry for a little mini-makeover! Is it a new interest, a new haircut or even redecorate the room that attracts? Sit down and forge plans together!

(Glitter, horoscope of the month for Gemini, p. 56)

Sometimes the close relationship between BFFs includes the creation of a shared world outside of the surrounding main world. Such a unique shared understanding sometimes includes more or less laughable or embarrassing situations that can be shared with a BFF. For example:

OMG how ... embarrassing! Began to guffaw. Not so long ago we had the English test. My best friend who is in another class went past outside our classrooms. She waved and I waved back a bit on the sly. But then she started making faces and I laughed myself to death! It was quite quiet in the classroom and my teacher asked me if I really thought that the examination was sooo fun. I was completely red in the face, and the whole class looked at me.

[A reader] (Glitter, p. 45)

With the most prized relationship held as a BFF who one can exchange confidences and share experiences with as a closely connected couple, there is an acknowledgement that some girls don't always find this easy. In order to address this, there is ample advice from the magazines concerning the achievement of this ideal. This is at the expense of providing an alternative representation of the different forms that friendships can take.

Such advice is evident across most of the magazines with various ways of providing friendship advice. For example *Top of the Pops* published a set of "essential friendship hacks!" or "rules" for the maintenance of good friendships and the enhancement of positive friendship feelings:

Rule 1. Be nice to each other
Taylor says...We just need to be good and kind to each other and not judge. It's so important to have friends that you trust. We have these big group texts where I'll just text them all about everything that's going on with my day.
We say... Never get involved in gossip-spreading or anything that makes someone else feel uninvolved or left out. Got issues? Talk them through with patience and kindness.

Rule 2. Cherish your oldest mates

Ellie says... I have friends who are famous and I have friends who are not famous, but those older connections are the particularly special ones for me.

Taylor says... Longevity is something very precious and rare in friendships.

We say... Don't ditch your bezzie cos you've found a new group of mates or assume you've nothing in common any more. Friendships do change but a shared history is pretty special.

Rule 3. Build new friendships

We say... Joining a club is a great way to meet new people. Smile and ask a question or pay a compliment. Something like, "I love your shoes, where are they from?" is an easy icebreaker.

Rule 4. Put mates before boys

Taylor says... There's no friction between me and the girls in our group. It's almost like a sisterhood has such a higher place on the list of priorities for us. And if we have the same taste in men – we don't hold that against each other.

We say... Would a boyfriend enjoy gossiping about Zoella's latest haul vlog? No. This is just one reason why girlfriends have an important role in your life – so don't dump 'em for a dude!

Rule 5. Be there for the highs...

We say... There's nothing sweeter than finding someone you totally 'get' (and who gets you). Chatting about crushes, putting the world to rights, or just cracking up together over internet raccoon videos – there's nowt better!

Rule 6. ... Be there for the lows

We say... it's not just about the LOLs. A true friend always offers a shoulder to cry on, judgment free. Now hug it out.

Rule 7. Laugh together – lots!

We say... What makes a best mate? Someone who regularly makes you laugh so much you almost pee yourself, of course!

(Top of the Pops, pp. 14–15)

Such advice is clear concerning what makes a 'good' friendship: exchanging information; maintaining old friendships due to shared history while still allowing space for new friendships; never choosing boyfriends over friends; and providing support through good times and bad.

Disruptions to 'good' friendships

While good friendships and the enjoyment of quality time spent with good friends is held as the ideal in all of the girls' magazines, there were several discussions evident that focused on disruptions to such ideals. The actual disruptions were considered along a dimension from gentle teasing to more serious challenges that involved being the focus of the group joke.

Along with minor friendship transgressions, we also see advice that centres on more serious disruptions. Such advice is often delivered via the problem page sections of the magazines, with key disruptions to friendships centring around boyfriends, sexuality, the management of friendship networks, and not 'doing' friendship correctly. These issues will be considered in the following sections.

The challenge of boyfriends

One of the main challenges to friendships was highlighted through the acquisition of a boyfriend, with particular complications surrounding mutual attraction to the same boy by BFFs. For example:

> OMG! Do you and your BFF fall in love with the same sweetie? Remember that your friendship is more important than a crush!
>
> *(Glitter, horoscope of the month for Cancer, p. 56)*

This dilemma is a common one portrayed in the magazines, and answers to such a dilemma typically focus on the special relationship between two friends, one that should always be prioritised over a boyfriend. However, further complications are also portrayed when the girl's BFF and new boyfriend do not get on and the girl is therefore required to manage the potentially challenging relationship between two close individuals. Such dynamics present difficulties in the maintenance of perceived loyalty between the friends. For example, the following issue was raised on a problem page in *Top of the Pops*:

> Bad BFF Behaviour
>
> Dear Gemma and Dr Radha,
>
> Every time my friends get boyfriends that I don't like, I keep my thoughts on them to myself. But when I get a boyfriend, they tell me straight away if they hate him and tell me to dump him! I feel like they just don't want me to be happy, but I'm not sure why.
>
> Rachel, email
>
> Gemma says: Sit your friends down and tell them exactly how their comments are upsetting you. It's worth explaining that, while you respect their opinions, you'd appreciate them giving any boy you like a chance before judging him. Suggest a double date. They're fun, less formal and your friends will be able to see how much your boyfriend means to you.
>
> *(Top of the Pops, p. 42)*

The advice, therefore, typically reinforces that friends are more important than boyfriends, and are therefore relationships that are worth working at to maintain.

The challenge of sexuality

In addition to being attracted to boys who are friends, as in the previous example, there is a further complexity for tween girls to manage, that of their own sexuality and their emerging identity as romantic sexual subjects. One of the common problem page letters focuses on issues of sexuality and the 'problem' of having a crush on your best friend. Very often the feelings are dismissed as 'immature' with the girl constructed as not really understanding her own feelings due to immaturity.

The challenge of 'doing friendship correctly'

Other expressions of disruptions to 'good' friendships are things not to do to friends; transgressing developmental tasks, such as emotional and social (gendered) development at a certain pace; not being supported by friends, for example, being drawn on while you are asleep (*Total Girl*, p. 18, p. 20); having friends who may over-do or possibly fake similarity, such as imitating the more popular girl too much (*Glitter*, p. 41); conflicts with friends who do not want to do the same thing; lack of disclosure; too little investment of time in friends; experiences of loneliness; and friends as bad role models. Having no friends at all is something the various problem pages also offer advice on.

Reflections

The meaning of popularity and untroubled girlhood needs to be understood as part of intra-gendered productions of hegemonic and subordinated femininities. Pyke and Johnson (2003) propose that hegemonic femininity is influenced by issues of race, class, sexuality and age in crafting a version of femininity that prioritises some ways of being a woman (or a girl) over others. Following Glenn (1999), Pyke and Johnson argue that in order to understand femininities that are positioned as marginalised, we must first understand the production of dominant or hegemonic femininities, such as ideal untroubled girls in the explored magazines.

Closely connected to the concept of hegemonic femininity are notions of homosociality. Homosociality, according to Lipman-Blumen (1976), promotes clear distinctions between women and men through segregation in social institutions, and the creation of expectations that serve to support the hegemonic ideals of men and women. Encouraged types of female homosociality and close female friendships are closely connected to notions of age and being a girl, drawing on important normative representations (Fox, 2002; Gunkel, 2010).

A girl typically considered to be popular among her peers is one who has the resources and skills to 'fit in' with her particular cultural context (Harris, 2004; Peirce, 1990). Drawing on Brown (2011), it can be argued that notions of popularity are intertwined with broader discourses about girls and girlhood. In the case of popularity within girls' friendships, there are different kinds of girl positions: the untroubled "friendly girl" (Xi et al., 2016) who is pretty and popular in a particular way and sociometrically considered well-liked, and the troubled "mean girl" (Xi et al., 2016; c.f. Ringrose, 2006) who may be pretty and popular in a different way that may draw on specific peer perceptions, commanding a specific kind of popularity and social status (c.f Eder, 1985; Xi et al., 2016). Thus, the notion of hegemonic femininity as produced in relation to a diverse range of other feminini-ties is useful when exploring what can be referred to as hegemonic young feminin-ity, stressing the meaning of being both 'pretty and popular' in particular ways as central markers of hegemonic young femininity.

The magazines portray quite explicit roles for young girls with respect to encour-aged versions of female sociality. Clear expectations are given concerning the nor-mative assumptions of the developmental tasks of becoming feminine and sociable in particular ways, reinforcing hegemonic femininities. The location for the devel-opment of such social skills is presented as within the group of same-sex friends, stressing the importance of female homosociality as part of hegemonic femininity, and within such a group, clear ideas concerning what are appropriate activities to engage in and the rank ordering of relationships are provided. For example, in line with a discourse of girl power (Griffin, 2004), friends should always outweigh the importance of boyfriends, and homosocial relationships are the prioritised form of 'doing relationships correctly'.

Such friendship ideals are also couched within understandings of the tasks of childhood, and of social and emotional development in particularly gendered ways. In several examples within the magazines, we see the importance of doing homo-social as well as heterosexual relationships 'correctly', with things at the right pace as set by both the group and dominant popular culture. The representations of ideal (untroubled) friendly girls as popular girls (as the centre of the group of friends) in the magazines also point towards the opposite: troubled girls, girls in the shadows who are not being mentioned and not being presented as a possible position for girls to adopt. While reproducing the ideal of being active, the passive and lonely girl, who does not take social initiatives, is not filled with energy, is not the centre of the circle of friends, does not demonstrate consideration for the well-being of friends, and does not have an intimate best friend, is produced as a troubled and possible socially and emotionally immature girl. In conclusion, we would argue that girls' magazines provide large-scale access to preferred socialities and young hegemonic femininity for tween and pre-tween girls. The broader social media may serve to further reinforce and prioritise particular ways of being a girl. Such dominant constructions of social female roles may therefore serve to prioritise par-ticular female roles over others, serving to marginalise those girls who cannot take up such prized positions.

References

Ahn, J. (2011). "You're my friend today, but not tomorrow": Learning to be friends among young US middle-class children. *American Ethnologist*, 38(2), 294–306.

Allen, J. P., Chango, J. & Szwedo, D. (2014). The adolescent relational dialectic and the peer roots of adult social functioning. *Child Development*, 85(1), 192–204.

Baiocco, R., Laghi, F., Schneider, B. H., Dalessio, M., Amichai-Hamburger, Y., Coplan, R. J., Koszycki, D. & Flament, M. (2011). Daily patterns of communication and contact between Italian early adolescents and their friends. *Cyberpsychology Behavior and Social Networking*, 14(7–8), 467–471.

Bank, B. J. (1994). Effects of national, school, and gender cultures on friendships among adolescents in Australia and the United States. *Youth & Society*, 25(4), 435–456.

Bauminger, N., Finzi-Dottan, R., Chason, S. & Har-Even, D. (2008). Intimacy in adolescent friendship: The roles of attachment, coherence, and self-disclosure. *Journal of Social and Personal Relationships*, 25(3), 409–428.

Blazek, M. (2011). Place, children's friendships, and the formation of gender identities in a Slovak urban neighbourhood. *Children's Geographies*, 9(3–4), 285–302.

Braun, V. & Clarke, V. (2006) Using thematic analysis in psychology. *Qualitative Research in Psychology*, 3(2), 77–101.

Brown, M. (2011). The sad, the mad and the bad: Co-existing discourses of girlhood. *Child and Youth Care Forum*, 40(2), 107–120.

Bunnell, T., Yea, S., Peake, L., Skelton, T. & Smith, M. (2012). Geographies of friendships. *Progress in Human Geography*, 36(4), 490–507.

Chan, A. & Poulin, F. (2007). Monthly changes in the composition of friendship networks in early adolescence. *Merrill-Palmer Quarterly-Journal of Developmental Psychology*, 53(4), 578–602.

Clark, L. & Tiggemann, M. (2006). Appearance culture in nine- to 12-year-old girls: Media and peer influences on body dissatisfaction. *Social Development*, 15(4), 628–643.

David-Barrett, T., Rotkirch, A., Carney, J., Izquierdo, I.B., Krems, J.A., Townley, D., McDaniell, E., Byrne-Smith, A. & Dunbar, R.I.M. (2015). Women favour dyadic relationships, but men prefer clubs: Cross-cultural evidence from social networking. *PLOS ONE*, 10(3).

Eder, D. (1985). The cycle of popularity: Interpersonal relations among female adolescents. *Sociology of Education*, 58(3), 154–165.

Fagan, M. (2006). Choirs and split voices: Female identity construction in Lorrie Moore's 'Who Will Run the Frog Hospital'? *College Literature*, 33(2), 52–69.

Fox, L. C. (2002). Geometries of nation-building: Triangulating female homosociality in Richardson's Wacousta. *Studies in Canadian Literature*, 27(2), 5–2.

Gaughan, M. (2006). The gender structure of adolescent peer influence on drinking. *Journal of Health and Social Behavior*, 47(1), 47–61.

Glenn, E. N. (1999). The social construction and institutionalization of gender and race. In M. Marx Ferree, J. Lorber & B. B. Hess, *Revisioning gender* (pp. 3–43). Thousand Oaks, CA: Sage.

Glick, G. C. & Rose, A. J. (2011). Prospective associations between friendship adjustment and social strategies: Friendship as a context for building social skills. *Developmental Psychology*, 47(4), 1117–1132.

Griffin, C. (2004). Good girls, bad girls: Anglocentrism and diversity in the constitution of contemporary girlhood. In Harris, A. (2004) (ed.), *All About the Girl – Culture, Power, and Identity* (pp.29–43). New York, London: Routledge.

Gunkel, H. (2010). 'I myself had a sweetie …': Re thinking female same sex intimacy beyond the institution of marriage and identity politics. *Social Dynamics: A Journal of African Studies*, 36(3), 531–546.

Harris, A. (2004). *All About the Girl – Culture, Power, and Identity*. New York and London: Routledge.

Jackson, S. (2005). 'I'm 15 and desperate for sex': 'Doing' and 'undoing' desire in letters to a teenage magazine. *Feminism & Psychology*, 15(3), 295–313.

Keener, E., Mehta, C. & Strough, J. (2013). Should educators and parents encourage other-gender interactions? Gender segregation and sexism. *Gender and Education*, 25(7), 818–833.

Kyratzis, A. (1999). Narrative identity: Preschoolers' self-construction through narrative in same-sex friendship group dramatic play. *Narrative Inquiry*, 9(2), 427–455.

Lam, C. B., McHale, S. M. & Crouter, A. C. (2014). Time with peers from middle childhood to late adolescence: Developmental course and adjustment correlates. *Child Development*, 85(4), 1677–1693.

Leppanen, J. M. & Hietanen, J. K. (2001). Emotion recognition and social adjustment in school-aged girls and boys. *Scandinavian Journal of Psychology*, 42(5), 429–435.

Leung, C. B. (2009). Collaborative narration in preadolescent girl talk: A Saturday luncheon conversation among three friends. *Journal of Pragmatics*, 41(7), 1341–1357.

Lipman-Blumen, J. (1976). Toward a homosocial theory of sex roles: An explanation of the sex segregation of social institutions. *Signs*, 1(3), 15–31.

MacDonald, F. (2014). Negotiations of identity and belonging: Beyond the ordinary obviousness of tween girls' everyday practices. *Girlhood Studies*, 7(2), 44–60.

Martz, L. (2014). Mary Neal and Emmeline Pethick: From mission to activism. *Women's History Review*, 23(4), 620–641.

Mehta, C. & Strough, J. (2010). Gender segregation and gender-typing in adolescence. *Sex Roles*, 63(3–4), 251–263.

Merten, D. E. (1999). Enculturation into secrecy among junior high school girls. *Journal of Contemporary Ethnography*, 28(2), 107–137.

Mestre, J. M., Guil, R., Lopes, P. N., Salovey, P. & Gil-Olarte, P. (2006). Emotional intelligence and social and academic adaptation to school. *Psicothema*, 18, 112–117.

Moller, K. J. & Allen, J. (2000). Connecting, resisting, and searching for safer places: Students respond to Mildred Taylor's The Friendship. *Journal of Literacy Research*, 32(2), 145–186.

Morris, K. & Fuller, M. (1999). Heterosexual relationships of young women in a rural environment. *British Journal of Sociology of Education*, 20(4), 531–543.

Mrug, S., Borch, C. & Cillessen, A. H. N. (2011). Other-sex friendships in late adolescence: Risky associations for substance use and sexual debut? *Journal of Youth and Adolescence*, 40(7), 875–888.

Oliva, A., Parra, A., Reina, M. C. (2014). Personal and contextual factors related to internalizing problems during adolescence. *Child & Youth Care Forum*, 43(4), 505–520.

Peirce, K. (1990). A feminist theoretical perspective on the socialization of teenage girls through Seventeen magazine. Sex Roles, 23(9/10), 491–500.

Pichler, P. (2005). Multifunctional teasing as a resource for identity construction in the talk of British Bangladeshi girls. *Journal of Sociolinguistics*, 10(2), 225–249.

Poulin, F. & Pedersen, S. (2007). Developmental changes in gender composition of friendship networks in adolescent girls and boys. *Developmental Psychology*, 43(6), 1484–1496.

Pyke, K. D. & Johnson, D. L. (2003). Asian American women and racialized femininities. "Doing" gender across cultural worlds. *Gender & Society*, 17(1), 33–53.

Ringrose, J. (2006). A new universal mean girl: Examining the discursive construction and social regulation of a new feminine pathology. *Feminism & Psychology*, 16(4), 405–424.

Rotenberg, K. J., Michalik, N., Eisenberg, N. & Betts, L. R. (2008). The relations among young children's peer-reported trustworthiness, inhibitory control, and preschool adjustment. *Early Childhood Research Quarterly*, 23(2), 288–298.

Rowsell, H. C., Ciarrochi, J., Heaven, P. C. L., Deane, F. P. (2014). The role of emotion identification skill in the formation of male and female friendships: A longitudinal study. *Journal of Adolescence*, 37(2), 103–111.

Salomon, A. & Strobel, M. G. (1997). Social network, interpersonal concerns and help-seeking in primary grade school children as a function of sex, performance and economic status. *European Journal of Psychology of Education*, 12(3), 331–347.

Thomas, J. J. (2012). Processes through which adolescents believe romantic relationships influence friendship quality. *The Journal of Psychology*, 146(6), 595–616.

van Den Berg, P., Paxton, S. J., Keery, H., Wall, M., Guo, J. & Neumark-Sztainer, D. (2007). Body dissatisfaction and body comparison with media images in males and females. *Body Image*, 4(3), 257–268.

Xi, J., Owens, L. & Feng, H. R. (2016). Friendly girls and mean girls: Social constructions of popularity among teenage girls in Shanghai. *Japanese Psychological Research*, 58(1), 42–53.

Zeijl, E., te Poel, Y., du Bois-Reymond, M., Ravesloot, J. & Meulman, J. J. (2000). The role of parents and peers in the leisure activities of young adolescents. *Journal of Leisure Research*, 32(3), 281–302.

Zucker, K. J., Wilson-Smith, D. N., Kurita, J. A. & Stern, A. (1995). Children's appraisals of sex-typed behavior in their peers. *Sex Roles*, 33(11–12), 703–725.

PART II
Locating development

5

'THE FAILED CHILD OF THE FAILING MOTHER'

Situating the development of child eating practices and the scrutiny of maternal foodwork

Maxine Woolhouse

Children's diets are argued to be central to their health and development (Birch, 1990), yet in 1990, Paul Rozin (1990) lamented the paucity of developmental psychological research into children's acquisition of dietary habits. However, recent years have witnessed an explosion of research investigating the development of children's eating patterns (and the like) coupled with maternal feeding practices, prompted by concerns around the putative 'child obesity epidemic'. Within this body of research and corresponding with the general trend in orthodox developmental psychology (Burman, 2008), it is mothers who are most subject to scrutiny, with their child's developing eating practices and body weight being held up as a barometer of the mother's competence; should the child be classed as 'overweight' and/or developing 'poor' dietary habits, she/he is deemed to have been failed by a failing mother and destined for a life of poor health. In contrast, wider systems and structures of inequality known to be pivotal in the formation of dietary habits (Charles & Kerr, 1998) are largely overlooked.

The key argument in this chapter is that the development of dietary practices, tastes, and so forth, *and* maternal feeding practices cannot be isolated from the specific social, cultural, economic and political conditions within which these practices take place. In particular, I argue for the necessity to take social class into account (see Day, Rickett & Woolhouse, 2014) along with other dimensions of difference, in attempting to make sense of the development of taste and eating-related practices. Moreover, failing to interrogate the structural and ideological contexts of eating and feeding practices not only produces yet another example of 'mother-blaming' (Jackson & Mannix, 2004), but also often stigmatises children who are positioned outside of the 'ideal' white, middle-class family norm. I begin this chapter with a brief discussion of some of the critiques offered by those such as Burman (1994, 2008) in relation to the framing of mothers as constituting the social world of the child in orthodox developmental research, and the implications this has for both children and mothers. I then move on to present a critical discussion of some of the developmental research on maternal feeding practices and children's eating habits, highlighting a number of problems with this body of work. Finally, I draw on a selection of critical and primarily discursive scholarship in this area to illustrate the locatedness of food and eating practices and how these cannot be adequately understood when viewed in isolation from economic circumstances *and* the classed, gendered and culture-specific meanings imbued within food practices.

In recent decades, orthodox developmental psychology has attracted a number of critics (e.g. Burman, 1994, 2008; Morss, 1996; Walkerdine, 1993), all of whom have brought to our attention a number of shortcomings in the fundamental assumptions underpinning the discipline. For purposes here, I focus on those pertaining to the way in which the individual and the social surroundings are theorised and conceived of, and more specifically, criticisms regarding the obfuscation of local and wider geopolitical and social spaces within which development takes place, in addition to dimensions of difference and the ways in which these contribute to the production of developmental psychological accounts that are partial, limited and unhelpful (Singer, 1993). By way of illustration, I focus specifically on developmental psychological literature concerning children's eating practices and maternal foodwork.

The positioning of mothers and children

A key argument presented by Burman (1994, 2008) is that in mainstream developmental psychology, the social world of the child commonly doesn't extend beyond 'the mother'. As such, this provides a narrow and impoverished understanding and produces individualistic accounts devoid of adequate consideration of the wider structures, processes and relations of power within which children and mothers (and mothering practices) are situated (Burman, 1994, 2008). A troubling consequence of this is 'mother blaming'; if mothers are conceived of as constituting the child's social world, then mothers are held accountable for virtually all aspects of their child's well-being (Burman, 1994, 2008; Jackson & Mannix, 2004; Kokkonen, 2009). However, not only is she held responsible for her child's 'outcomes', she is positioned as culpable for her own life circumstances, such as experiencing poverty, abandonment or abuse (Jackson, 2000), perhaps especially those circumstances deemed to have detrimental effects on the 'life chances' of her child/ren. Alongside this, children are implied as victims of their mothers and as facing a bleak future unless the mother can make the 'appropriate' changes. Such modes of understanding are politically convenient in that they reflect and bolster neoliberal rationalities, whereby individuals are expected to take responsibility for all aspects of their lives with minimal state intervention, and are thus held accountable for the consequences of the 'choices' they make (Crawford, 2006).

Whilst it can be argued that all mothers are interpellated within a discourse of mother-blame, as Jackson and Mannix (2004) remind us, it is *particular* mothers who will be subject to a more piercing judgemental gaze, and held up as more likely to be responsible for their children's 'shortcomings'. In the UK context at least, these include single mothers, black and minority ethnic mothers, lesbian mothers, working-class mothers (Phoenix & Woollett, 1991) and those in paid employment (Lewis, 1991). However, the particular meanings attached to and therefore judgements made of different groups of mothers and their children differ according to cultural and geopolitical locations. For example, the extent to which mothers of pre-school children are expected to return to work or not varies considerably across the globe (Charles & Cech, 2010).

The scrutiny of the development of children's eating habits and maternal feeding practices in a discursive climate of 'childhood obesity'

As Wright, Maher and Tanner (2015) note, it is mothers who are placed under most scrutiny and held responsible for shaping the eating practices of their children, and relatedly, as responsible for their current and future health. Furthermore, in academic literature, mass media and in the popular cultural imagination, maternal food practices are saturated with class-based rhetoric. For example, poor and working-class mothers are commonly assumed to be ignorant of practices that purportedly will 'protect against childhood obesity' (Wright et al., 2015), and are deemed as 'high-risk' families who make 'bad choices' (e.g. see Gross, Mendelsohn, Fierman, Hauser & Messito, 2014; Hernandez, Thompson, Cheng & Serwint, 2012). On the other hand, middle-class mothers are subject to accusations that they lack the time to provide a healthy environment due to, for example, maternal employment (Maher, Fraser & Wright, 2010). I argue then that this domain of research represents the crystallisation of a number of contemporary, potent and pervasive discourses around the 'epidemic of childhood obesity', mothering, social class, vulnerable children, and so forth, and therefore powerfully illustrates some of the limitations of mainstream developmental psychology and the detrimental effects these may have for those groups that are implicated in this body of research.

Surveying a selection of the developmental research in the area of child eating and maternal feeding practices brings to our attention a number of themes, which I argue to be problematic. First of all, it is notable how the 'social context' is primarily reduced to mother-child relations. Although most authors begin with references to "*parental* feeding practices" [my emphasis] and the like (Gregory, Paxton & Brozovic, 2010, p. 1), these are soon replaced with references to *mothers* (e.g. Gregory et al., 2010; Hays, Power & Olvera, 2001; Rodgers et al., 2013) implying that 'parent' and 'mother' are synonymous. For example, Rodgers et al., (2013, p. 2) state

> As feeding practices are potentially modifiable risk factors [in child obesity], understanding relationships between parent feeding practices and child weight and eating behaviors is of importance. However, to date, there has been a lack of clearly defined constructs describing maternal feeding practices.
> *(Rodgers et al., 2013, p. 2)*

This conflation of parents and mothers, notable in this extract, has a number of consequences. First, it is assumed that fathers play little role in the feeding of children or more generally in family-related foodwork. Whilst it may be the case that mothers continue to do the bulk of this work (Moisio, Arnould & Price, 2004), that isn't to say that fathers have no bearing on food practices (in households where mother and father cohabit). For example, Valentine (1999) argues that even when food is purchased and prepared by mothers, food choices are often based on the tastes and preferences of their partners and children.

Second, this exclusive focus on mothers means it is they who are held accountable for their perceived inadequacies and the supposed consequences these have on their child. For example, in a prospective study examining the relationship between maternal feeding practices and weight gain in young children, Rodgers et al. (2013, p. 7) state that their findings "support the importance of maternal feeding practices in relation to child weight gain and the development of obesogenic eating behaviors in young children. They provide evidence of the importance of considering maternal feeding practices in relation to obesity in childhood". The only other 'factors' involved in children's weight gain considered by the authors are "other maternal variables" (p. 9). In other words, it is almost exclusively mothers who are positioned as pivotal in producing 'childhood obesity' and consequently are the sole targets of intervention.

A third problem with the exclusive scrutiny of mothers and their feeding practices is that, with its intense individualism, it obfuscates the complex sociocultural, political and economic environments within which mothering takes place and functions as a convenient distraction from wider structural inequalities, discursive conditions, and the unequal relations of power within which women as mothers are positioned (Arendell, 2000). Furthermore, the complex and multiple ways in which mothers are interpellated into contradictory discourses around mothering, food, health, choice, risk, childhood obesity, and so forth, are disregarded. For example, Rodgers et al. (2013) reportedly found that maternal instrumental and emotional feeding, restricting foods and encouraging children to eat more are associated with child weight gain and eating behaviours that promote obesity. On the other hand, the maternal monitoring of high calorie foods aids in the development of healthy eating habits. However, what the authors fail to interrogate are the myriad of complex and contradictory cultural meanings invoked here. Regarded as an important expression of femininity (Fürst, 1997), feeding children may be a symbolic act of care and nurturance for mothers (Daniels, Glorieux, Minnen & van Tienoven, 2012) and constitutes them as 'good mothers' (Locke, 2015). However, in contrast, positioned as the gatekeeper to the child's diet (Gregory et al., 2010), and therefore the child's current and future health (Stang & Loth, 2011), mothers are expected to make the 'right' choices (Locke, 2015), negotiating the tensions, for example, between discretely monitoring food consumption without being coercive and controlling (Wright et al., 2015). Thus, failing to consider the perilous discursive terrain and structural conditions within which mothering and foodwork takes place results in a depleted account of the development of children's dietary patterns, weight, and so forth, and simply becomes yet another example of implicit mother-blaming.

Of further note is the way in which infants and children are presented in this literature. The child is largely reduced to a body mass index (BMI) score, a weight category (e.g. underweight, normal, overweight, obese) and a number of 'eating behaviours/characteristics' such as emotional eating, tendency to overeat, fussiness, and so forth (e.g. Gregory et al., 2010; Hernandez et al., 2012; Rodgers et al., 2013), with little or no attempt to situate children's eating practices and bodies within the immediate or wider sociocultural and political context. In addition, those children deemed to exhibit problematic eating behaviours and/or those cast as 'overweight' are positioned as 'at risk' of developing a host of life-threatening health problems in later life.

Food practices and social class

Food practices are inextricably linked with social class (Atkinson & Deeming, 2015), structured by the volume and forms of capital (e.g. cultural, social and economic) at our disposal (Bourdieu, 1984). In other words, our food practices are generally reflective of our financial resources, and expressive of identities, values, and aspirations – that is *if* we are sufficiently distanced from economic necessity (e.g. see Atkinson & Deeming, 2015). It might be expected then that psychological research on maternal feeding practices, the formation of children's dietary habits, and so forth, would engage in some form of sympathetic, class-based analysis when attempting to interpret findings. However, in the 'mainstream' literature this seems far from the case. It appears that social class is either indirectly referenced through the provision of some related demographic data (e.g. education/income/occupation) with little or no discussion around this data offered (e.g. Rodgers et al., 2013), or class (typically coded as 'low' or 'high' income) is treated as a key variable where attempts are made to link income with an array of maternal feeding practices and food-related attitudes (e.g. Gross et al., 2014; Hays et al., 2001). As an example of the first-case scenario, Rodgers et al. (2013) examined the relationship between a variety of different maternal feeding practices and child weight gain over a one-year period and the development of so-called child 'obesogenic' eating behaviours. The authors reported data regarding mothers' educational attainment and income levels and commented that "Mothers, on average were well-educated, and had a medium household income" (p. 3). (In fact, over 70 per cent of mothers were educated to university level and 75 per cent had a household income exceeding $60,000). However, of note is the absence of discussion around social class in attempting to make sense of the findings. It seems that this is a prime example of the normalisation and invisibility of middle-classness; it is only the working-classes who are marked out as classed, as if class has no bearing in the production of middle-class subjectivities and lifestyles (Day et al., 2014).

In contrast, there are many examples of studies that include samples of 'low-income' mothers whose children are deemed to be at 'high-risk' of child obesity;

these mothers also tend to be drawn from black and minority ethnic (BME) populations in the United States (e.g. see Gross et al., 2014; Hays et al., 2001). Such
studies are typically premised on the argument that children from low-income
(especially BME) families are more likely to become 'obese' and therefore the
feeding practices of mothers in such families need to be identified and (ultimately)
corrected. For example, Hughes et al. (2005) aimed to develop a measure to identify styles of feeding specifically in caregivers of low-income US minority children. Four patterns of feeding styles were identified – authoritarian, authoritative,
indulgent and uninvolved. The authoritarian style of feeding is related to high
levels of control (e.g. pressurising the child to eat, restricting food, etc. [Hughes
et al., 2005]) and low levels of responsiveness to the child, and was reportedly the
most common one found among caregivers in the study (over one-third of African
American and Hispanic parents). This style of feeding is said to be associated with
'problems' such as the child not recognising satiety cues when eating energy-dense
foods (Johnson & Birch, 1993, cited in Hughes et al., 2005). The authors argue that
gaining a better understanding of this feeding style and identifying specific feeding
behaviours as a target of change may be helpful. They also note that approximately
15 per cent of the sample exhibited "an authoritative feeding style" (Hughes et al.,
2005, p. 90) characterised by exercising "appropriate control" (p. 90) over the
feeding environment but relying on "child-centered techniques to do so" (p. 90).
This child-centred approach to feeding is held up by the authors as ideal, whereby
children may lean towards consuming healthy foods prompted by internal rather
than external (i.e. parental) control.

Remarkable here is the evaluative language and tone of approval used to describe
the practices of the so-called authoritative parents – they exercise "appropriate"
and "considerable control" over their child's eating, but "control" is qualified by
this being "child-centred" (Hughes et al., 2005, p. 90). As Burman argues (1994,
2008), in spite of developmental psychology's claims to be scientific (and therefore
objective and value-free), it slips into moral prescription and therefore serves to
regulate mothering practices. Child-centred parenting is very much set up as the
ideal (Arendell, 2000; Hays, 1996) and this extends to child feeding practices where
parents (i.e. mothers) are expected to feed on demand in response to the child's
'natural' appetite but, simultaneously, discretely exercise control over the types of
food made available in order to provide a 'healthy eating' environment (Locke,
2015). Drawing on Walkerdine and Lucey (1989), Phoenix and Woollett (1991)
note how mothers are expected to raise children to be self-regulating by exercising control, but not overtly, and cultivate self-regulation in children "...without
appearing to do so" (p. 18). However, as noted earlier, this model of good mothering is constructed around the white (Phoenix & Woollett, 1991), married (Arendell, 2000), middle-class mother (Singer, 1993; Walkerdine & Lucey, 1989) who
may have access to the various forms of necessary capital to engage in such idealised
mothering practices in ways which mothers who are differently located (for example, through class, income, 'race', sexuality, marital status, dis/ability, etc.) do not
(Arendell, 2000).

To summarise, a number of themes are discernible in the mainstream developmental psychological literature related to maternal feeding practices and children's diets (and/or body mass indices, etc.), which I argue to be problematic. First, infants and children featured in this body of research are reduced to categories of weights, measurements, BMI scores and sometimes a limited number of discrete 'eating behaviours'. Furthermore, those children deemed as falling into problematic categories (e.g. 'obese' or 'emotional eaters') are positioned as destined for a life of negative health outcomes. Second, it is striking how the social context is generally reduced to the mother and mother–child relations (Burman, 1994, 2008). In addition to assuming that it is only *mothers* who are involved in feeding children, this literature also obscures the wider sociopolitical, economic and discursive conditions within which maternal foodwork takes place. This, at least implicitly, leads to mother-blaming whereby mothers are held accountable for their perceived shortcomings in the child feeding arena and are therefore the main target of intervention (e.g. see Chan, Magarey & Daniels, 2011).

Third, social class is typically conceptualised as socio-economic status (SES) through the collection and reporting of data regarding maternal education, income and/or occupation (e.g. Gregory et al., 2010; Hernandez et al., 2012; Moroshko & Brennan, 2013; Rodgers et al., 2013). However, as Day et al. (2014) have argued, socio-economic status alone provides an over-simplified understanding of social class; whilst such information is a useful indicator of access to economic and social capital, it tells us nothing about how class is experienced and 'plays out' in our everyday lives (Day et al., 2014) and how, for example, we might be differently positioned according to class within and through a variety of discourses (e.g. see Wright et al., 2015).

Finally of note is that, in contrast to the bulk of research conducted in psychology more generally where social class has been neglected (Day et al., 2014; Ostrove & Cole, 2003), low-income mothers *are* commonly included in the sample on the premise that children of low-income mothers are deemed 'high-risk' in terms of 'developing obesity' (Gross et al., 2014). Thus, this area of research represents a prime example of what Woollett and Phoenix (1997, p. 278) refer to as a "normalised absence/pathological presence". Within this literature, low-income mothers' food-related practices (especially mothers of colour) are implicitly framed as inadequate and detrimental to the child's future health, and therefore in need of remedy. For example, Hernandez et al. (2012) suggest that focusing on improving parenting strategies to avoid food being used to manipulate child behaviour may be particularly beneficial for low-income parents "…where limited support systems may predispose them to placating their child with food" (p. 667). Whilst there is some (albeit limited) acknowledgement here of the circumstances within which foodwork is undertaken (i.e. "limited support systems" p. 667), the target of intervention remains at the level of individual parents (by improving their parenting skills) rather than calls for change at the wider structural level.

It can be argued then that mainstream developmental psychological literature in this domain reflects and reproduces neoliberal sentiments by pitching what is deemed to be a social problem (i.e. the development of 'unhealthy' eating patterns and 'child obesity') at the level of the individual. However, it is mothers and their children, particularly poor mothers and mothers of colour who are constructed as especially problematic, that have become the prime targets of change (Boero, 2007). Framed within scientific discourse, such work purports to be apolitical and value-free, yet its individualising effects and the pathologising of gender, ethnicity and class suggests this to be far from the case.

What this points to then is the need for an interrogation of the specific historical, cultural, material and discursive locatedness of the formation of children's eating practices and maternal foodwork. This includes a critical examination of the various meanings attached to food and eating practices according to the particular conditions under which these take place. As such, I now turn my attention to a review of a selection of critical and discursive work in this area which, I argue, attempts to locate development within particular socio-economic, political and cultural spaces and serves to address the limitations of the work reviewed above.

Situating child eating practices and maternal foodwork

Feeding and child eating practices and the meanings attached to these are shaped by the resources available to mothers (e.g. finance, time, social support, and so forth). However, as Wright et al. (2015) argue, contemporary neoliberal discourses are negotiated in various ways depending on how parents/mothers are socially located. In other words, discourses may 'speak to us' differently according to our particular class positionings and of course according to other dimensions of difference.

To illustrate, Wright et al. (2015) interviewed middle- and working-class mothers of pre-school children in Australia about their everyday food practices and understandings of obesity and health. They found that the mothers' differing social locations and access to resources shaped their feeding practices and how they articulated and experienced neoliberal discourses around maternal responsibility and child feeding. For example, although family meals were "...a minefield to be negotiated for most of the mothers" (p. 427), they were a particular source of anxiety for middle-class mothers who, through having the economic means to do so, attempted to accommodate individual child preferences along with considering nutritional needs, health, the household economy and values around mothering and "responsible citizenship" (p. 427). A key consideration was providing foods that were perceived as ensuring current and future health. In contrast, for the working-class mothers, meals were less about catering to individual tastes and more about offering what was available and had been prepared. That doesn't mean to say that they weren't aware of the middle-class emphasis on individual choice, just that it wasn't a value they shared, with them considering it to be "unfair" (p. 428) and more important for everyone to eat the same meal. For the working-class mothers, the meanings around foodwork also extended beyond concerns over nutrition and health; eating and cooking together was about strengthening and reinforcing family relationships, sometimes in the aftermath of relationship breakdowns.

In a similar study, Woolhouse (2012) interviewed working- and middle-class mothers and their teenage daughters (in the United Kingdom) about food, eating and body management practices. As with the Wright et al. study (2015), there were notable classed differences through the ways in which mothers and daughters positioned themselves within dominant discourses around food, health and (in the case of mothers) maternal foodwork. For example, many of the working-class mothers pointed to the multiple constraints they contended with when attempting to achieve what they recognised as 'the ideal' in terms of maternal foodwork:

Asha (Mother): it's difficult because like […] Paul [husband] will be on […] he […] he does alternate shifts […] like one week he'll be on 'earlies' un one week he'll be on 'lates' […] so there'll be every other week […] Marella's home at four, I finish at four so I'm home about ten past four […] so […] there'll just be me un Marella so we'll […] I'll cook […] un I'll have to cook for like […] an hour after I'm in […] un sometimes I'll just cook for Marella un then I'll eat later […] sometimes it can be really awkward actually 'cos I'll cook about three different things in one night […] erm […] un other times it's like […] you either eat it or you don't eat [laughs] that kind of thing 'cos otherwise it's just too much messing about […] erm […] un on those weeks sometimes we do end up with a lot of takeaways don't we? 'cos it's just a bit easier […] un we shouldn't but […] but we do […] un weekends we kind of

Marella (Daughter): well there's just like them little takeaway shops down t'road

Here, Asha points to the complexities of everyday life where family members are in and out of the house at different times of the day and night due to work or other commitments, and the ease of availability of takeaways (as indicated by Marella). The ideal of the whole family sitting down together for an evening meal cooked from scratch by the mother (e.g. Backett-Milburn, Wills, Gregory & Lawton, 2006), an ideal built around white, educated, middle-class values (Boero, 2007), is elusive in this account. Asha is fully aware of discourses around 'junk food and health risks' (etc.), notable when in reference to takeaways she says 'un we shouldn't', but she also points to a host of reasons why takeaways may sometimes be a practical solution in negotiating a complicated family life.

In a similar vein, one of the working-class single mothers in the study (also in full-time paid employment) highlighted how extensive time spent cooking (when time and money are precious resources) is often not worthwhile and, despite cultural assumptions to the contrary (Fürst, 1997), isn't an enjoyable activity for all mothers:

Diane (mother): yeah completely, I think if you've […] if you do a Sunday dinner un you've made a lot of effort un it's taking you forever un you've

	had this joint of beef in all day or whatever [...] un they [the kids] don't eat it [...] you do think 'why did I bother?' [...] I could have made beans on toast in five minutes
Diane:	then [...] I couldn't [...] I don't know [...] un I do think there's a culture now of [...] it all being about home-cooked stuff [...] you know [...] 'you be the next Jamie Oliver' or [...] 'have you tried this, this un this' [...] this [...] I don't know you feel I say to people 'I hate cooking' un I do hate cooking, I absolutely detest it [...] but [...] it's like saying 'I can't read' you know 'what do you mean you don't like cooking?'

Here, Diane points to the cultural expectation that not only will mothers devote significant time to 'cooking from scratch' for their children but also that they should gain pleasure and fulfilment through this. Moreover, Diane draws attention to maternal foodwork as a performance of social class wherein mothers who aren't inspired by 'celebrity chefs' and, what's more, declare a dislike of cooking, are positioned as lacking in cultural capital ("it's like saying 'I can't read'") and treated with suspicion and incredulity.

Constructions of the good/ideal mother, and therefore optimal child development, are infused with neoliberal sentiments around individual responsibility and choice, and class-based assumptions of the availability of resources (Kukla, 2006). This is particularly salient when it comes to advice around infant feeding. In the United Kingdom and elsewhere, breastfeeding has been vociferously promoted as the best type of feeding practice (Faircloth, 2010), whilst formula feeding is regarded as the 'risky choice' (Keenan & Stapleton, 2010) and mothers who 'choose' to bottle feed are framed as selfish and irresponsible (Murphy, 1999). Typically in breastfeeding promotional campaigns, the social and economic constraints to breastfeeding plus the multitude of historical and cultural meanings attached to it are overlooked. In a critical examination of the National Breastfeeding Awareness Campaign (launched in the United States in 2004), Wolf (2007) draws attention to the ways in which the 'breast is best/formula is risky' message is saturated with cultural and class-based assumptions about the resources available to mothers and the meanings they attach to breast or bottle feeding. For example, Wolf cites the work of Blum (1999) who found that working-class African American women didn't conceive of good mothering as an exclusive mother-baby relationship; rather, the raising of a child was deemed a shared responsibility among older siblings and other family members. As such, bottle-feeding was more conducive to this end. The importance of returning to work to support the family was also emphasised, something which, again, didn't allow for breastfeeding. Wolf (2007) points out that, in efforts to encourage black and working-class mothers to breastfeed, public health campaigns offer advice on and promote the practice of expressing milk whilst at work. However, as Wolf argues, this advice is based on assumptions that the nature of the work, the employer and the working environment will all allow for time out to use a breast pump which, for many women in low paid and insecure jobs, is simply not the case. Finally, Blum (1999, cited in Wolf, 2007) also found that for some of the African American women in her research, the legacy of slavery and the enforced wet nursing of white women's children, in addition to racist derogatory meanings attached to black women's bodies, meant that breastfeeding didn't signify what Kukla (2006, p. 161) argues is the image normally sold to us of "a joyous natural bonding experience".

In a further illustration of the role of class-based identities and socio-economic circumstances in the formation of food practices, Backett-Milburn et al. (2006, 2010) conducted interviews with working- and middle-class families living in Eastern Scotland about their eating practices in the context of their everyday lives and their understandings of health and healthy behaviours. In the study with working-class families, the sample comprised of household members predominantly responsible for family food provision (mostly mothers). All the families had at least one young teenager. A common theme in the talk of the participants was that they regarded "good eaters" (Backett-Milburn et al., 2006, p. 628) as teenagers who don't complain about the food prepared for them (as opposed to 'fussy eaters') and who would eat everything offered to them rather than defining a 'good eater' as someone who eats 'healthy' foods. Similarly, given the limited food budgets available to these families, there was greater concern about teenagers wasting food than there was about the exact nutritional content of the food consumed. Of particular note was that interviewees accepted the diminishing control they had over their teenagers' diets (due to their increasing independence) and simply saw this as part of their growing up; of much greater concern to the carers were other potential 'risks', such as smoking, alcohol, drugs, sex and "mixing with a bad crowd" (p. 629). Finally, it was also noted how the carers were far more worried about thinness (and teen preoccupation with thinness) than they were about fatness, often referring disparagingly to thin people as "stick insects" (p. 630). Similar sentiments were also observed in a study by Woolhouse, Day, Rickett and Milnes (2012) in which working-class teenage girls constructed preoccupations with thinness as associated with 'posh' girls, vanity and superficiality, something from which the participants were keen to distance themselves.

In much contrast, Backett-Milburn et al.'s (2010) study with middle-class families revealed little reference to economic constraints and the types of challenges faced from the immediate environment talked about by the working-class participants. Instead, surveillance of and influence over their teenagers' diets were prominent aspects of their talk; even those parents who didn't think their children's diets were nutritionally ideal subscribed to the idea that change was possible with appropriate parenting strategies. Portion sizes were controlled and comments were made if parents thought that their child was eating too much or too little. Parents also checked on what their children had eaten outside of the home. Much emphasis was placed on educating their children about healthy diets and cultivating their tastes towards more "adult" and "cosmopolitan" foods (p. 1320), something which the authors argued to be part of the production of their imagined future middle-class adult identities and lifestyles (Backett-Milburn et al., 2010). In short, the food practices of these middle-class families were not only afforded through their "distance from necessity" (Atkinson & Deeming, 2015, p. 890), but were also expressions and displays of middle-class identities and class aspirations, signalling 'who they were' and importantly, 'who they were not' (Backett-Milburn et al., 2010).

Concluding remarks

In this chapter I have aimed to draw attention to a number of shortcomings in 'mainstream' developmental psychology through an examination of a selection of literature in the area of developing child eating habits and maternal feeding practices. This, I argued, is a domain that represents the crystallisation of a number of these shortcomings, and therefore serves as a particularly illuminating example of the potential implications and negative consequences for the various groups of people who are interpellated into the discourses produced and reproduced in and through this body of work.

A snapshot of some of the critical literature in this domain, as reviewed above, brings to the fore how the development of children's dietary practices and maternal feeding is very much context-dependent, located in particular cultural, political and geographical spaces and tied to economic and material resources available. For example, as Kukla's (2006) research highlighted, the meanings attached to practices promoted as 'ideal' by health professionals, governments, and the like (e.g. breastfeeding), may differ considerably according to economic circumstances (e.g. mothers needing to return to work), cultural values (e.g. the importance of shared child-rearing), historical legacies (e.g. slavery and the enforced wet nursing of white women's children), and so forth. Similarly, Woolhouse et al.'s study (2012) highlighted the complexities of family life and the constraints placed on the consumption of regular healthy meals, particularly in socio-economic environments where convenience foods are readily available and accessible. For working-class families and those with limited economic means, as Backett-Milburn et al.'s (2006) research indicated, 'healthy eaters' may be (re)understood as children who eat what is provided for them, who don't waste food and aren't preoccupied with 'thinness', something which is associated with privilege (Woolhouse et al., 2012).

As such, the literature reviewed in this chapter points to the variety of contexts within which children develop, and specifically the sociocultural, political and economic environments within which eating practices are forged. However well-intentioned, mainstream research in this domain pays scant attention to the wider structural forces *and* particular localised meanings that shape and constrain feeding practices and the development of children's dietary habits; rather, such research is infused with neoliberal assumptions about individual choice and education (or lack of), and tends towards pathologising cultural values and practices that don't reflect those of the white middle-classes. In turn, this unwittingly results in some groups of children being positioned as having being failed and as condemned to a future of life-threatening health conditions through the failing practices and values of their mothers.

References

Arendell, T. (2000). Conceiving and investigating motherhood: The decade's scholarship. *Journal of Marriage and the Family*, 62, 1192–1207.

Atkinson, W. & Deeming, C. (2015). Class and cuisine in contemporary Britain: The social space, the space of food and their homology. *The Sociological Review*, 63, 876–896.

Backett-Milburn, K., Wills, W. J., Gregory, S. & Lawton, J. (2006). Making sense of eating, weight and risk in the early teenage years: Views and concerns of parents in poorer socio-economic circumstances. *Social Science & Medicine*, 63(3): 624–635.

Backett-Milburn, K., Wills, W. J., Roberts, M. & Lawton, J. (2010). Food, eating and taste: Parents' perspectives on the making of the middle class teenager. *Social Science and Medicine*, 71(7), 1316–1323.

Birch, L. (1990). Development of food acceptance patterns. *Developmental Psychology*, 26(40), 515–519.

Blum, L. M. (1999). *At the Breast: Ideologies of Breastfeeding and Motherhood in the Contemporary United States*. Boston: Beacon.

Boero, N. (2007). All the news that's fat to print: The American "obesity epidemic" and the media. *Qualitative Sociology*, 30, 41–60.

Bourdieu, P. (1984). *Distinction*. London: Routledge.

Burman, E. (1994). *Deconstructing Developmental Psychology*. London: Routledge.

Burman, E. (2008). *Deconstructing Developmental Psychology* (2nd Edition). Hove: Routledge.

Chan, L., Magarey, A. M. & Daniels, M. A. (2011). Maternal feeding practices and feeding behaviours of Australian children aged 12–36 months. *Maternal and Child Health Journal*, 15, 1363–1371.

Charles, M. & Cech, E. (2010). Beliefs about maternal employment. In J. Treas & S. Drobnič (Eds.), *Dividing the Domestic. Men, Women, & Household Work in Cross-national Perspective* (pp.147–174). California: Stanford University Press.

Charles, N. & Kerr, M. (1998). *Women, Food and Families*. Manchester: Manchester University Press.

Crawford, R. (2006). Health as a meaningful social practice. *Health. An Interdisciplinary Journal for the Social Study of Health, Illness and Medicine*, 10(4), 401–420.

Daniels, S., Glorieux, I., Minnen, J. & van Tienoven, T. P. (2012). More than preparing a meal? Concerning the meanings of home cooking. *Appetite*, 58, 1050–1056.

Day, K., Rickett, B. & Woolhouse, M. (2014). Class dismissed: Putting social class on the critical psychological agenda. *Social and Personality Psychology Compass*, 8(8), 397–407.

Faircloth, C.R. (2010). 'If they want to risk the health and well-being of their child, that's up to them': Long-term breastfeeding, risk and maternal identity. *Health, Risk & Society*, 12(4), 357–367.

Fürst, E. L. (1997). Cooking and femininity. *Women's Studies International Forum*, 20(3), 441–449.

Gregory, J. E., Paxton, S. J. & Brozovic, A. M. (2010). Maternal feeding practices, child eating behaviour and body mass index in preschool-aged children: A prospective analysis. *International Journal of Behavioral Nutrition and Physical Activity*, 7(55), 1–10.

Gross, R. S., Mendelsohn, A. L., Fierman, A. H., Hauser, N. R., & Messito, M. J. (2014). Maternal infant feeding behaviours and disparities in early child obesity. *Child Obesity*, 10(2), 145–152.

Hays, S. (1996). *The cultural contradictions of motherhood*. New Haven, CT: Yale University Press.

Hays, J., Power, T. G. & Olvera, N. (2001). Effects of maternal socialization strategies on children's nutrition knowledge and behaviour. *Applied Developmental Psychology*, 22, 421–437.

Hernandez, R. G., Thompson, D. A., Cheng, T. L. & Serwint, J. R. (2012). Early childhood obesity: How do low-income parents of pre-schoolers rank known risk factors? *Clinical Pediatrics*, 51(7), 663–670.

Hughes, S. O., Power, T. G., Orlet Fisher, J., Mueller, S. & Nicklas, T. A. (2005). Revisiting a neglected construct: Parenting styles in a child-feeding context. *Appetite*, 44, 83–92.

Jackson, D. (2000). Understanding women's health through Australian women's writings: A feminist exploration (Unpublished doctoral dissertation). Flinders University of South Australia, Adelaide, SA, Australia.

Jackson, D. & Mannix, J. (2004). Giving voice to the burden of blame: A feminist study of mothers' experiences of mother blaming. *International Journal of Nursing Practice*, 10(4), 150–158.

Johnson, S. & Birch, L. (1993). *Parenting style and regulation of food intake in children. Abstracts for the biennial meeting for the society for research in children development*. Chicago, IL: Chicago University Press.

Keenan, J. & Stapleton, H. (2010). Bonny babies? Motherhood and nurturing in the age of obesity. *Health, Risk & Society*, 12(4), 369–383.

Kokkonen, R. (2009). The fat child – A sign of 'bad' motherhood? An analysis of explanations for children's fatness on a Finnish website. *Journal of Community & Applied Social Psychology*, 19(5), 336–347.

Kukla, R. (2006). Ethics and ideology in breastfeeding advocacy campaigns. *Hypatia*, 21(1), 157–180.

Lewis, S. (1991). Motherhood and employment: The impact of social and organizational values. In A. Phoenix, A. Woollett, & E. Lloyd (Eds.), *Motherhood: Meanings, Practices and Ideologies* (pp. 195–215). London: Sage.

Locke, A. (2015). Agency, 'good motherhood' and 'a load of mush': Constructions of baby-led weaning in the press. *Women's Studies International Forum*, 53, 139–146.

Maher, J., Fraser, S. & Wright, J. (2010). Framing the mother: Childhood obesity, maternal responsibility and care. *Journal of Gender Studies*, 19(3), 233–247.

Moisio, R., Arnould, E. & Price, L. (2004). Between mothers and markets: Constructing family identity through homemade food. *Journal of Consumer Culture*, 4(3), 361–384.

Moroshko, I. & Brennan, L. (2013). Maternal controlling feeding behaviours and child eating in preschool-aged children. *Nutrition & Dietetics*, 70, 49–53.

Morss, J. R. (1996). *Growing Critical: Alternatives to Developmental Psychology*. London: Routledge.

Murphy, E. (1999). 'Breast is best': Infant feeding decisions and maternal deviance. *Sociology of Health & Illness*, 21(2), 187–208.

Ostrove, J. & Cole, E. (2003). Privileging class: Toward a critical psychology of social class in the context of education. *Journal of Social Issues*, 59(4), 677–692.

Phoenix, A. & Woollett, H. (1991). Motherhood: Social construction, politics and psychology. In A. Phoenix, A. Woollett & E. Lloyd (Eds.), *Motherhood: Meanings, Practices and Ideologies* (pp. 13–27). London: Sage.

Rodgers, R. F., Paxton, S. J., Massey, R., Campbell, K. J., Wertheim, E. R., Skouteris, H. & Gibbons, K. (2013). Maternal feeding practices predict weight gain and obesogenic eating behaviours in young children: A prospective study. *International Journal of Behavioral Nutrition and Physical Activity*, 10(24), 1–10.

Rozin, P. (1990). Development in the food domain. *Developmental Psychology*, 26(4), 555–562.

Singer, E. (1993). Shared care for children. *Theory & Psychology*, 3(4), 429–449.

Stang, J. & Loth, J. A. (2011). Parenting style and child feeding practices: Potential mitigating factors in the etiology of childhood obesity. *Journal of the American Dietetic Association*, 111(9), 1301–1305.

Valentine, G. (1999). Eating in: Home, consumption and identity. *Sociological Review*, 47(3), 492–531.

Walkerdine, V. (1993). Beyond developmentalism? *Theory & Psychology*, 3(4), 451–469.

Walkerdine, V. & Lucey, H. (1989). *Democracy in the Kitchen: Regulating Mothers and Socialising Daughters*. London: Virago.

Wolf, J. (2007). Is breast really best? Risk and total motherhood in the national breastfeeding campaign. *Journal of Health Politics, Policy and Law*, 32(4), 595–636.

Woolhouse, M. (2012). Mothers' and daughters' discursive constructions of food, eating and femininity (Unpublished doctoral thesis) Leeds Beckett University, Leeds, UK.

Woolhouse, M., Day, K., Rickett, B. & Milnes, K. (2012). 'Cos girls aren't supposed to eat like pigs are they?' Young women negotiating gendered discursive constructions of food and eating. *Journal of Health Psychology*, 17(1), 46–56.

Woollett, A. & Phoenix, A. (1997). Deconstructing developmental psychology accounts of mothering. *Feminism & Psychology*, 7(2), 275–282.

Wright, J., Maher, J. & Tanner, C. (2015). Social class, anxieties and mothers' foodwork. *Sociology of Health & Illness*, 37(3), 422–436.

6

FAMILY RELATIONSHIPS AND TROUBLED MASCULINITIES

The experience of young men in contact with social care services

Martin Robb, Brid Featherstone, Sandy Ruxton and Michael R.M. Ward

Introduction

The so-called 'problem' of boys has become a key focus of public and political anxiety, and of policy and practice interventions in the United Kingdom and elsewhere in the past few decades. Concerns have encompassed boys' apparent educational underachievement relative to that of girls, high rates of suicide and mental health problems, and offending and antisocial behaviour (Featherstone, Rivett & Scourfield, 2007; Roberts, 2014; Ruxton, 2009; Ward, 2015). Indeed, boys have increasingly been defined in media debate and public policy as 'at risk' and as a 'risk' to others (Syal, 2013).

The family relationships of boys and young men have been a major component of this concern about the state of young masculinity, with a common theme in the media and political rhetoric being the supposed absence of fathers from the lives of many boys and young men, and more generally the apparent lack of male role models in the lives of boys today, with particular concerns being expressed about the impact on boys from working-class and black and minority ethnic backgrounds (Cushman, 2008; Dennis & Erdos, 1992; Murray, 1990; Reach, 2007). Examples of this 'male role model' discourse have included interventions by politicians from across the political spectrum (Abbott, 2013; Lammy, 2011; Mahadevan, 2011;), and reports published by think tanks such as the Centre for Social Justice, which in 2013 claimed not only that more boys than ever were growing up without a father figure, but that whole communities were in danger of turning into 'men deserts' (Centre for Social Justice, 2013). This rhetoric has had practical implications resulting in initiatives under recent UK governments of all political colours to encourage fathers' involvement in family life, to organise mentoring schemes particularly for black and working-class boys and to recruit more men to work in services with children and young people (Dermott, 2012; Featherstone, 2009; Robb, 2010).

The 'male role model' discourse has become a kind of unchallenged common sense in debates about the needs of boys and young men. However, it can be argued

that this discourse relies on a simplistic understanding of young men's development, and on a social learning model that ignores the part played by a complex
web of influences in the development of young masculine identities, including a
range of family, peer and other relationships (Barton, 2016; Robb, 2007; Ruxton,
2015, forthcoming; Tarrant et al., 2015). Theorists such as Connell (1995) have
argued that individuals do not 'learn' their adult gender identity by internalising
social expectations. Rather, gender identity is made up of a complex set of practices and relations and is negotiated by active subjects in social encounters located
in specific social contexts, subject to dominant notions of how men and women
are supposed to be (Hicks, 2008). Moreover, it can be argued that the discourse is
in danger of overlooking the important role played by women, including mothers, other female relatives and female professionals, in the lives of many vulnerable
young men, as well as the complexities and ambiguities of boys' family relationships
more generally.

In this chapter, we draw on the findings of a study exploring gender identities
and practices in work with young men using social care services to present an
account of young men's family relationships that resists the reductive generalisa-
tions that, we would argue, characterise much current debate.

The study

Beyond Male Role Models: Gender Identities and Work with Young Men was a two-year
study undertaken by a team of researchers based at the Open University (UK) in
association with Action for Children, a charity providing services to children, young
people and families throughout the United Kingdom. The study was funded by the
Economic and Social Research Council (Grant No: ES/K005863). The research
involved interviewing service users aged 16 to 26 and practitioners working with
them at centres in London, the West of Scotland, the West of England and North
Wales. Services included projects working with ex-offenders, young people leaving
care, disabled young people and young carers. Fifty male service users, 14 female
service users, 12 male staff and 17 female staff participated in the study, which
included semi-structured interviews and focus group discussions (Robb et al., 2015).

Although the main focus of the research was on relationships between young
men and support workers, in the course of telling their stories and accounting for
their experience, young male service users revealed a good deal about their family relationships and the part they played in their development, in particular the
development of their gender identities. This chapter sets out to summarise what we
discovered, and to discuss the broader implications for an understanding of the lives
of vulnerable boys and young men.

Complexity and contradiction in young men's
family relationships

Our study found that, by contrast with the rather simplistic ways in which boys'
experiences and needs are described in the dominant policy discourse, the ways

in which young men in contact with social care services talked about their family relationships were marked by a deep ambivalence, and often by apparently contradictory experiences and attitudes. On the one hand, and to some extent echoing the dominant rhetoric, it seemed undeniable that 'family' had often been a contributory cause of the problems that many of the young men had faced. However, at the same time, young men often remained emotionally attached to their families and regarded them as a source of support and continuity in difficult times and through often traumatic experiences. Moreover, for some young men, the continuity of family ties, and in some cases starting new families of their own, formed an important part of how they envisaged their futures.

To a certain extent, the finding that young men saw their family relationships as a major source of their problems confirms the conventional stereotype of dysfunctional families and intergenerationally transmitted problems (Murray, 1990). Certainly, a key component of what we have termed the 'male role model' discourse has been a sense that the absence of stable family relationships is one of the key causes of the problems faced by many of today's boys and young men. However, the experiences and perspectives of the young men in our study were rather more complex, nuanced and ambivalent than these simplistic explanations sometimes suggest.

Perhaps unsurprisingly, many of our interviewees, both young male service users and those working with them, highlighted the detrimental impact of family breakdown and fractured family relationships on their lives. Support workers described the family lives of the young men they worked with as 'hectic' or 'chaotic', referring specifically to issues resulting from parents divorcing or separating, fathers being non-resident and mothers forming new partnerships, as Billy, a worker in Dorset, explained:

> Often young people we take, their lives are very hectic and there's no structure to it. Often from broken families [...] just with mum or whatever or just with dad and hasn't got one of the other parents around or whatever. Or maybe mum's remarried and the man she's married has got children himself and then the young person we are working with almost feels like pushed out of the way, all that kind of stuff, so that's quite common.

An example of young men feeling neglected or excluded in re-formed family structures, with very practical consequences, was given by Terry, a young male service user in Scotland:

Int: How did you end up homeless?
Terry: Well I don't get on with my step-dad.
[...]
Int: So did you have to sleep rough or – ?
Terry: Aye I had to for a week, last winter.

For some of the young men we interviewed, their own problems were exacerbated by the fact that one or both of their parents had themselves been in trouble, for example as a result of offending or addiction, and were thus either physically absent from home, or if present, then unable to adequately carry out their role as parents. More generally, there was a sense in our data of young men inheriting or reproducing problems experienced in preceding generations. Sometimes this intergenerational influence was inseparable from problems shared by the wider local community, locked into a repeating cycle of disadvantage. This seemed to be particularly true for the young men living in a deindustrialised region in the West of Scotland, as articulated by Roy, a support worker:

> I think the whole West of Scotland suffers from the drink culture, and I would say the drugs culture is more prevalent than it used to be, but there is certainly a lot of 'look after yourself'. I am one of three brothers and my dad had his dad die when he was nine, and his mum died when he was born, and he was the youngest of eleven kids, so at fifteen he ended up living in dosshouses, walking five miles to work and things like this.

Against this background, young men's families could often act as a catalyst or a route into trouble, rather than as a protection against it, particularly if other family members were already involved in risky behaviour. Adam, another young male service user in the West of Scotland, described how he became involved in the local gang culture:

Int: Oh, you were in a gang were you?

Adam: Aye, looked up to them, never had any big brothers or that, did have an older brother, but he was a junkie, yer know.

Int: So with the gangs stuff then, how did you get involved in it?

Adam: All my family was involved, brought up with it, my pals were in it.

Superficially, Adam's claim that he "looked up to" gang members echoes one of the key claims of the 'male role model' discourse: that the absence of male role models within the family leads to young men seeking substitutes in gang culture. However, in Adam's case, it should be noted that it was actually other (older, male) family members who were the catalyst for his own involvement.

At the same time, and as a cautionary note, it is worth making the point that young men themselves did not always see their own experience in such deterministic terms. Max, a support worker from the West of Scotland, who shared a similar background to the young men he worked with, was asked whether he had had a troubled upbringing:

> Well no, I have always had my mum and all the rest of it, but it's my choices in life, I went with the wrong group, it was nobody else choices by my own, I wasnee forced or anything, I wasnee forced into being in a gang, I wasnee forced into doing drugs and I got myself into jail.

In the light of these experiences of family troubles, it is perhaps surprising and somewhat paradoxical that many young men also emphasised the importance of family relationships in their lives. Family ties often continued to be regarded as a vital source of support, even when the actual experience of family life had been disrupted or traumatic, as expressed by these young male service users in the West of Scotland:

Ralph: All my family are my pals.
Burt: People who are gonna stick by ye, no matter what ye do.
Johnson: That's it man, I took my mam for granted, unbelievable.
Ralph: My wee brother and sister are like my bairns anyway.
Burt: That's still your family, still your blood.

This rhetorical emphasis on the overriding importance of blood ties has traditionally been a feature of working-class life (Blackshaw, 2003; Winslow, 2001). It can be understood, perhaps, in terms of regarding 'family' as a refuge from and a bulwark against the impermanence of other social relationships, or in Christopher Lasch's words – a haven in a heartless world (Lasch, 1995). However, the precise nature of young men's attachment to family members, and of the support offered by them, presents a complicated picture that resists easy stereotypes.

Attachment and ambivalence: Fathers, mothers and others

One of the areas in which we found young men's ambivalence about family ties particularly keenly expressed was in what they said about their relationships with their fathers. Young men frequently described their fathers as having been physically absent from their lives as they were growing up. The experience of Adam, a young service user from Scotland, was fairly typical:

Int: And where are you living at the moment? What's your kind of situation?
Adam: With my mam and sister.
Int: OK, so just your mam and your sister, so you're kind of the man of the house then?
Adam: (Laughs) I've always been the man of the house.
Int: Ah OK, so your dad's not about then?
Adam: Nah, he's never been about.

Even when fathers were physically present, relationships could be problematic and many young men expressed deeply conflicted feelings about their fathers. On the one hand, some communicated a sense of respect for their fathers, especially if they could be seen as doing the 'right thing', such as providing for their families. Eddie, another service user from the West of Scotland, put it in these terms:

Int: Are there any guys you look up to then? Or people I should say?
Eddie: Aye, me father.
[...]

Int: Why do you look up to him then?

Eddie: Just because he worked most days, he's got asbestosis now, because he used
to do pipe covering years ago, work every f---ing day of his life, until I
turned about sixteen or so, when he was f--ed, just got big respect for the
guy, put food on the table, aye, big respect for him man.

It is worth noting that this interview took place in the post-industrial West of
Scotland, where the young men we interviewed remained attached to quite conventional working-class masculine aspirations, despite the absence of traditional
jobs and the fact that their own family lives had hardly adhered to conventional
patterns. Eddie admired his father for his success in conforming to those traditionally masculine working-class aspirations. At the same time, there was very little
evidence, either in Scotland or in the other locations we visited, of young men
admiring their fathers for having a 'hands on' role in family life.

The respect that Eddie expressed for his father was shared by some other young
men, but that respect was often half-hearted and in many cases a complete lack of
filial respect was evident. However, paradoxically, young men often expressed a
sense of residual attachment to their fathers, suggesting a disappointed desire for a
closer relationship. There were echoes in this of earlier studies by Mac an Ghaill
(1994) and Frosh et al. (2002), both of which found a similar yearning by boys for
a greater emotional connection with their fathers. This ambivalent combination of
attachment and distance, of affection and dislike, was powerfully encapsulated by
Harry, a young man at a project for care leavers in Cornwall:

> I haven't chatted to him in, what is it, ten and a half years [...] And I will
> always love him, because he is my dad, but I don't have any physical, or any
> face-to-face contact with him, because you know, I don't respect him and
> don't like him and just love him based on the fact that he is my dad.

However, despite any residual ties of affection that may have existed between
young men and their fathers, what came across very clearly was a determination not
to follow their fathers' examples or repeat their mistakes. There is an echo here of
what one of us found when interviewing a very different group of men – 'involved'
middle-class fathers – who articulated a similar sense of ambivalence, combining
a grudging respect for their own fathers with a definite aspiration to be a different
kind of father and a different kind of man (Robb, 2004).

Our sense that the 'male role model' discourse tends to overlook the positive
contribution made by women to boys' development was reinforced by the ways
in which many young men in our study described their relationships with their
mothers and other female relatives. Many of the young men spoke about having
strong female influences in their lives. If fathers were frequently described as not
present or as unreliable, then mothers were often spoken of as providing a more
reliable and consistent source of support, and many of the young men lived with
their mothers rather than their fathers. Like Adam, who was quoted earlier as saying

that his father had never been around and that he had always lived with his "mam and sister", Frankie, another Scottish service user, contrasted his feelings towards his mother and father:

> I've stayed with my mam all my life no, me mam's brand new, yer know [...] she's like sound, yer know, easy going, ah but I do stay with my dad now man, pain in the arse, but not much you can do, you know what I mean?

In some cases, the relationship of care and support between mother and son was mutual and reciprocal, as in this example from the West of Scotland:

Int: And where do you live Davey? [...] By yourself or - ?
Davey: With me mam.
Int: Ok, and how's that? [...]
Davey: It's all right aye, she's kinda not well, so I kinda look after her as well.

It is important not to overemphasise this closeness, since some young men reported quite difficult relationships with their mothers, and in other cases mothers were themselves not around or were preoccupied with their own problems. Moreover, it could be argued that, in some cases, young men spoke more about their relationships with their mothers than their fathers simply because their mothers were physically present in the home, while fathers were, for whatever reason, not living with the family. Nevertheless, a picture emerges of many young men valuing the consistency and stability of care and support offered by their mothers, and of mothers providing them with a model of adult care that, as a consequence, they also looked for and valued in their support workers. Once again, there are echoes here of the finding by Frosh et al. that mothers tended to be "more sensitive and emotionally closer to [boys] than their fathers who were seen to be more jokey, but also more distant and detached" (Frosh et al., 2002).

Grandmothers also played an important role in the lives of some young men, particularly when neither parent was living with them, or if there were other problems at home. 'Nans' and 'grans' seemed able to offer an alternative form of support, at a useful emotional distance from the more intense and often conflicted relationships with fathers and mothers. Here is Robert, a worker and former service user in Scotland, talking about his relationship with his grandmother:

Int: Oh, you live with your gran do you?
Robert: Aye. [...] I'm really close to her. I was at my girlfriends there for a bit but me papa died last week [...] so we've been looking after the funeral, so I've been back at my gran's [...] I've always stayed with my gran [...] since an early age. [...] I was always back and forward to my mum's but she's always had my brothers there [...] and me nephew and things like that so it was always crowded [...] so I was always to my gran's.

Tom, an older male worker from the West of Scotland, who, like Max and Robert, came from the same kind of background as many young service users, described the part played by his grandmother in supporting him through his own troubled childhood:

Int: Oh OK, you were in care then?

Tom: Aye, brought up in care, lived with my gran, my parents were drug and alcohol dependent, my gran then took me off my parents […] I was a only like a baby, couple of months old […] Yeah I lived with my gran up until I was 13, then my gran died […] So I went with my gran first, and then my mum and dad had my other brothers and then they got took into care and me and my gran fought for them and we got them out of care and to stay with us.

We can conclude from this that, in the context of fathers' absence or of difficult relationships with fathers, mothers and other female relatives often provide a more consistent form of care and support for young men 'at risk'. The 'male role model' discourse, echoing conventional developmental theory, seems to assume that the support offered to boys by women, and particularly that provided by lone mothers, is somehow inadequate and that a vital influence is lacking if a father or father figure is not present in a young man's life. Women are frequently left to provide stability and consistency when a father is physically absent from a child's life, but often end up being blamed for problems caused by that absence (Daniel & Taylor, 2006). However, our findings echo those of other studies that have highlighted the positive role of mothers and grandmothers in the lives of boys and young men (Reay, 2002; Reeves, 2008b). 'Male role model' explanations assume that only men can 'model' the qualities that boys need to ensure their transition to a positive adult masculine identity, despite research showing that positive father and mother involvement includes common factors (O'Brien, 2005). But what if the only men in a boy's life are absent, or if they are physically present but emotionally distant and modelling an inconsistent, unreliable or even aggressive masculinity, while the main models of consistency and care in a young man's life are female?

Young fatherhood and the transition to responsible adult masculinity

One area in which researchers have demonstrated that female relatives have an important role to play in young men's lives is in the transition to young fatherhood. Jane Reeves' research with disadvantaged young fathers highlighted the key role of grandmothers in encouraging young men to stay with their partners and take responsibility for their children, while Gavin Swann concluded that the mothers of girlfriends are the primary gatekeepers determining whether a young father will be able to play an active role in his child's life (Reeves, 2008a; Swann, 2015). A number of the young men that we interviewed for this study were themselves fathers and it appeared that, perhaps contradicting easy stereotypes, many took their new responsibilities seriously. Eddie and Adam, service users in the West of Scotland, spoke about their experience as young fathers:

Int: And are you in a relationship at the moment?
Eddie: Aye, got a wee bairn as well [...] a three year old, yeah three in March.
...
Int: Now have you got any plans for the future, say, where you want to be?
Adam: Just get a f----ng decent job, I got a wee child to provide for [...] She'll be in two in January.

Of course, it is important not to generalise too widely from these experiences. Even within our own study, there were examples of young men who were not in contact with children they had fathered. In a focus group with young fathers at a project in South London, one young man said "I've got one, he's two…I don't get to see him", while another participant said "I've got a daughter and she's about two months now…I don't get to see her that much". However, for other young men, caring for their children was obviously an important and transformative experience. For some, becoming a father was not their first experience of caring for children, and they spoke about taking on quasi-paternal roles within their families, particularly when one or both parents were living elsewhere. As Ralph, a young service user in the West of Scotland, put it: "My wee brother and sister are like my bairns anyway". This kind of sibling care is more usually associated with older sisters rather than older brothers (there is a memorable example of this in British politician Alan Johnson's powerful memoir of working-class childhood: Johnson, 2014), so there is a challenge here to the stereotype of gender roles within families, as well as a sense that boys as well as girls might learn the caring skills needed for parenthood at an early age (see also Robb, 2001).

The evidence of our study appears to contradict dominant discourses surrounding young fatherhood which, intersecting with problematising discourses about young masculinity, tend to focus on the failures of young men to take responsibility for children they have fathered. Although it is important not to confuse young men's rhetoric with their actual performance as fathers (for a more complete picture, it would be important to interview the mothers of their children), our conclusion was that many young men in contact with services took their responsibilities as fathers seriously and saw fatherhood as an opportunity to move away from a problematic past and exchange it for a more responsible adult masculine identity. To some extent, our findings echoed those of other studies that have demonstrated the positive role of young fatherhood in enabling young men to desist from 'risky' behaviour (Reeves, 2008b; Speak, Cameron & Gilroy, 1997).

At the same time, however, many young men reported difficulties in negotiating a route from the risky young masculine identities that had created problems for them in the past towards a new identity as a reliable parent and provider for their child. A number of the young fathers that we interviewed described the problems they experienced in juggling disparate masculine identities and conflicting sets of relationships. One of the key findings of our study was that many young men, particularly those from poor or disadvantaged communities, remain embedded in local cultures of hypermasculinity, characterised generally by violence, excessive alcohol consumption and aggressive sexuality, but with significant differences depending on geography and local context (Robb et al., 2015; Ward, 2014, 2015). This finding tends to contradict both the widespread notion that contemporary young masculinities have become somehow 'softer' and also the assumption that young gender identities are now universal rather than local, being shaped largely by a globalised media culture (Anderson, 2009; Blanchard, McCormack & Peterson, 2015).

Extracting oneself from this kind of hypermasculine culture, even when motivated by the powerful emotions unleashed by the experience of fatherhood, remained a difficult and ongoing process for the young men we interviewed, and there was a pervasive sense of the fragility of newly espoused identities. An understanding of young identities as plural, fluid and negotiated, as opposed to a simplistic, straight-line notion of adolescent development, can help us to understand the experiences that these young men described (Robb, 2007). Here, it is also important to highlight the crucial role played by care and support services in providing a 'third space' away from both the intensity of family relationships and the hypermasculine atmosphere of the street, where young men from troubled backgrounds could negotiate the transition to different and more positive and productive adult masculine identities.

In a focus group at a project in the West of Scotland, Burt and Johnson talked about the difficulties in negotiating their new identities as young fathers:

Burt: Obviously I got bairns and that, so I've had to grow up […] For me now my life's about getting a job, family, basically, in a nutshell it is family, that is like, very, very important […] I'm trying to be a respectful person, I don't wanna walk down the street, and seeing all that stuff, because when I am walking down the street with my wee boy, if I've been doing that at the weekend, rolling about with people, then I am walking down the street and I might bump into these people you know.

Johnson: And they might not even care you got yer bairns with yer.

Burt: Exactly! You've got their risks, you've also got, I can be walking down the street on a Friday night, and singing songs and I'll get 'Who you looking at, yer dafty', you know what I mean, and that image, other mums and dads maybe walking down the street who are out for a wee quiet drink at the weekend and then they see me walking down the street day with my wee boy, what they gonna think? They're gonna think, that's the boy I seen yesterday kicking stuff about and smashing things, fighting with people, and he's walking down the street with a bairn, what kind of dad's he gonna be?

There is a real sense in Burt's narrative of the challenge of managing different aspects of his identity, including different kinds of masculinity in different contexts, and of how easily his new identity as a young father could be threatened and overwhelmed by the former identity associated with a local culture of hypermasculine behaviour. To understand what Burt is describing, we need a notion of adolescent development, particularly of the development of gender identity as something that is continually negotiated and renegotiated in social and relational contexts (Connell, 1995; Robb, 2007).

In other words, while the experience of young fatherhood can certainly open up the possibility of alternative and more positive masculine identities for young men from troubled backgrounds, the process of achieving that new identity is by no means easy or straightforward. It involves a continuing struggle between often competing identities and sets of relationships, and can often only be successfully achieved with the support and scaffolding of care and support services.

At the same time, the investment in young fatherhood evident in our interviews with young men reflected the continuing importance of family ties, attachments and relationships in their lives. Despite the fact that many of these young men had themselves experienced fractured family relationships, in particular troubled relationships with their own parents, they still saw fatherhood, and forming a family of their own, as an important part of their future and as a route to a responsible adult masculinity. In other words, despite the disrupted and perhaps atypical nature of their transitions to adulthood, by comparison with the majority of the population, these young men often wanted the same things that other boys and young men aspire to, including stable and loving family relationships.

Conclusion

Our research demonstrates that family relationships play an important but at the same time complex and often contradictory role in the lives of young men in contact with social care services. As such, our findings challenge the reductive simplicities of the 'male role model' discourse and the developmental theories that underpin it. On the one hand, troubled or disrupted family relationships have often been a key factor in the problems that young men have faced growing up. However, despite this, family ties remain as a vital source of emotional attachment and support for many. The relationships that vulnerable or 'at risk' young men have with their fathers are often deeply ambivalent, while in many cases mothers and grandmothers play a vital stabilising role in young men's lives. The experience of becoming a father can itself be a catalyst for helping young men to leave behind a troubled past, but the difficulties of negotiating a path away from local cultures of hypermasculinity, and the continuing need for social care services to provide support for that process, should not be underestimated.

References

Abbott, D. (2013). 'Britain's crisis of masculinity', Demos Twentieth Birthday. Lecture available at http://www.demos.co.uk/files/DianeAbbottspeech16May2013.pdf (accessed 24 April 2016).

Anderson, E. (2009). *Inclusive Masculinity: The Changing Nature of Masculinities*. Abingdon: Routledge.

Barton, J. (2016). 'Why consistent carers are more important than male role models for boys', *Huffington Post*. 16.02.16. Available at www.huffingtonpost.co.uk/2016/02/16/consistent-carers-more-important-than-male-role-models-for-boys_n_9156800.html.

Blackshaw, T. (2003). *Leisure Life, Myth, Masculinity and Modernity*. London: Routledge.

Blanchard, C., McCormack, M. & Peterson, P. (2015). Inclusive masculinities in a working-class sixth form in Northeast England', *Journal of Contemporary Ethnography*, Advance online publication.

Centre for Social Justice (2013). *Fractured Families: Why Stability Matters*. London.

Connell, R. W. (1995). *Masculinities*. Cambridge: The Polity Press.

Cushman, P. (2008). So what exactly do you want? What principals mean when they say "male role model", *Gender and Education*, 20(2), 123–136.

Daniel, B. & Taylor, J. (2006). Gender and child neglect: Theory, research and policy', *Critical Social Policy*, 26(2), 426–439.

Dennis, N. & Erdos, G. (1992). *Families without Fatherhood*. London: IEA Health and Welfare Unit.

Dermott, E. (2012). "Troops to teachers": Solving the problem of working-class masculinity in the classroom? *Critical Social Policy*, 32(2), 223–241.

Featherstone, B. (2009). *Contemporary Fathering: Theory, Policy and Practice*. Bristol: The Policy Press.

Featherstone, B., Rivett, M. & Scourfield, J. (2007). *Working with Men in Health and Social Care*. London: Sage.

Frosh, S., Phoenix, A. & Pattman, R. (2002). *Young Masculinities*. Basingstoke: Palgrave.

Hicks, S. (2008). Gender role models....who needs 'em'? *Qualitative Social Work*, 7(1), 43–59.

Johnson, A. (2014). *This Boy: A Memoir of a Childhood*. London: Corgi.

Lammy, D. (2011). *Out of the Ashes: Britain after the Riots*. London: Guardian Books.

Lasch, C. (1995). *Haven in a Heartless World: The Family Besieged*. New York: Norton.

Mac an Ghaill, M. (1994). *The Making of Men: Masculinities, Sexualities and Schooling*. Buckingham: Open University Press.

Mahadevan, J. (2011). Riots blamed on absent fathers and poor school discipline, *Children & Young People Now*. Available at: www.cypnow.co.uk/cyp/news/1049472/riots-blamed-absent-fathers-poor-school-discipline (accessed 28 April 2016).

Murray, C. (1990). *The Emerging British Underclass*. London: IEA.

O'Brien, M. (2005). *Shared Caring: Bringing Fathers into the Frame*. Norwich: East Anglia.

Reach (2007). *An Independent Report to Government on Raising the Aspirations and Attainment of Black Boys and Young Black Men*. London: The Stationery Office.

Reay, D. (2002). Shaun's story: Troubling discourses of white working-class masculinities, *Gender and Education*, 14(3), 221–234.

Reeves, J. (Ed.) (2008a). *Inter-Professional Approaches to Young Fathers*. Keswick: M&K Update Ltd.

Reeves, J. (2008b). Recklessness, rescue and responsibility: Fatherhood as a factor of desistance amongst young men in the criminal justice system. In J. Reeves (Ed.), *Inter-professional Approaches to Young Fathers* (pp. 215–219). Keswick: M&K Update Ltd.

Robb, M. (2001). Men working in childcare. In P. Foley, J. Roche & S. Tucker (Eds.), *Children in Society: Contemporary Theory, Policy and Practice* (pp. 230–238). Basingstoke: Palgrave/The Open University.

Robb, M. (2004). Exploring fatherhood: Masculinity and intersubjectivity in the research process, *Journal of Social Work Practice*, 18(3), 395–406.

Robb, M. (2007). Gender. In M. J. Kehily, *Understanding Youth: Perspectives, Identities and Practices*. London: Sage/The Open University.

Robb, M. (2010). Men wanted? Gender and the children's workforce. In M. Robb & R. Thomson (Eds.), *Critical Practice with Children and Young People* (pp.185–199). Bristol: Policy Press/The Open University.

Robb, M., Featherstone, B., Ruxton, A. & Ward, M. (2015). *Beyond Male Role Models: Gender Identities and Work with Young Men: Report*. Milton Keynes: The Open University.

Roberts, S. (Ed.) (2014). *Debating Modern Masculinities, Change, Continuity Crisis?* Basingstoke: Palgrave MacMillan.

Ruxton, S. (2009). *Men, Masculinities and Equality in Public Policy*. London: Coalition on Men and Boys.

Ruxton, S. (2015). Do boys need male role models?, *Huffington Post*. 30.10.15. Available at www.huffingtonpost.co.uk/sandy-ruxton/male-role-models_b_8416328.html.

Ruxton, S. (forthcoming). Beyond male role models: Gender identities and work with young men in the UK. In Kulkarni, M. (Ed.) *An Exploration of Global Masculinities*. London: Routledge.

Speak, S., Cameron, S. & Gilroy, R. (1997). *Young Single Fathers: Participation in Fatherhood – Bridges and Barriers*. London: Family Policy Studies Centre.

Swann, G. (2015). *Breaking down Barriers: Developing an Approach to Include Fathers in Children's Social Care*, Professional doctorate thesis, University of East London.

Syal, R. (2013). 'British male identity crisis spurring machismo and heartlessness', *The Guardian* [Online]. 14.05.13. Available at http://www.theguardian.com/politics/2013/may/14/male-identity-crisis-machismo-abbott (accessed 28 April 2016).

Tarrant, A., Terry, G., Ward, M. R. M., Ruxton, S., Robb, M. & Featherstone, B. (2015). Are male role models really the solution? Interrogating the "war on boys" through the lens of the "male role model" discourse, *Boyhood Studies*, 8(1), 60–83.

Ward, M. R. M. (2014). "You get a reputation if you're from the valleys": The stigmatization of place in young working-class men's lives. In T. Thurnell and M. Casey, *Men, Masculinities, Travel and Tourism* (pp. 89–104). Basingstoke: Palgrave MacMillan.

Ward, M. R. M. (2015). *From Labouring to Learning: Working-Class Masculinities, Education and De-Industrialization*. Basingstoke: Palgrave Macmillan.

Winlow, S. (2001). *Badfellas: Crime, Tradition and New Masculinities*, Oxford: Berg.

7

BEYOND VULNERABILITY

Working with children who have experienced domestic violence

Jane Callaghan, Joanne Alexander and Lisa Fellin

This chapter explores children's experiences of domestic violence. Academic research in this area tends to focus on children as damaged by domestic violence, with an extensive consideration of the negative impact on children's mental health, social, interpersonal and educational outcomes. This literature establishes children living with domestic violence as a vulnerable group, in need of significant intervention and support. This construct of vulnerability extends into professional talk about children's lives, with mental health, social work and domestic violence support professionals describing children as vulnerable, damaged and needy – often inevitably so. In contrast, we argue that framing children as 'vulnerable' functions to undermine an understanding of their located capacity for agency, and can render children voiceless in specific contexts. Gatekeeping practices intended to protect vulnerable children have an unintended consequence of preventing them from articulating their own experience. We present examples that challenge the positioning of children who experience domestic violence as vulnerable and damaged, and that highlight young people's capacity to articulate their experiences of violence, its impact, their coping practices and their capacity for agency. In doing so, we challenge the notion of a single developmental trajectory for the construction of healthy or adaptive identities (Burman, 2016; James & Prout, 2015). This notion constructs a sense of normal childhood reliant on a well-functioning, nuclear family and a stable family home in which to grow and develop. Such a construction implicitly 'others' children who experience domestic violence, and this sense of them as having different and problematic childhoods entrenches the idea that they are passive witnesses, damaged by their experiences. In contrast, we argue that children who experience domestic violence find ways of managing their familial experiences using a range of paradoxical resiliencies. Such resiliencies contribute to the maintenance of a sense of agency for children, constituted within the constraints and enabling elements of family life, home and other material spaces. Children's experiences of violence do not occur in a social vacuum, nor do the resources they develop to cope with that violence: both are located within the lived realities and social constructions of childhood, family life and the spaces and places they inhabit.

Passive and silent: The academic and professional construction of children's experiences

The negative psychological, social and educational outcomes of children's experiences of domestic violence are now well-documented in social science research. Children who experience domestic violence are at greater risk of a range of mental health difficulties (Meltzer, Doos, Vostanis, Ford & Goodman, 2009) and poorer health outcomes (Hornor, 2005). There is an association between 'exposure' to domestic violence and other forms of child abuse (Finkelhor, Turner, Ormrod & Hamby, 2009), including an elevated risk of being murdered by the perpetrating parent (Devaney, 2008; Jaffe, Crooks & Wolfe, 2003). Children who experience domestic violence are also more likely to experience a range of educational difficulties (Byrne & Taylor, 2007), and are more likely to be involved in bullying, both as victim and aggressor (Baldry, 2003). It has been suggested that some of these challenges are a result of neurological changes as a consequence of early exposure to violence (Peckins, Dockray, Eckenrode, Heaton & Susman, 2012; Saltzman, Holden, & Holahan, 2005).

Whilst the negative impact of domestic violence on children is indisputable, we suggest that the over-focus in psychological literature on the damage done produces an individualising and pathologising account that renders children as passive witnesses, and argue that this is ultimately unhelpful to their recovery (Callaghan & Alexander, 2015). They are described as 'witnesses' who are 'exposed' to domestic violence, and damaged by that exposure – language that extends dominant ideas of children as passive recipients of adult behaviour (parenting, teaching, etc.) (James and Prout, 2015). The language used to describe children who live with domestic violence strips away a sense of them as meaning-making beings (Callaghan, Alexander, Mavrou, Fellin, & Sixsmith, 2016) who have a capacity to experience what is happening in their families and to find ways to respond to and resist the coercive interactions that characterise those experiences (Callaghan, Alexander, Sixsmith & Fellin, 2016b; Katz, 2015). In addition, much of the research on the mental health and well-being of children who experience violence has been conducted using quantitative measures, often with adult informants, with the effect that children's voices are often omitted from such research entirely (Callaghan, 2015; Eriksson & Näsman, 2012; Eriksson, 2012; Øverlien, 2009). As a consequence, this research renders children as passive in two ways – both through the way they are described, as damaged objects, collateral damage in adult violent interactions, and through the denial of their capacity to articulate and reflect on their own experiences.

Research that focuses on children's actions and strategies for coping has tended to focus on a traditional approach to resilience as an individual 'coping despite adversity' (see, for example, Gewirtz & Edleson, 2007; Howell, 2011; Martinez-Torteya, Anne Bogat, von Eye & Levendosky, 2009). Children's coping is still framed in this approach as relatively passive. The factors that are seen as 'making' children resilient include temperament (Martinez-Torteya et al., 2009), positive and supportive educational contexts and supportive friends and/or parents (Kassis, Artz & Moldenhauer, 2013; Kassis, Artz, Scambor, C., Scambor, E., & Moldenhauer, 2013), the chronicity of the violence (Martinez-Torteya et al., 2009), the child's relationship with peers and their social skills (Gewirtz & Edleson, 2007) and the child's emotional self-control (Gewirtz & Edleson, 2007; Kassis, Artz, Scambor, et al., 2013). However, mental health literature focuses very strongly on the coping, parenting practice (Gewirtz & Edleson, 2007; Gewirtz, Forgatch & Wieling, 2008; Kassis, Artz & Moldenhauer, 2013) and mental health of mothers (Levendosky, Leahy, Bogat, Davidson & von Eye, 2006; Martinez-Torteya et al., 2009; Whitaker, Orzol & Kahn, 2006) in determining children's resilience. Children's well-being and mental health, therefore, is ultimately understood as being dependent on good mothering (Bancroft & Silverman, 2002; Lapierre, 2008) in a literature that overwhelmingly assumes that women are the victims and men the perpetrators of domestic violence. This produces a mother-blaming discourse that locates victimised women as responsible for children's mental health, and removes the focus away from male violence and its implications for women and children (Callaghan, 2015) as well as from other contextual, social, service and policy issues (Callaghan, Fellin & Warner-Gale, 2016). These different contextual levels are obscured by these victim-blaming and individualising discourses, which reiterate developmental psychology's preoccupation with the facilitating role of the mother (Hays, 1996; Shirani, Henwood & Coltart, 2011). They also reproduce a model of parenting commonplace in developmental psychology that positions children as passive recipients of parenting practice (Burman, 2016), neglecting the relational and intersubjective nature of children's experiences of parenting and of coping (Callaghan, Alexander, & Fellin, 2016; Cooper & Vetere, 2008; Katz, 2015; Swanston, Bowyer & Vetere, 2014). In contrast, we argue that children's coping and resilience is relational, contextual and locally produced, and that children are agentic in the way they manage, live with and recover from domestic violence.

Throughout this chapter, we draw on the small but significant body of qualitative literature on domestic violence, which focuses increasingly on the importance of understanding children's direct accounts of their experiences (Bowyer, Swanston & Vetere, 2013; Mullender et al., 2003) and on recognising and supporting children's capacity for agency (Callaghan et al., 2016b; Eriksson & Näsman, 2012; Katz & Windecker-Nelson, 2006; Øverlien, 2014). We anchor our argument in examples from published papers and reports from Understanding Agency and Resilience Strategies (UNARS), a European Commission funded project set in Italy, Greece, Spain and the United Kingdom. This two-year project involved individual interviews with 107 children and young people (aged 8–18) about their experiences of living with domestic violence, focus groups with carers and professionals, and a policy analysis. Using the insights gained from these methods, we developed a therapeutic group-based intervention for young people focused on building on their existing coping skills, and a training programme for professionals who work with families affected by domestic violence. The examples we use in this chapter are drawn from published work based on our interviews with children and young people.

Talking about it: Children's ability to articulate and reflect on their experiences

Reading academic research and policy documents in the twenty-first century, one might be forgiven for imagining that the problem of children's representation and voice in research and service development and delivery has been resolved. Slogans like 'no decision about me without me' and the emphasis, for instance, in research funding applications on meaningful participation by children in all aspects of research, suggests that empowered and vocal children are engaged in all these processes. These developments have resulted in a growing recognition of children's capacity to reflect on their experience, and their right to be heard (Einarsdottir, Dockett & Perry, 2009; Skelton, 2008). However, research and practice in violence work in particular still privilege adult voices (Callaghan, Alexander, Mavrou, et al., 2016; McGee, 2000; Øverlien, 2009).

One of the things that really surprised us as we developed our work with children was the extent of the gatekeeping we experienced, in all four European countries. We had expected adults to be cautious about children's involvement, but the challenges we had in recruitment extended beyond that to the significant blocking of children's participation. McGee (2000) suggests that some of this reluctance arises from the illusion that children 'do not know' about the violence, and need to be sheltered from that knowledge, whilst Lombard (2015) found that professionals expressed reluctance to 'open a can of worms' – a reluctance to ask children about the violence in case it led to the disclosure of emotional and other difficulties that support services are poorly equipped to manage and contain. Both these viewpoints rest on a presumption of 'innocent childhood' (Burman, 2016), idealising children as vulnerable, helpless and in need of protection, discourses that were reiterated in our focus group interviews with professionals who worked in the domestic violence sphere (Callaghan & Alexander, 2015). This denied children the right to be heard about their experiences, as they were deemed 'too vulnerable' to participate, effectively reinforcing a view of their passivity, lack of agency and lack of emotional competence (Alexander, Callaghan, Fellin & Sixsmith, 2016; Callaghan, Alexander, Sixsmith, et al., 2016a). This is illustrated very clearly in our analysis of children's practices of disclosure about domestic violence (Callaghan, Alexander, Mavrou, et al., 2016). Many of the children we interviewed reported that they had made a conscious choice not to tell others about the violence they were experiencing, because they had experiences of not being taken seriously, or of their accounts being disbelieved or dismissed. They suggested that they were 'only children' and unlikely to be heard. This is poignantly described by Elda (17, Italy):

Elda: I felt helpless, passive and fragile
Int: What made you feel that way?

Elda: My age
Int: Why?
Elda: It is a constraint. No one listens to you if you're a little girl.

In this extract, it is clear that Elda's helplessness is not 'personal'; she is not suggesting that she is a passive, fragile or helpless person. Rather, she suggests that her sense of passivity was constituted in her interactions with adults – that her age and her positioning as a 'little girl' functionally silenced her, making her unable to help herself. Elda's vulnerability, helplessness and passivity is accomplished relationally (Callaghan, Alexander, Mavrou, et al., 2016). It is clear that it is not (just) the violence in her family that disempowers her; rather, it is the failure of adults to hear her account – this failure to hear silences disempowers children, increasing their sense of isolation and their challenges with trust (Buckley, Holt, & Whelan, 2007).

In a context where coercion and violence often already silences children, our professional failure to allow children to speak, and to listen when they do, teaches children that their experiences and accounts are not valued (Vetere & Cooper, 2005). This can place children at risk, as, for example, their views of violent encounters are not sought, and their disquiet about post-separation contact is not heard (Morrison, 2015). Further, in a culture where a therapeutic discourse of personal development predominates, and children's wellness is seen as being dependent on their willingness to 'talk about' and 'talk through' their experiences (Callaghan, Fellin & Warner-Gale, 2016; Burman, 2016), silencing this group of children positions them even more strongly as pathologised and deviant, and prevents their articulation of the complex ways in which they are able to cope and retain a sense of agency. Despite these constraining adult discourses, we found that the children we interviewed were extremely articulate, and able to tell us their stories in phenomenologically dense, complex and detailed ways. They were also not unduly distressed by the interviews, and were able to reflect on their experiences of coping with violence and those of other people, as well as to critically comment on contextual, policy and service issues. They were able to explain very difficult experiences to the interviewers, and to make use of vivid images, metaphors and even humour. Most children also appeared to find the interviews supportive and even enjoyable, and generally appreciated the opportunity to speak openly – often for the first time - about their experiences, and reported that it was an empowering experience. In common with Evang & Øverlien (2014), we also found that the children were very active in the interviews, making clear decisions about what to say and how, and taking control of the interviews in various ways (e.g. one young boy took the recording device away from the interviewer, and held it up to his mouth to ensure that points that were particularly important to him were heard).

Hearing children's stories requires that we listen to more than just their words. Extra-normative experiences – experiences that sit outside the range of taken-for-granted experiences of childhood – are often not easy to put into words, and are recounted in "constrained articulations" (Callaghan, Gambo & Fellin, 2015). To hear children's accounts of such experiences requires that we listen not just to what they say, but how they say it, how they embody their stories, how they act, and what they will not say (Callaghan et al., 2015). It is important to recognise the limitations of voice, and that we can only say that which it is contextually possible to articulate (Unterhalter, 2012); it is difficult to talk about experiences that are culturally extra-normative and for which there is not an easily available language. In addition, such experiences are often inarticulable as 'family secrets', which children often feel they are not allowed to discuss. For example, in the next extract, Rachel (11, UK) talks about having to step in and tell her parents to stop fighting because they were upsetting her little brother (Callaghan, Alexander, Sixsmith, et al., 2016b). When asked how she felt, she says:

> [erm] I felt that, […] I don't really know a word to describe it really [umm] for them, for me to have to tell them to stop and them not stopping themselves, it was quite like, [….] I don't really know a word to say it [erm] […]

She lacks access to a language to express the experience of having to intervene to ask a parent to behave like a parent. The experience she is communicating here is not merely the content of 'I had to tell them to stop', but also the lived experience of the contextual demand that she care for her brother in a context where her parents were failing to do so. In her hesitations and the breakdown of her speech, she communicates more about that experience than her words do. The experience is communicated as constrained articulation in the silences, the style of speech, and the way she held her body as she spoke, and not so much in the speech itself.

Embodying agency and resistance

When considering how victims cope with violence and how they maintain a sense of self in the wake of coercive control and physical attacks, psychological research has tended to focus its attention on emotions, cognitive styles, social skills and social support, and thus has fragmented victims' (coherent) lived experiences into separate components (e.g. cognition, emotion, personality) (Galbusera & Fellin, 2014). In focusing separately on the intrapsychic and interpersonal factors, such research has largely neglected the experience of violence as something that is embodied and that occurs in material space (Callaghan & Clark, 2007). Violence and control are physical and material experiences, and it therefore makes sense that our resistance to such control and violence might also take place in embodied ways. Our heteronormative, patriarchal and ableist assumptions about family life tend to presume that women and children are both emotionally weaker and less physically competent, and we overlook or underestimate how they might use their bodies and the spaces of home and the outdoors in agentic ways that are protective and resistant.

In our interviews with children, 'home' was an important but fraught space for children. Home is culturally constituted as a place of safety in the Western imagination (Mallett, 2004) and as the 'right' place in which to raise children (Dorrer, McIntosh, Punch & Emond, 2010). However, homes are often more complex and ambiguous spaces for individuals, particularly when characterised by conflict, emotional upheaval or violence (Graesch, 2004; Harden, 2000; Wilson, Houmøller & Bernays, 2012). Home is not always a space in which children feel a sense of 'belonging', but can be an ambiguous space that creates "belonging and/or ... a sense of marginalisation and estrangement" (Mallett, 2004, p. 84). This was certainly the experience of home that the children we interviewed described: on the one hand, they talked about home as dangerous, threatening and unpredictable; on the other hand, it was a space (or there were spaces within the home) that they felt they could reclaim, and in which they could re-constitute a sense of control and agency (Alexander et al., 2016). This is illustrated in the next extract from an article we wrote (Callaghan et al., 2016a) on children's embodied experiences of domestic violence, where we argue that through children's sense of themselves as corporeal agents, their experience of the home is constituted as both a space of oppression and of resistance. This relates to the grounded and embodied nature of their being in the world, with familial and relational experiences of self constituted in embodied language, not in the abstract and decontextualised text: body and language are intertwined and inseparable (Merleau-Ponty, 1964).

Emma (16):   Yeah, it was like you had a high rise bed, had like a desk and a wardrobe ... That kind of thing, so you'd have like a little gap behind there, used to have a little light down there [laughs].

Int: So you literally hid in there?

Emma: Yeah, [pointing to her drawing of a map of house] so like where my room is in here, the bed would be against this wall and I'll have a chest of drawers there and I used to hide behind this little, there, where my bed used to have a gap behind... and sometimes he'd come in my room and start shouting at me but he wouldn't know where I am [laughs].

If we only focused on the elements of coercion, control and fear when reading this extract, we might overlook the way that Emma uses the material spaces of home to resist the perpetrator's controlling and oppressive behaviours. She has found a way to 'escape' within the physical spaces and materials of the home, inverting the sense of the home as a dangerous space by creating within it homely spaces of safety. This use of dens and hiding places was described to us by many of the children we spoke to, in all four European countries. Children described ways that they made their dens safe and homely by populating them with objects they associated with friends and loved ones, or with comfort. Emma's story illustrates how she used the small, constrained space to stabilise the unsafety of the home. These small, safe spaces were often in children's rooms or in outside rooms (e.g. sheds) – spaces that they defined as their own, and where the perpetrator did not often go. Emma has restored some (very limited) sense of control over one space in the home, undoing in the smallest way what Wardhaugh (1999) has described as the experience of being 'homeless at home'. Even though she is frightened and hiding, she nonetheless finds in this experience some expression of agency and resistance. She sees herself as 'fooling' the perpetrator, as successfully evading him ("he wouldn't know where I am"). This sense of her 'gesture of defiance' (Hebdige, 1979, p. 4) is expressed in her laugh, as she describes how he does not know where she is. Trawick (2007), talking about children living through the 1997–98 armed conflict in Sri Lanka, noted that children described the worst parts of their experiences not as the exposure to violence, but as the loss of control over their use of space and their loss of autonomous movement. Restoring some sense of mastery over the home space, however small that might be, is a powerful resistance to the loss of control children experience when violence and coercive control occurs (Callaghan, Alexander & Fellin, 2016).

Untangling children's sense of their own agency and capacity for resistance from the dominant representation of them as passive witnesses to violence, or as helpless victims, requires that we attend carefully to their experiences and sense-making, and that we understand how they make use of space and place. Attending only to their cognitive or affective processes, or measuring their capacity for 'resilience' through standardised questionnaires, will not enable us to access or understand their located and contextual experiences of agency and resistance. Children's use of space and place is important in understanding their experience of the world (Holloway & Valentine, 2000), and in making sense of how they grow and change over time. For some young people, 'home' isn't a straightforwardly positive space, rather it is a space they make and remake, and for others, 'home' does not match adult definitions of what home is. For instance, some of the young people we spoke to who had transitioned from refuge into 'settled housing' felt nostalgic about the refuge space, which they saw as 'home'. The people they bonded with in refuge were experienced as 'family', because of the sense of connection, protection and community they built together within the refuge environment. Children do not live their emotional lives intrapsychically, rather their emotional experiences are materio-psychosocial. Their resistances to domestic violence and coercive control exist not just in their inner worlds, or in their relationships with others, but also in their embodied, spatial and material worlds. This has powerful implications for those who wish to intervene and support children during and after domestic violence, but these implications are often under-theorised in social and mental health work with children and families (Callaghan, Fellin & Alexander, 2016). It also has important implications for our understanding of childhood more generally, challenging ideas that children are passive recipients of adult behaviour (care, or abuse).

Emotional and relational responses to violence

Literature on children's mental health and psychological development when they experience domestic violence has documented extensively the negative psychological effect of domestic violence on children. One of the mechanisms through which this damage is presumed to occur is through the impact of domestic violence on children's emotional development. Located within a 'deficit model'

(Mullender et al., 2003), this research tends to presume that children who experience domestic violence will have difficulties with emotional recognition and regulation, and sets out to test this hypothesis in a range of ways. For instance, after administering a picture stimulus story-telling task with two groups of children (one group that had experienced domestic violence, and another that had not), Logan and Graham-Bermann (1999) found that, whilst all children expressed more negative emotion than positive, and all children were more likely to identify and express non-affiliative than affiliative emotion, children from families where domestic violence had occurred were less likely to express affiliative emotions. They concluded that children who have experienced domestic violence may have an inhibited ability to express emotions in a relational context. Similarly, in a study of children who had experienced 'inter-adult violence', Maughan and Cicchetti (2002) found significantly more children from families affected by domestic violence had dysregulated emotion patterns (Katz, Hessler, & Annest, 2007). Does children's emotional competence mediate the relationship between domestic violence exposure and later social and behavioural adjustment? Katz et al. (2007) found that children from homes with higher rates of domestic violence were less emotionally aware and had higher rates of emotional dysregulation, and that these emotional difficulties mediated the relationship between domestic violence 'exposure' and internalising problems as well as social difficulties. Based on these kinds of findings, researchers have concluded that children who experience domestic violence are more likely to be 'emotionally incompetent' (Katz et al., 2007).

What unites these studies is the acontextual approach taken to understanding and measuring children's emotions as individual and isolated processes. In the Logan and Graham-Bermann study, the researchers coded emotional content in the stories simply as 'positive' or 'negative', 'affiliative' or 'non-affiliative'. This strips out the meaning of the emotions described, and the context in which they are located, reducing them to abstract and isolated categories produced by the researchers. Using a story task and assuming that it is a realistic measure of children's real-worlds is a further factor when considering the validity of this approach. Maughan and Cicchetti staged angry, neutral and conciliatory interactions between a researcher and the child's mother, in an experimental setting. Given that the children in the study had observed significant violence at home, the ethics of this experiment is surely questionable, and it seems likely that watching a stranger argue with their mother would understandably be more distressing for children who have experienced domestic violence. Placing the child in an unfamiliar context and subjecting them to such a stressor surely makes their struggle in controlling and regulating their emotion reasonable and understandable. The artificiality of the situation also presumably made the interaction puzzling for the observing child, who presumably could see no cues for the hostile interaction witnessed. In the Katz et al. study, children's emotions were measured using the child and adolescent meta-emotion interview, a 20–40 minute structured interview in which they were asked 16 questions about anger, and then the same 16 questions about sadness. Questions included items such as: "'What does it look like when you are angry? Is there anything you do to get over feeling angry? Can you give me a recent example of a time when you were angry? In that incident, what happened, who did and said what, how did you get over your anger?"' (Katz et al., 2007, p. 570). Asking children such abstract questions assumes that emotions can be reasonably isolated from their social, material and relational context, and are appropriately understood in such a disembodied, intellectual way. None of these approaches take seriously the located nature of children's meaning-making, or the contextual-relational experience of emotions (Ugazio, 2013). Abstracting emotion from the context in which emotions are felt and lived simply cannot be a valid measure. Emotions are central and dynamic elements of people's experiences, a way of feeling and knowing that is constituted in context and interaction. Such knowledge and feeling is always grounded in a world of contextual meaning and practice (Polanyi and Van Den Berg, 1996).

In contrast to this reading of children as 'emotionally incompetent', our research has explored the complex, nuanced and highly located emotional work that children do when they experience domestic violence. Emotions are understood in our work as embodied, relational and contextually located (Callaghan, Fellin, Alexander, Mavrou & Papathassiou, 2017). Children are acutely attuned to their relational context, constantly scanning adult reactions and working to 'read' their emotions to respond in a way that will keep them and others safe. As Swanston et al. (2014) suggest, children are like "miniature radar devices" as they are always engaged in an attempt to predict the unpredictable. Consider, for instance, this extract (Callaghan et al., 2016a):

> Lucy (13) I'd always hesitate of what I would say…even if I said "Hello," I'd always think before like, is he just going to shut me out? Is he going to respond in a nice way, or be angry or anything like that? I'd always think ahead of what I was saying.

Whilst Lucy may not be labelling emotions, she does describe herself as acutely attuned to the emotions of those around her. She is engaged in constant monitoring and reflection, adapting her own emotional responses to the perceived mood of the perpetrator. Consider the complexity of the emotional and social world that children who experience domestic violence inhabit. After all, familial relationships where there is violence are not just characterised by violence, but by a range of difficult and complicated interactions, allegiances and secrets. If we look once again at Rachel's quote, we begin to see the challenges of attempting to capture children's rich emotional experiences in language:

Rachel: [erm] I felt that, […] I don't really know a word to describe it really [umm] for them, for me to have to tell them to stop and them not stopping themselves, it was quite like, […] I don't really know a word to say it [erm] […]

Rachel is aware that there is no language available in everyday English to describe this experience. Indeed in any language, it is difficult to conceptualise how a child might communicate this. Rachel is able to narrate the experience through a kind of "constrained articulation" (Callaghan et al., 2015). Her emotions are expressed not in what she can say, but rather what she cannot say – they are contained in the silence, and in the breakdown in articulation. As she says so eloquently "I do not know a word to say it". How could such emotional experiences be conveyed in a fixed response questionnaire, or in an abstract set of responses to a structured interview about a particular labelled emotion? The emotional worlds of children who experience violence are extra-normative, and not easily accessible to everyday language and labelling. This does not mean that they are emotionally incompetent – rather, they show evidence of great awareness of their own and others' emotions, very detailed and complex emotional labour, consideration for others, and management of their own emotional reactions (Callaghan, Fellin, Alexander, Mavrou & Papathanassiou, 2016).

Developmental and psychological literature on emotions therefore suggests that children who experience domestic violence lack the ability to regulate their emotions. This is because mainstream developmental theory depends on notions of competence, rooted in assumptions of age-linked maturation that occurs within the child in interactions with more competent adults. In contrast, the children we spoke to were able to self-soothe (Callaghan, Fellin, Alexander, Mavrou & Papathanassiou, 2016). This was often achieved through their use of material space and objects – they would hide themselves in small, quiet spaces, where they could feel safe and could calm themselves down. They would use outdoors spaces – sheds and trees – as places to reflect. Paul (9) describes how, when he's upset, he goes outside:

> there's like this slide. And I go to that. And sometimes I like to climb on it, and go to the top. And there's like a tree. And I go and sit there for a while.
>
> *(Paul, 9)*

This is a highly competent but very located strategy for managing emotional distress. In taking himself out of the situation he is stressed by, he is giving himself the space and time to reflect. In taking up a high space, he is creating both a sense of safety (being out of the way of conflict) and a meditative or reflexive space. He puts a little distance between himself and the world while he calms himself down.

These extracts illustrate that children have complex emotional coping strategies that enable them to maintain a sense of agency, to manage their emotional responses and to self-soothe. They are reflexive emotional labourers, working to care for themselves and for those around them. Of course, we are not suggesting that they cannot be volatile, distressed or angry, nor are we suggesting that their reactions are not sometimes indicative of the harm domestic violence has done to them. However, we are suggesting that in using methods that neglect children's own articulations of their lived experiences of violence, psychological researchers are imposing adult and normative versions of what it means to be 'emotionally competent' that do not take into account the complexity of the relational context in which children who live with domestic violence function. The effect of this is that they underestimate children's capacity to reflect on, articulate and cope with difficult emotion. This underestimation further underscores and confirms the presumption built into developmental theory that adults and children are different categories of being (Burman, 2016). Whilst children's coping strategies in these situations are not always optimal, they do offer a starting point from which to build that makes sense to the child, and that fits in the narrative of their lives. Emotion coaching or emotional skills training that is rooted in abstract and decontextualised readings of 'good ways' to do emotions (Katz & Windecker-Nelson, 2006) cannot be sufficiently sensitive to, or respectful of, the work children have already done to enable themselves to cope with the difficult and at times overwhelming emotions they feel when domestic violence occurs.

Conclusions

In this chapter we have summarised the qualitative body of literature on domestic violence, including extracts from our own published work in this area, to show how it challenges the positioning of children who experience domestic violence as only vulnerable and damaged. The dominance of the idea that experiences of domestic violence place children at risk of pathology and of the intergenerational transmission of violence reiterates the developmental assumption that only normative, nuclear family practices produce 'normal' children, and that there is a single, universal way to 'do' childhood. By illustrating the diverse forms of experience and coping that children in contexts of domestic violence live through and enact, we have deconstructed the assumption of a single normative developmental trajectory for children's well-being and functioning, constructed as an individual and acontextual journey (Burman, 2016; James & Prout, 2015). We have argued that children who experience domestic violence create multiple, sophisticated and idiosyncratic ways of managing their personal and familial experiences. These act as situated resiliencies, and operate on both a verbal and embodied level. Their resilience and resistance strategies are located and embedded in the very environments in which they live (Ungar, 2015, Ungar, Ghazinour and Richter, 2013) and reflect their life contexts and experiences, rather than following a particular and universalised resilience that might be defined as 'health despite adversity'. Children's resources are built on the constraints they have experienced – they cope in context, not in some abstract and universal sense; as a consequence, these resiliencies can thus seem paradoxical in their manifestation.

This assumption of vulnerability is maintained by caregiver and professional discourses about children's damages and deficits, which further fuel the self-fulfilling prophecies of intergenerational transmission, rather than attempting to deconstruct it by envisaging alternative stories of competence, creativity and resilience. In contrast, we have argued that helping children to share, notice and value their located and contextual competence and skills – despite the family, professional, institutional and policy hindrances they face – will foster hope and confidence in their abilities to build stronger and healthier identities and relations. This emphasises the

importance of seeing children not as isolated developing individuals, but as growing up in a way that is connected to their social interactions and context, and the
value of an approach to children's lives that is located socially and geographically.

Our chapter has also highlighted young people's capacity to articulate their experiences of violence, its impact, their coping practices and their capacity for agency.
These voices and experiences are often neglected and further silenced by adults and
professionals´ assumptions about children´s vulnerability and the potential traumatic effect of telling their story. Constructing children as 'vulnerable' functions to
further undermine their sense of agency, control and self-esteem, and perpetuates
their feeling of being voiceless and powerless in their life contexts. Gatekeeping
practices intended to protect vulnerable children have an unintended consequence
of preventing them from articulating their own experience. In contrast, our data
suggests that interviews can be affirming, empowering and constructive experiences of being heard and listened to.

References

Alexander, J. H., Callaghan, J. E. M., Fellin, L. C. & Sixsmith, J. (2016). Children's corporeal agency and use of space in situations of domestic violence. In J. Horton & B. Evans
(Eds.), *Geographies of Children and Young People. Play, Recreation, Health and Well Being*
(pp. 1–21). Singapore: Springer.

Baldry, A. C. (2003). Bullying in schools and exposure to domestic violence. *Child Abuse &
Neglect*, 27(7), 713–732. http://doi.org/10.1016/S0145-2134(03)00114-5.

Bancroft, R. & Silverman, J. (2002). *The Batterer as Parent. The Impact of Domestic Violence on
Family Dynamics*. London: Sage.

Bowyer, L., Swanston, J. & Vetere, A. (2013). "Eventually you just get used to it": An inter-
pretative phenomenological analysis of 10–16 year-old girls' experiences of the transition
into temporary accommodation after exposure to domestic violence perpetrated by men
against their mothers. *Clinical Child Psychology and Psychiatry*, 20(2), 304–323. http://doi.
org/10.1177/1359104513508963.

Buckley, H., Holt, S. & Whelan, S. (2007). Listen to me! Children's experiences of domestic
violence. *Child Abuse Review*, 16(5), 296–310.

Burman, E. (2016). *Deconstructing Developmental Psychology* (Third Edition). Hove: Routledge.

Byrne, D. & Taylor, B. (2007). Children at risk from domestic violence and their educational attainment: Perspectives of education welfare officers, social workers and teachers.
Child Care in Practice, 13(3), 185–201. http://doi.org/10.1080/13575270701353465.

Callaghan, J. E. M. (2015). Mothers and children? Representations of mothers in research on
children's outcomes in domestic violence. *Psychology of Women Section Review*, (16), 2–5.

Callaghan, J. E. M. & Alexander, J. H. (2015). *Understanding Agency and Resistance Strategies:
Children's Experiences of Domestic Violence Report*. Northampton. Available at www.unars.
co.uk.

Callaghan, J. E. M., Alexander, J. H. & Fellin, L. C. (2016) Children's embodied experience of living with domestic violence: 'I'd go into my panic, and shake, really bad',
Subjectivity. Online ahead of publication.

Callaghan, J. E. M., Alexander, J. H., Mavrou, S., Fellin, L. C. & Sixsmith, J. (2016).
Practices of telling, and not telling: The management of disclosure in children's accounts
of domestic violence. *Journal of Child and Family Studies*. In Press.

Callaghan, J. E. M., Alexander, J. H., Sixsmith, J. & Fellin, L. C. (2016a). Beyond "witnessing": Children's experiences of coercive control in domestic violence and abuse. *Journal of Interpersonal Violence*. Online ahead of publication. http://doi.org/10.1177/0886260515618946.

Callaghan, J. E. M., Alexander, J. H., Sixsmith, J. & Fellin, L. C. (2016b). Children's experiences of domestic violence and abuse: Siblings' accounts of relational coping. *Journal of Clinical Child Psychology and Psychiatry*, 21(4).

Callaghan, J. E. M. & Clark, J. (2007). Feminist theory and conflict. In K. Ratele (Ed.), *Intergroup Relations: A South African Perspective* (pp. 87–110). Cape Town: Juta.

Callaghan, J. E. M., Fellin, L. C. & Alexander, J. H. (2016). Mental health of looked-after children: Embodiment and use of space. In J. Horton, B. Evans & T. Skelton (Eds.), *Play, Recreation, Health and Well Being; Vol. 9 of Skelton, T. (Ed.) Geographies of Children and Young People*. Singapore: Springer.

Callaghan, J. E. M., Fellin, L. C., Alexander, J., Mavrou, S. & Papathanassiou, M. (2016). Children's experiences of domestic violence: Embodiment, context and emotional competence. *Psychology and Violence*. Online ahead of publication. http://dx.doi.org/10.1037/vio0000108

Callaghan, J. E. M., Fellin, L. C. & Warner-Gale, F. (2017). A critical analysis of child and adolescent mental health services policy in England. *Clinical Child Psychology and Psychiatry*, 22(1): 109–127. http://doi.org/10.1177/1359104516640318. Online Ahead of Publication.

Callaghan, J. E. M., Fellin, L. C., Alexander, J., Mavrou, S. & Papathanassiou, M. (2017). Children's Experiences of Domestic Violence: Embodiment, Context and Emotional Competence. *Psychology and Violence (APA)*. Online ahead of publication. http://dx.doi.org/10.1037/vio0000108.

Callaghan, J. E. M., Gambo, Y. & Fellin, L. C. (2015). Hearing the silences: Adult Nigerian women's accounts of "early marriages." *Feminism & Psychology*, 25(4), 506–527. http://doi.org/10.1177/0959353515590691.

Cooper, J. & Vetere, A. (2008). *Domestic Violence and Family Safety: A Systemic Approach to Working with Violence in Families*. Chichester: Wiley and Sons.

Devaney, J. (2008). Chronic child abuse and domestic violence: Children and families with long-term and complex needs. *Child & Family Social Work*, 13(4), 443–453. http://doi.org/10.1111/j.1365-2206.2008.00559.x.

Dorrer, N., McIntosh, I., Punch, S. & Emond, R. (2010). Children and food practices in residential care: Ambivalence in the "institutional" home. *Children's Geographies*, 8(3), 247–259. http://doi.org/10.1080/14733285.2010.494863.

Einarsdottir, J., Dockett, S. & Perry, B. (2009). Making meaning: Children's perspectives expressed through drawings. *Early Child Development and Care*, 179(2), 217–232. http://doi.org/10.1080/03004430802666999.

Eriksson, M. (2012). Participation for children exposed to domestic violence? Social workers' approaches and children's strategies. *European Journal of Social Work*, 15(2), 205–221. http://doi.org/10.1080/13691457.2010.513963.

Eriksson, M. & Näsman, E. (2012). Interviews with children exposed to violence. *Children & Society*, 26(1), 63–73. http://doi.org/10.1111/j.1099-0860.2010.00322.x.

Evang, A. & Øverlien, C. (2014). "If you look, you have to leave": Young children regulating research interviews about experiences of domestic violence. *Journal of Early Childhood Research*, 13(2), 113–125. http://doi.org/10.1177/1476718X14538595.

Finkelhor, D., Turner, H., Ormrod, R. & Hamby, S. L. (2009). Violence, abuse, and crime exposure in a national sample of children and youth. *Pediatrics*, 124(5), 1411–23. http://doi.org/10.1542/peds.2009-0467.

Galbusera, L. and Fellin, L. (2014). The intersubjective endeavour of psychopathological research: methodological reflections on a second-person perspective approach. *Frontiers in Psychology*, 5, 1150–213.

Gewirtz, A. H. & Edleson, J. L. (2007). Young children's exposure to intimate partner violence: Towards a developmental risk and resilience framework for research and intervention. *Journal of Family Violence*, 22(3), 151–163. http://doi.org/10.1007/s10896-007-9065-3.

Gewirtz, A. H., Forgatch, M. & Wieling, E. (2008). Parenting practices as potential mechanisms for child adjustment following mass trauma. *Journal of Marital and Family Therapy*, 34(2), 177–92. http://doi.org/10.1111/j.1752-0606.2008.00063.x.

Graesch, A. P. (2004). Notions of family embedded in the house. *Anthropology News*, 45(6), 20.

Harden, J. (2000). There's no place like home: The public/private distinction in children's theorizing of risk and safety. *Childhood*, 7(1), 43–59.

Hays, S. (1996). *The Cultural Contradictions of Motherhood*. New Haven: Yale University Press.

Hebdige, D. (1979). *Subculture: The Meaning of Style*. London: Accents.

Holloway, S. I. & Valentine, G. (2000). *Children's Geographies: Playing, Living, Learning*. London: Routledge.

Hornor, G. (2005). Domestic violence and children. *Journal of Pediatric Health Care: Official Publication of National Association of Pediatric Nurse Associates & Practitioners*, 19(4), 206–12. http://doi.org/10.1016/j.pedhc.2005.02.002.

Howell, K. H. (2011). Resilience and psychopathology in children exposed to family violence. *Aggression and Violent Behavior*, 16(6), 562–569. http://doi.org/10.1016/j.avb.2011.09.001.

Jaffe, P. G., Crooks, C. V & Wolfe, D. A. (2003). Legal and policy responses to children exposed to domestic violence: The need to evaluate intended and unintended consequences. *Clinical Child and Family Psychology Review*, 6(3), 205–13. Available at www.ncbi.nlm.nih.gov/pubmed/14620580.

James, A. & Prout, A. (2015). *Constructing and Reconstructing Childhood: Contemporary Issues in the Sociological Study of Childhood*. London: Routledge.

Kassis, W., Artz, S. & Moldenhauer, S. (2013). Laying down the family burden: A cross-cultural analysis of resilience in the midst of family violence. *Child & Youth Services*, 34(1), 37–63. http://doi.org/10.1080/0145935X.2013.766067.

Kassis, W., Artz, S., Scambor, C., Scambor, E. & Moldenhauer, S. (2013). Finding the way out: A non-dichotomous understanding of violence and depression resilience of adolescents who are exposed to family violence. *Child Abuse & Neglect*, 37(2–3), 181–99. http://doi.org/10.1016/j.chiabu.2012.11.001.

Katz, E. (2015). Domestic violence, children's agency and mother-child relationships: Towards a more advanced model. *Children & Society*, 29(1), 69–79. http://doi.org/10.1111/chso.12023.

Katz, L. F., Hessler, D. M. & Annest, A. (2007). Domestic violence, emotional competence, and child adjustment. *Social Development*, 16(3), 513–538. http://doi.org/10.1111/j.1467-9507.2007.00401.x.

Katz, L. F. & Windecker-Nelson, B. (2006). Domestic violence, emotion coaching, and child adjustment. *Journal of Family Psychology: JFP: Journal of the Division of Family Psychology of the American Psychological Association (Division 43)*, 20(1), 56–67. http://doi.org/10.1037/0893-3200.20.1.56.

Lapierre, S. (2008). Mothering in the context of domestic violence: The pervasiveness of a deficit model of mothering. *Child and Family Social Work*, 13(4), 454–463. http://doi.org/10.1111/j.1365-2206.2008.00563.x.

Levendosky, A. A., Leahy, K. L., Bogat, G. A., Davidson, W. S. & von Eye, A. (2006). Domestic violence, maternal parenting, maternal mental health, and infant externalizing behavior. *Journal of Family Psychology*, 20(4), 544–52. http://doi.org/10.1037/0893-3200.20.4.544.

Logan, D. E. & Graham-Bermann, S. A. (1999). Emotion expression in children exposed to family violence. *Journal of Emotional Abuse*, 1(3), 39–64. http://doi.org/10.1300/J135v01n03.

Lombard, N. (2015). *Young People's Understanding of Violence Against Women*. Farnham: Ashgate.

Mallett, S. (2004). Understanding home: A critical review of the literature. *Sociological Review*, 52(1), 64–89.

Martinez-Torteya, C., Anne Bogat, G., von Eye, A. & Levendosky, A. A. (2009). Resilience among children exposed to domestic violence: The role of risk and protective factors. *Child Development*, 80(2), 562–77. http://doi.org/10.1111/j.1467-8624.2009.01279.x.

Maughan, A. & Cicchetti, D. (2002). Impact of child maltreatment and interadult violence on children's emotion regulation abilities and socioemotional adjustment, *Child Development*, 73(5), 1525–1542.

McGee, C. (2000). *Childhood Experiences of Domestic Violence*. London: Jessica Kingsley.

Meltzer, H., Doos, L., Vostanis, P., Ford, T. & Goodman, R. (2009). The mental health of children who witness domestic violence. *Child & Family Social Work*, 14(4), 491–501. http://doi.org/10.1111/j.1365-2206.2009.00633.x.

Merleau-Ponty, M. (1964). *The primacy of perception: And other essays on phenomenological psychology, the philosophy of art, history, and politics*. Illinois, USA: Northwestern University Press.

Morrison, F. (2015). "All over now?" The ongoing relational consequences of domestic abuse through children's contact arrangements. *Child Abuse Review*, 24(4), 274–284.

Mullender, A., Hague, G., Imam, U. F., Kelly, L., Malos, E. & Regan, L. (2003). *Children's Perspectives on Domestic Violence*. London: Sage.

Øverlien, C. (2009). Children exposed to domestic violence: Conclusions from the literature and challenges ahead. *Journal of Social Work*, 10(1), 80–97. http://doi.org/10.1177/1468017309350663.

Øverlien, C. (2014). "He didn't mean to hit mom, I think': Positioning, agency and point in adolescents' narratives about domestic violence. *Child & Family Social Work*, 19(2), 156–164. http://doi.org/10.1111/j.1365-2206.2012.00886.x.

Polanyi, L. and Van den Berg, M. H. (1996). Discourse structure and discourse interpretation. in *Proceedings of the tenth Amsterdam Colloqium*, 113–31.

Peckins, M. K., Dockray, S., Eckenrode, J. L., Heaton, J. & Susman, E. J. (2012). The longitudinal impact of exposure to violence on cortisol reactivity in adolescents. *The Journal of Adolescent Health: Official Publication of the Society for Adolescent Medicine*, 51(4), 366–72. http://doi.org/10.1016/j.jadohealth.2012.01.005.

Saltzman, K. M., Holden, G. W. & Holahan, C. J. (2005). The psychobiology of children exposed to marital violence. *Journal of Clinical Child and Adolescent Psychology: The Official Journal for the Society of Clinical Child and Adolescent Psychology, American Psychological Association, Division 53*, 34(1), 129–39. http://doi.org/10.1207/s15374424jccp3401_12.

Shirani, F., Henwood, K. & Coltart, C. (2011). Meeting the challenges of intensive parenting culture: Gender, risk management and the moral parent. *Sociology*, 46(1), 25–40. http://doi.org/10.1177/0038038511416169.

Skelton, T. (2008). Research with children and young people: Exploring the tensions between ethics, competence and participation. *Children's Geographies*, 6(1), 21–36.

Swanston, J., Bowyer, L. & Vetere, A. (2014). Towards a richer understanding of school-age children's experiences of domestic violence: The voices of children and their mothers. *Clinical Child Psychology and Psychiatry*, 19(2), 184–201. http://doi.org/10.1177/1359104513485082.

Trawick, M. (2007). Freedom to move: A bike trip with Menan. In K. Malone (Ed.), *Child space: An Anthropological Exploration of Young People's Use of Space* (pp. 21–40). New Delhi: Concept Publishing Company.

Ugazio, V. (2013). *Semantic Polarities and Psychopathologies in the Family: Permitted and Forbidden Stories*. London: Routledge.

Ungar, M., Ghazinour, M. & Richter, J. (2013). What is Resilience Within the Ecology of Human Development? *Journal of Child Psychology and Psychiatry*, 54(4), 348–66. DOI: 10.1111/jcpp.12025.

Ungar, M. (2015). Varied patterns of family resilience in challenging contexts. *Journal of Marital and Family Therapy*. 42(1), 19–31. DOI: 10.1111/jmft.12124.

Unterhalter, E. (2012). Inequality, capabilities and poverty in four African countries: Girls' voice, schooling, and strategies for institutional change. *Cambridge Journal of Education*, 42(3), 307–325. http://doi.org/10.1080/0305764X.2012.706253.

Vetere, A. & Cooper, J. (2005). *Narrative Therapies with Children and their Families: A Practitioner's Guide to Concepts and Approaches*. London: Routledge.

Wardhaugh, J. (1999). The unaccommodated woman: Home, homelessness and identity. *The Sociological Review*, 47(1), 91–109. http://doi.org/10.1111/1467-954X.00164.

Whitaker, R. C., Orzol, S. M. & Kahn, R. S. (2006). Maternal mental health, substance use, and domestic violence in the year after delivery and subsequent behavior problems in children at age 3 years. *Archives of General Psychiatry*, 63(5), 551–60. http://doi.org/10.1001/archpsyc.63.5.551.

Wilson, S., Houmøller, K. & Bernays, S. (2012). "Home, and not some house": Young people's sensory construction of family relationships in domestic spaces. *Children's Geographies*, 10(1), 95–107. http://doi.org/10.1080/14733285.2011.638172.

PART III
The limits of childhood

8

INDEPENDENT MIGRANT CHILDREN, HUMANITARIAN WORK AND STATECRAFT

Mapping the connections in South Africa

Stanford Taonatose Mahati[1] and Ingrid Palmary

Introduction

In this chapter we will explore the implications of the ways that the independent migrant child has been produced through humanitarian interventions and how these are connected to constructions of gender and nation. We use the term 'independent child migrants' rather than 'unaccompanied migrant children' because it acknowledges that children's migration choices are a consequence of family livelihood decisions that facilitate children's movement rather than a failure of adults to accompany or protect them. Following Cheney's (2005, p. 5) claim that "[i]t is important to consider the ways that both childhood and the aid industry are depoliticised in popular discourse, despite the fact that both domains are rife with politics", this chapter discusses the function of discourses of sexuality, humanitarianism and nationality, and their consequences for girls who migrate independently of adult carers.

To achieve this, the chapter draws on a series of research projects with migrant children on South Africa's borders, with a focus on research that was conducted on the South Africa/Zimbabwe border. We work from the assumption that a plethora of discourses around child migration produce different childhoods for different children, in contrast to the often taken-for-granted notion of universal childhood (see Boyden, 2003). Rather, understandings of childhood vary historically and culturally (Prout & James, 1997). Consequently, the idea that there is a 'global' or indeed an 'African' child is rejected by many childhood scholars as it presumes "a false commonality of experience" (Ansell, 2009, p. 194; see also Alipio, Lu & Yeoh, 2015). As a result, this chapter is informed by the 'new social studies of childhood' approach that sees childhood as socially constructed (see Ansell, 2009; Holloway & Valentine, 2000) and historically and contextually produced. Emphasising and reflecting on the importance of social context, we unpack some of the gendered understandings of childhood in Musina and the discursive features of various, at times contradictory, understandings of independent child migrants who are interacting with humanitarian agencies. In addition, in the words of Bourdillon (2011, p. 98), we draw attention to "the dangers of local and global ideals and stereotypes" of childhood.

The context

Musina town on the South African border with Zimbabwe has, since the beginning of this new millennium, been the home to large numbers of (mostly) Zimbabwean migrants. As the economic and political conditions in Zimbabwe have deteriorated, and large numbers of Zimbabweans have moved to South Africa, there has been increasing attention of many kinds paid to movement on this border. In particular, there has been increasing policing of the border with the army being deployed at times to prevent undocumented migration as well as a number of humanitarian agencies such as Save the Children, Médecins Sans Frontières (MSF) or Doctors without Borders, among others, setting up operations in the area. Several of these humanitarian agencies have responded to the needs of children and their responses have included shelters for children (one for boys and one for girls), support to children trying to access education and food provision within the shelters. In addition, family tracing and reunification has been an important part of the humanitarian response. Often these services have been extremely underfunded and conditions in shelters have been overcrowded and the food quality very poor.

In addition, Musina is well-known to be very violent. Gangs known locally as *Magumaguma* assist people to cross the border irregularly, but are also notorious for rape, theft and other kinds of violence. In particular, there have been concerns about a range of sexualised forms of violence, including rape, sexual coercion, sex work and so on, in the border area (De Sas Kropiwnicki, 2010; Palmary, 2009). The presumed interconnections of these forms of sexual violence and their consequences will be explored in the pages to follow. Suffice to say that sexualised violence is a central concern within the context of an increase in the number of child migrants without their parents and guardians.

Like the thousands of adults who used various avenues to escape from the harsh socio-economic and political situation in Zimbabwe, a large population of independent child migrants are responding to economic and political challenges by moving to neighbouring countries such as South Africa (Clacherty, 2003; Palmary, 2009). In other work, Mahati (2015) has documented more broadly how, due to their age and other factors such as nationality and citizenship, these children are not seen as full participants in society (see also James, 2011), limiting, for example, their entitlements to work. Here, however, we focus on just one discursive production of migrant children, which is their gendered and sexualised national representation.

Gender childhood and nation

It is increasingly accepted that childhood is gendered. In this volume, Robb et al. (2015) question the ways in which gendered assumptions about the care of boys simplify and reproduce gender. Other authors such as Bhana and Pattman (2011) have noted how, for example, gender shapes HIV interventions in school in ways that are not only gendered but racialised. This is in keeping with work of Walkerdine (1990) and others who show how notions of gender shape how girls are responded to in educational settings.

In addition, there has been a substantial literature linking gender and nationalism over the past 30 years. In particular, this literature has noted the ways in which women and children are positioned as being at the heart of the national project. A number of authors have noted how war is justified through the protection of the family (Yuval-Davis, 1993) and how notions of national pride are rooted in the morality of family life (Summers, 1991). Despite this very long tradition of work that unpacks the connections between gender and nation, relatively little work has been done to consider how childhood is evoked as part of the national project. A significant exception is the work of Stephens (1997), which explored some of these connections. The author notes that:

> A major challenge for the social sciences in decades to come is exploration of the ways these differentiating identities – male or female, adult or child, citizen of this or that nation – support, legitimate and reinforce, as well as challenge and partially contradict one another.
>
> *(Stephens, 1997, p. 6)*

Nevertheless there have been remarkably few efforts to take up this challenge. Most significant for our purposes here is the work of Burman (1995), who shows how notions of the north and south are intertwined in aid appeals as well as how these map onto notions of gender and culture. Far from being separate realms, the connections between the imagined child of the global north and the global south are rooted in relationships of mutual construction shaped by inequality. Following a similar argument, Fassin (2012) notes:

> On the one hand, moral sentiments are focused mainly on the poorest, most unfortunate, most vulnerable individuals: the politics of compassion is a politics of inequality. On the other hand, the condition of possibility of moral sentiments is generally the recognition of others as fellows: the politics of compassion is a politics of solidarity. This tension between inequality and solidarity, between a relation of domination and a relation of assistance, is constitutive of all humanitarian government.
>
> *(Fassin, 2012, p. 3)*

Here we explore this interconnectedness between childhood, gender and the nation in the context of humanitarian interventions in South Africa in order to move forward the theme in this section of the book, namely, the locatedness of notions of development and their implications for the nature of support children receive. This means that there is necessarily a focus on the unequal and sometimes global relationships of north and south that structure humanitarianism. However, this is complicated by our focus on 'south–south' migration between South Africa and Zimbabwe as we will elaborate. Furthermore, we focus on the sexualisation of children in this border zone. Whilst there has been some attention paid to childhood and sexuality, much of what has been written in the African context has been problem-focused, particularly on HIV and sexual abuse. Here, rather than rehearse these debates, we focus on the consequences of such problematised emphasis on children's sexuality. Several writers have noted the slide between victimisation and pathologisation (Dudley-Marling & Lucas, 2009). The phenomenon of the movement of children without their parents or guardians, including across national borders, is one that has generated a great deal of anxiety and has questioned models of appropriate childhood (Mahati, 2015). A number of scholars including Mahati (2015) and Bourdillon (2010) have argued that 'out of home' children, like migrant children and so-called street children, are seen as non-conformist and contrary to normal childhood. In other words, they are seen as both vulnerable and deviants. The need to unpack notions of victimisation and pathologisation remains important. We do so in this chapter by considering how nationality shapes the discursive production of independent child migrants and the impact this has for their assistance. We show how discourses on children, childhood and what is considered to be a proper child deserving of care and support have been accentuated by ideas of nationality and citizenship.

Nationality and citizenship, relatively new and powerful concepts in Africa, are often used as tools to create difference amongst people as well as sameness (Billig, 1995). Evidence will be presented in this chapter which shows that nationality can, despite efforts by the South African state's progressive child protection laws, often wittingly or unwittingly, enhance or limit opportunities for different people, in this case foreign migrant children. There is abundant literature which indicates that nationality is a powerful tool in shaping how local and foreign people are perceived and treated by state and non-state actors (see Landau, 2006; Landau, 2012). It is the function and consequence of the discourse of nationality in humanitarian work and statecraft that needs to be critically analysed and challenged. This chapter simultaneously shows the complexities around humanitarian work and nationalism that also influence the migration experiences of young migrants who are searching for livelihoods and other things in the host country.

Methodology

This chapter focuses on one of the central findings from a nine-month ethnographic study in Musina. This study was, however, part of a bigger study of three borderland areas as well as a number of more policy-oriented studies (see Crawley, 2011). Here we draw particularly on interviews conducted with humanitarian workers who worked in 'places of safety' for children as well as with independent migrant children to explore the meanings they attached to the migration of children, its risks and its significances. As stated earlier, the work proceeded from the position that children are social actors (James, Jenks & Prout, 1998) and that they actively "engage with the world around them" (Alipio et al., 2015, p. 258; James, Jenks & Prout, 1998). We focus here on one central discourse that emerged from the research, namely, the nationalisation of childhood.

The work in Musina was conducted primarily at two children's shelters as well as with children who did not live in the shelters but lived on the streets or in many different kinds of accommodation. The first author had access to the shelters during all times of the day and night, particularly at the shelter for boys as he is a man and had some restrictions at the girls' shelter in line with their child protection rules as well as for ethical reasons (see Mahati, 2015). The author was able to spend extended periods of time observing the interactions of children and humanitarian workers. There were many intersecting points of disagreement between these two groups. Most of these centred on children's desire to work, which was in contrast to humanitarian workers' desire for them to be in school. However, one central and surprising aspect of the conflict between humanitarian workers and children was the sexualisation of migrant girls. In the section that follows, we unpack how the migration of children was sexualised in ways that supported nationalist notions of morality and pathology and the consequences thereof.

Sexual and 'nationalised' childhoods

In this section, we provide an insight into the way in which childhoods were produced as sexualised and therefore also as not sufficiently childlike (Kehily, 2009). Generally, there is a lack of gendered accounts of the experiences of migrant children (Sirriyeh, 2010), but more notably there is limited attention paid to childhood sexualities with childhood often being deemed to be an asexual phase of life (Crawley, 2011). It was clear during the research that the sexualisation of girls, through a blurred notion of abuse and promiscuity, had significant consequences for the support that independent migrant girls received and the life opportunities they had.

This became evident to the first author when, early on in the research, a local man dropped a letter off at a church shelter for girls in which he complained that he had been "abused" by a young Zimbabwean migrant woman who lived there. He accused the woman of "liking money so much", implying she seduced him for money. He appealed to the church and the church management to intervene before his "pay day" and put a stop to the woman's practice of "only loving him when he [had] money". As the female humanitarian worker and the first author were discussing this letter, the humanitarian worker became incensed when she saw some migrant girls dressed in tight fitting jeans and mini-skirts leaving the shelter, claiming that they were going to do 'piece jobs'[2]. She commented to the researcher who is Zimbabwean: "children from your country like men a lot". As the field-work progressed, we realised that her views were shared by many humanitarian workers. They often expressed weariness in continuously trying to stop "these Zimbabwean girls" from "loitering in the streets" where they claimed these girls experience sexual exploitation, engage in pre-marital sex, contract sexually transmitted infections and have unplanned pregnancies.

The distinction between sexual abuse, which was rife in this border area, and girls' promiscuity was remarkably blurred. At times, humanitarian workers overtly blamed independent migrant girls for putting their lives at risk or facilitating their sexual abuse by "crossing the border" and "leaving your parents", acts seen as opposing normal girlhood. We observed humanitarian workers asking the girls: "*Knowing* that you are a *girl* why did you migrate?" In this way, girls who had migrated to South Africa were frequently accused of being reckless and inviting abuse. This contrasted sharply with the characterisation of migrant boys whose migration was tolerated, and sometimes even celebrated, because they were seen to be taking up masculine responsibilities of economic provision and exploring new territories. Whilst the boys were no doubt stigmatised in other ways (such as being accused of being criminals or *Magumaguma*), this gendered characterisation of girls' movement was stark.

Humanitarian workers were quite rightly concerned that almost every day a number of girls were being raped along the border with Zimbabwe, but this concern was expressed as exasperation over why girls continued to migrate rather than over why girls continued to be abused. Consequently, as Gordon (1988, p. 58) observed, the survivors of sexual abuse are changed from "innocent betrayed to sex delinquent". The fact that sexual offences against girls and women have reached crisis level in South Africa was obscured and instead humanitarian workers questioned why *munhu wemukadzi* [a woman or girl] dared cross the border or "be out there".

The notion that girls were not sexually innocent in turn led to their representation as adults due to their transgression of the norms of childhood. The status and privilege of childhood was withdrawn from children seen to have appropriated adult behaviour. For instance, a female humanitarian worker had this to say about a 13-year-old girl:

> Compared to her, you [the researcher] might be a minor. She knows so *many things* about sex and the different styles [of having sex]. She might know a lot more than you. That one is an *adult* and is the one who can tell you about sex.
>
> *(own emphasis)*

As this topic was explored further, it became clear that Musina was in the grip of a moral panic about the sexuality of Zimbabwean migrant girls. Writing from a very different context, Rubin (1984) notes that:

> It is precisely at times like these, where we live with the possibility of unthinkable destruction, that people are likely to become dangerously crazy about sexuality. Disputes over sexual behaviour often become the vehicles for displacing social anxieties, and discharging their attendant emotional intensity.
>
> *(p. 100)*

This does indeed capture the context of Musina whereby the practice of unprecedented movement of children and anxieties about its consequences was displaced onto a concern with girls' morality. However, as Fahs, Dudy and Stage (2013) note, moral panic functions to deflect attention away from broader sociopolitical issues that are arguably more important. Thus, the moral focus on the sexuality of migrant girls deflects from their abuses, which are created through state structures such as border control and the lack of monitoring of exploitative working conditions. Most notably it was the moral panic in the area that allowed abuse to slide into accusations against migrant girls.

Inventing pathologised sexualities

There were two important ways that the morality of migrant girls was constructed as problematic. The first was because of girls' desire to work. As mentioned earlier, poverty was a primary reason for children's migration and work was often their primary purpose for being in South Africa. However, for girls who sought work, the accusation of prostitution hung over them constantly. In particular, migrant girls who wore new and trendy clothing or who bought fast food were accused of engaging in transactional sex or sex work[3]. If we contrast this with the migrant children who attended school rather than working, this accusation was not levelled against them and they were seen to be more moral and to come from better families than girls who worked or looked for work. In one example, when the first author accompanied a social worker to find children who were being illegally detained in the detention centre in Musina, the social worker complained that it was not worth trying to identify girls who were detained and take them to the place of safety because "they quickly leave the shelter to stay with boyfriends".

People from poor economies have generally been devalued even as they are seen as vulnerable. Generally, humanitarian workers viewed children from Zimbabwe as poorer than South African children. As a consequence, any perceived opulence of migrant children, such as buying and wearing expensive clothes, triggered resentment amongst humanitarian workers and these children were seen as not deserving of support.

The second way in which the moral panic in Musina displaced the problems facing migrant girls was in the way that sexuality was nationalised and seen as a failing of Zimbabwe as a nation. Stephens (1997) reminds us that childhood is a political matter and nationality featured centrally in the everyday practices of humanitarian workers, shaping and producing different childhoods for different children. It resulted in Zimbabwean childhoods being "lived and experienced differently" to a normalised South African childhood (Goldstein, 1998, p. 389). Far from girls being cast as solely responsible for their immorality, Zimbabwe as a nation was portrayed as negligent. Humanitarian workers often derisively asked, "What type of country are these children coming from?" This is similar to what Neil Howard found in Benin, where "the view of rural parenting practices is unambiguously negative" (Howard, 2012, p. 6) and normative models of childhood render the majority of childhoods problematic. Zimbabwean parents and the government were seen as "ignorant and irresponsible" (Howard, 2012, p. 5). On one hand, this representation of migrant children as victims of a failing state worked as a tool for mobilising support for them. On the other hand, it served to create a country-based moral hierarchy. Based on differences in the moral standing of different nationalities, this moral hierarchy worked to cast Zimbabwean children as inevitably less moral. Humanitarian workers lamented that parents, relatives and the Zimbabwean government "must be ashamed" of failing to take care of its children. The creation of a moral South African nation thus draws on the idea of an immoral Zimbabwean nation (see Palmary 2016 for more). Humanitarian workers went to extraordinary lengths to make sure that the children remained conscious of their nationality and to ensure that they felt different to South African children. They worked from the myth that nation maps onto culture in meaningful ways (see Malkki, 1992). For example, we observed humanitarian workers from Zimbabwe holding discussions with independent children about 'their culture', which was always framed as national culture, and singing the Zimbabwean national anthem as a way of strengthening their sense of national identity. One of these humanitarian workers explained why they did that:

> We said even if they are unaccompanied they must know our culture and where they are coming from because they are not going to remain in this situation of being unaccompanied. They are growing up and they will become parents in this country. But they have to identify with a country, with a culture.

We describe this as humanitarian nationalism. The emphasis on nationality as the source of culture and moral reasoning as well as the identification of migrant children as needing specialised and separate interventions though international humanitarian organisations (rather than the same kinds of services South African children receive) functioned to reinforce the nation as a natural and meaningful entity (see Torpey, 2000). In everyday practices, such as singing the national anthem or providing separate and non-state services to migrant children, national difference becomes reinscribed and real.

In addition, children were held up as icons of their nation. On several occasions, the humanitarian workers who were Zimbabwean scathingly criticised the migrant girls for "tarnishing our image as Zimbabweans". Of note is that at some moments, for example when responding to independent children seen as behaving inappropriately, there were differences between humanitarian workers from Zimbabwe and South Africa. For example, humanitarian workers from Zimbabwe were more inclined to ascribe what they proudly regarded as independent migrant children's good traits of working hard, being respectful and attending school to their Zimbabwean nationality. On the other hand, some humanitarian workers (particularly South Africans) tended to attribute what they regarded as bad behaviour, such as independent migrant girls' perceived promiscuousness and mobility, to their Zimbabwean nationality. Such representations, both good and bad, served as tools for demanding that the independent children change their behaviour so that it could become consistent with "Zimbabweanness". Thus, nationality often structured the representations of independent children and shaped practices towards these children. We turn now to a consideration of the consequences of the moral panic regarding the sexuality of independent migrant girls.

The impact of sexualised nationalisms

Many authors have noted the pathologisation of women and girls who experience sexual violence. However, in this instance, the consequences of characterising girls as sexually deviant were shaped by the humanitarian environment. Returning to the example we introduced earlier in this chapter of the man who dropped off a letter complaining of women who "abused" him, his formulation of the problem absolved the man of any responsibility, positioning him as powerless in the face of the girls' 'hyper-sexuality'. Using a similar line of reason, humanitarian workers focused almost exclusively on the morality of migrant girls rather than the abuses they faced. In this section, we explore some of the ways in which the moral panic in Musina operated as a "political strategy of social[ly] ordering" (Robinson, 2008, p. 123) for migrant girls.

One of the most significant consequences was in relation to girls' work. As mentioned in the context section, most Zimbabwean children who move to South Africa usually do so with a desire to work given the economic difficulties they experience in Zimbabwe. However, a heightened concern with girls' sexual safety and promiscuity was used to justify preventing them from working. Migrant girls and humanitarian and state workers claimed that some local men were taking advantage of the desperation of migrant girls who moved from house to house begging for part-time work, by calling them to their houses and asking them to do household chores and then sexually abusing them. This was not untrue and as one of the girls noted, "We take a chance but many girls are being sexually abused or escape from being abused".

However, the failure to monitor working conditions resulted in independent migrant girls from Zimbabwe working in especially risky environments, including private homes, the streets and the border area. But they were being discursively constructed as irresponsible for putting themselves at risk of abuse and sexual exploitation. The framing of the problem as one of girls' recklessness closed down protection services that might make work safer for girls and instead limited their economic opportunities. And so, rather ironically, the way that girls' abuse was cast as a moral panic worked to slow down efforts to support migrant girls.

Another equally concerning consequence was that it resulted in the withdrawal of child protection services and legitimised harsh discipline and control (see also Meyer, 2007) against children. Migrant girls who were labelled sexual deviants were often expelled from shelters so as to 'protect other innocent girls' from being corrupted. Humanitarian workers argued that the sexuality of such girls, sometimes inferred from them having smart clothing or dressing 'inappropriately', was dangerous and therefore warranted exclusion from their shelters. This idea of preventing 'deviant' girls from corrupting innocent girls served to legitimise exclusionary practices in humanitarian work by humanitarian workers.

Beyond these consequences, the difficulties girls faced during migration were attributed to their essential qualities, rather than to the gendered practices in the borderland. For example, migrant girls' risk of sexual violence was conflated with their inability to deal with the adversity associated with migration. One humanitarian worker explained that:

> [T]heir [referring to boys] physical and biological make up makes them to have more resistance and resilience to circumstances like going for a long period without bathing.

In contrast, clearly in line with the view that femininity is also made up of biologically generated factors, they argued that it is difficult for girls not to bath for a number of days as they menstruate. The idea of girls' biological vulnerability denied them the life-changing opportunities (such as work) that boys could access (see Clark-Kazak, 2011). In addition, boys' presence on the street where work was available (such as waiting outside shops to assist with carrying bags) was tolerated whereas for girls, in the name of their safety, were required to remain at the shelters. Unlike boys, independent migrant girls, having been constructed as vulnerable and hyper-sexual, were closely monitored and their movement restricted. In this way, humanitarian workers often reproduced the idea of confining women to the private sphere of the home and worked to suppress independent migrant girls' economic and sexual expression. For example, they prohibited all the young girls below 18 years from leaving the place of safety's premises at certain times (such as after sunset). Rules governing the temporary place of safety included having set times for being inside the shelters and prohibiting children from sleeping out. Migrant girls complained bitterly about these restrictions, which they argued forced them to have poor and inadequate food because it prevented them from doing 'piece jobs' through which they could supplement their food. In the end, this rule was overturned for a number of reasons. First, there was a great deal of resistance from migrant girls, and the humanitarian workers had difficulties enforcing the rule prohibiting girls from going out of the shelter. However, more importantly, the places of safety, which were poorly funded and offered inadequate material support for independent children, made it impossible for girls to be entirely dependent on the shelters. This created a contradictory situation where girls outside of the shelter were disapproved of and sometimes treated harshly, but both humanitarian workers and girls knew that leaving the shelter was also a necessity.

A further consequence was that there was an extensive emphasis among humanitarian workers on returning girls to Zimbabwe. For example, one female humanitarian worker felt that "They [independent migrant girls] should have stayed at home and protected themselves instead of putting themselves at risk". However, this ignores the fact that, for many of the girls, home was a place of poverty and few opportunities and this was precisely the reason for their movement in the first place.

In the case of most of the children we interviewed, their parents were aware that they were in South Africa and migration formed an essential part of the family's livelihood strategy. This is not to deny that migration is difficult or dangerous, but rather that a simple return ignores the broader sociopolitical reasons why children move.

Conclusions

This study has explored some of the interconnections between childhood, nationality and humanitarian work, and the ways in which these are reproduced in borderlands. The border that we have chosen to focus on is not necessarily typical of borderlands in South Africa, but rather is one where there has been extensive state and humanitarian intervention. As such, it offers a useful example of the consequences of these kinds of interventions and their possible and impossible practices.

Evidence presented in this chapter shows that the category of childhood is highly politicised in such a context. Humanitarian workers and independent child migrants interact with and interpret the border zone and its apparatus in complex, shifting and sometimes contradictory ways. The politicisation of migrant children generates complexities and contradictions in the construction of the South African and Zimbabwean nation.

The chapter has shown that contradictory and politicised discourses around childhood exist, which function at different moments and produce different childhoods for different children. Migrant children experienced many different childhoods as childhood has "multiple and unstable constructions" (Burman, 2008, p. 116). This buttresses James, Jenks and Prout's (1998) point that childhood is situated in time and space and "is changed at different times and contexts" (cited in Thørnblad & Holtan, 2013, p. 3). The context of a borderland where there is widespread but criminalised migration creates very particular sets of conditions for the gendered production of childhood.

We have shown that the extensive sexual violence in Musina can be understood as a moral crisis for a number of reasons. First, it represents a way of displacing anxieties during times of social upheaval, focusing on the sexual morality of migrant girls rather than the broader sociopolitical conditions that produce extensive sexual violence in the area. Second, the borderland is often an area where the myth of nationality is exposed as people live across geographical regions. In these contexts, nationality as an identity is often harshly policed. In the case of this study, migration was constructed as a male practice that girls (as a consequence of both age and gender) had no place in. This was achieved through notions of home that ignored the desperate poverty that caused young people, both boys and girls, to move and which meant that child migration was often a well-thought-out family strategy. Because of the expectation that girls should not leave 'home', any indication of girls working or having material objects above absolute poverty levels was taken to be evidence of their sexual promiscuity. As Nyangairi (2010) has noted, for Zimbabwean women who sold sex in Johannesburg, just the very fact of leaving 'home' meant that accusations of being a prostitute hung over them. For independent migrant girls, evidence of earning money, such as having better food or clothing than the shelters provided, was taken to be indicative of their promiscuity.

Ironically, the harsh treatment of migrant girls described above draws heavily from advocacy that has emphasised the vulnerability of girls who migrate. However, by framing their vulnerability as essential to girlhood, rather than as a consequence of social and political structures, the solutions are seen to lie in the behaviour of girls rather than in their protection in, for example, the workplace.

The study revealed that the nationalised and gendered representation of migrant children led to the unequal treatment of different children. We have shown the very material consequences of the moral panic in Musina. For example, girls' access to support was heavily shaped by their willingness to enact a poverty stricken and nationalised moral position. The fact that humanitarian workers were willing to remove girls who did not take up this position from the shelter meant that girls had to choose between poverty in the shelter or stigmatisation if they ventured outside of the shelter. In negotiating this, there was no space for girls' migration to be conceptualised as successful. Whereas for boys earning money was evidence of a successful migration, for girls it was equated with immorality. This is consistent with previous research on migration and sexuality (see Brockerhoff & Biddlecom, 1999; Haram, 2004), which shows a gendered conflation of mobility and immorality. Since the notion that the right place for women and girls is the home continues to prevail, they reproduced the view that mobility, particularly across national borders, was not good for their moral well-being.

In addition, girls were seen as icons of the nation and the failures of Zimbabwean girls were conflated with the failings of the Zimbabwean state. As Stephens (1997) notes, this construction of the nation requires considerable ideological labour. Nowhere is this more the case than on borderlands where life is lived across borders and the boundaries of the nation often have little significance. What we have documented in this chapter represents the everyday practices that perform this ideological work.

It is important to note that humanitarian workers were working in poverty stricken and violent contexts themselves. Thus, although this chapter relies on a critique of their gendered and nationalist practices, we would not want to suggest that this reflects a simple illustration of bad practice among humanitarian workers. In many instances, the responses that they implemented such as limiting girls' work and movement were the only ones available to them. Given that border regimes and state services were not within their power to control, we would read the actions of humanitarian workers not as examples of abusive or uncaring practices, but rather as ones of making meaning within a context that is constrained by notions of sexual and state violence.

Notes

1   Stanford Mahati's study in Musina, South Africa, was funded by the ZEIT-Stiftung und Gerd Bucerius "Settling Into Motion" Programme, the National Research Fund (NRF) and the Atlantic Philanthropies.

2   'Piece jobs' are temporary casual jobs, usually working in a residential garden or house-
     hold although sometimes on farms.
3   The ways that certain acts were defined as transactional sex rather than "love" as well as
     their conflation with sex work is a complex topic that is beyond the scope of this paper
     but requires more careful unpacking to avoid taking these constructs for granted.

References

Alipio, C., Lu, M. C. & Yeoh, B. S. (2015). Asian children and transnational migration.
    Children's Geographies, 13(3), 255–262.

Ansell, N. (2009). Childhood and the politics of scale: Descaling children's geographies?
    Progress in Human Geography, 33(2), 190–209.

Bhana, D. & Pattman, R. (2011). Girls want money, boys want virgins: The materiality of
    love amongst South African township youth in the context of HIV and AIDS. *Culture,
    Health & Sexuality*, 13(8), 961–972.

Billig, M. (1995). *Banal Nationalism*. London: Sage.

Bourdillon, M. (2011). A challenge for globalised thinking: How does children's work relate
    to their development? *South African Review of Sociology*, 42(1), 97–115.

Bourdillon, M. F. (2010). *Rights and Wrongs of Children's Work*. Rutgers University Press.

Boyden, J. (2003). Children under fire: Challenging assumptions about children's resilience.
    Children Youth and Environments, 13(1), 1–29.

Brockerhoff, M. & Biddlecom, A. E. (1999). Migration, sexual behavior and the risk of HIV
    in Kenya. *International Migration Review*, 33(4), 833–856.

Burman, E. (1995). Developing differences: Gender, childhood and economic development.
    Children & Society, 9(3), 121–141.

Burman, E. (2008). *Developments: Child, Image, Nation*. London: Routledge.

Cheney, C. (2005). *Brothers Gonna Work it Out: Sexual politics in the Golden Age of Rap
    Nationalism*. New York, London: NYU Press.

Clacherty, G. (2003). *LoveLife: Promoting Sexual Health and Healthy Lifestyles*. Johannesburg:
    Clacherty and Associates.

Clark-Kazak, C. R. (2011). *Recounting Migration: Political Narratives of Congolese Young People
    in Uganda*. Montreal: McGill-Queen's Press-MQUP.

Crawley, H. (2011). "Asexual, apolitical beings": The interpretation of children's identities
    and experiences in the UK asylum system. *Journal of Ethnic and Migration Studies*, 37(8),
    1171–1184.

De Sas Kropiwnicki, Z. (2010). *Wolves in Sheep's Skin: A Rapid Assessment of Human
    Trafficking in Musina, Limpopo Province of South Africa*. International Organization for
    Migration: Pretoria.

Dudley-Marling, C. & Lucas, K. (2009). Pathologizing the language and culture of poor
    children. *Language Arts*, 86(5), 362–370.

Fahs, B., Dudy, M. L. & Stage, S. (2013). *The Moral Panics of Sexuality*. New York: Palgrave
    Macmillan.

Fassin, D. (2012). *Humanitarian Reason: A Moral History of the Present*. Berkeley, CA:
    University of California Press.

Goldstein, L. S. (1998). More than gentle smiles and warm hugs: Applying the ethic of care
    to early childhood education. *Journal of Research in Childhood Education*, 12(2), 244–261.

Gordon, L. (1988). The politics of child sexual abuse: Notes from American history. *Feminist
    Review*, (28), 56–64.

Haram, L. (2004). 'Prostitutes' or modern women? Negotiating respectability in Northern
    Tanzania. In S. Arnfred (Ed.), *Re-Thinking Sexualities in Africa* (pp. 211–232). Uppsala:
    The Nordic Africa Institute.

Holloway, S. L. & Valentine, G. (2000). Spatiality and the new social studies of childhood. *Sociology*, 34(4), 763–783.

Howard, N. (2012). Protecting children from trafficking in Benin: In need of politics and participation. *Development in Practice*, 22(4), 460–472.

James, A. (2011). To be (come) or not to be (come): Understanding children's citizenship. *The Annals of the American Academy of Political and Social Science*, 633(1), 167–179.

James, A., Jenks, C. & Prout, A. (1998). *Theorizing Childhood*. London: Polity.

Kehily, M. J. (2009). Children, young people and sexuality. In H. Montgomery and M. Kellett (Eds.), *Children and Young People's Worlds, Developing Frameworks for Integrated Practice* (pp. 219–236). Bristol: Policy Press.

Landau, L. B. (2006). Protection and dignity in Johannesburg: Shortcomings of South Africa's urban refugee policy. *Journal of Refugee Studies*, 19(3), 308–327.

Landau, L. B. (2012). *Exorcising the Demons Within: Xenophobia, Violence and Statecraft in Contemporary South Africa*. Johannesburg: Wits University Press.

Mahati, S. T. (2015). *The representations of childhood and vulnerability: Independent child migrants in humanitarian work*. University of the Witwatersrand, Johannesburg. Available at http://wiredspace.wits.ac.za/handle/10539/18304.

Malkki, L. (1992). National geographic: The rooting of peoples and the territorialization of national identity among scholars and refugees. *Cultural Anthropology*, 7(1), 24–44.

Meyer, A. (2007). The moral rhetoric of childhood. *Childhood*, 14(1), 85–104.

Nyangairi, B. (2010). *Migrant women in sex work: Trajectories and perceptions of Zimbabwean sex workers in Hillbrow, South Africa*. Available at http://wiredspace.wits.ac.za/handle/10539/8381.

Palmary, I. (2009). For better implementation of migrant children's rights in South Africa. *Report for UNICEF, Forced Migration Studies Programme, Johannesburg*, 11.

Palmary, I. (2016). Gender, Sexuality and Migration in South Africa: Governing Morality. London: Palgrave.

Prout, A. & James, A. (1997). A new paradigm for the sociology of childhood? Provenance, promise and problems. In A. Prout & A. James (Eds.), *Constructing and Reconstructing Childhood: Contemporary Issues in the Sociological Study of Childhood* (pp. 7–32). London: Routledge.

Robinson, K. H. (2008). In the name of 'childhood innocence': A discursive exploration of the moral panic associated with childhood and sexuality. *Cultural Studies Review*, 14(2), 113.

Rubin, G. (1984). Thinking sex: Notes for a radical theory of the politics of sexuality. In H. Abelove, M. A. Barale & D. Halperin (Eds.), *Social Perspectives in Lesbian and Gay Studies: A Reader* (pp. 150–187). New York: Routledge.

Sirriyeh, A. (2010). Home journeys: Im/mobilities in young refugee and asylum-seeking women's negotiations of home. *Childhood*, 17(2), 213–227.

Stephens, S. (1997). Editorial introduction: Children and nationalism. *Childhood: A Global Journal of Child Research*, 4(1), 5–17.

Summers, C. (1991). Intimate colonialism: The imperial production of reproduction in Uganda, 1907–1925. *Signs*, 16(4), 787–807.

Thørnblad, R. & Holtan, A. (2013). Kinship foster children: Actors in their encounter with the child protection system. *Qualitative Social Work*, 12(3), 307–322.

Torpey, J. (2000). The Invention of the Passport: Surveillance, Citizenship and the State. Cambridge: Cambridge University Press.

Walkerdine, V. (1990). *Schoolgirl Fictions*. London, New York: Verso Books.

Yuval-Davis, N. (1993). Gender and nation. *Ethnic and Racial Studies*, 16(4), 621–632.

9

WORKING CHILDREN

*Lindsay O'Dell, Sarah Crafter, Guida de Abreu
and Tony Cline*

"YES to work – NO to exploitation! YES to dignified work – NO to undignified
conditions! YES to work – NO to marginalisation! YES to work – NO to discrimination!" – Statement from the fifth meeting of Latin American working children
(cited in Liebel, 2004, p. 21).

Introduction

In this chapter we discuss children's engagement in work and how normative
understandings of childhood as a time for play, formal schooling and socialisation
play out in debates about and experiences of child workers. Ideas about children's
development, taken up in national and international policy, frame the debate about
working children and distinguishing between work and school, with the view that
work is very much at the limits or margins of normative childhood.

Debates about whether children should work or not draw on particular ideas
about childhood as distinct from adulthood and as a period of vulnerability that
requires adult protection, or at least supervision (see Crafter et al., 2009; Burman,
2008). From this perspective, child workers are constructed as in need of protection. We discuss how children's engagement in work is constructed, in particular
the distinction made in much of the literature, and in policy and practice, between
labour and work, childhood and adulthood, and between the global north and
south. The chapter focuses on how dominant constructions of the developing child
(drawn largely from the global north) make particular assumptions about the kind
of work children should, if at all, be engaging in. The chapter also interrogates the
assumption that 'work' is a paid activity that takes place outside the home through
a discussion of children who are young carers to family members. The symbolic and
actual limits of childhood are played out in public debate and legislation internationally about the role of work, including care work, in children's lives.

Children and work

There has been a great deal of international research to identify the scale of the 'problem' of children working. International organisations such as the International Labour Organisation (ILO), through their International Programme on the Elimination of Child Labour (IPEC), have used surveys from across the world to estimate the number of the world's children who work. The ILO (2013a, viii) notes that "There are some 264 million children ages 5 to 17 in economic activity in the world in 2012 (16.7 per cent). This is 42 million fewer than in 2008".

The ILO distinguishes 'economic activity' from child labour, which they define as illegal working practices as articulated through national legislation and ILO statutes. IPEC estimate 168 million children to be involved in child labour in 2012, about half of these in hazardous conditions, or what they term a 'worse form of child labour' (ILO, 2013b, viii). There are an estimated 300,000 "children associated with armed forces and groups" internationally (warchild.org, n.d.). The statistics provided in these reports are likely to underestimate the number of working children as many children work illegally and are therefore very difficult to research (Dayiogiu, 2012; McKechnie et al., 1998). Dayioglu (2012) has argued that the way in which questions are asked in surveys, such as the Child Labor Survey, determine the level of work captured across different countries. For example, rates of agricultural work are high in Africa but are lower in countries such as Moldova. Dayioglu suggests that this is because commercial agriculture is more widespread in Moldova and therefore family work on farms may not be recognised as children's work.

It is evident that particular kinds of work put children (and adults) at immediate risk of harm. Research by the ILO (2013b) reported that in a one-year period, 106.4 million children aged between 5 and 17 experienced a work-related injury and 15.1 million of these required subsequent medical attention. There are obvious health risks for children, such as exposure to risks associated with prostitution, including HIV/AIDS (Forasteri 1997), or those who work in agricultural settings where there is a risk of exposure to dangerous pesticides and heavy machinery (Forasteri, 1997; McKechnie et al., 1998). The ILO (2013b) report on the hazards of child labour focused on physical harm, but there are also psychosocial hazards to consider (Wood, 2004). The psychological effects of being trained to be a soldier (often by giving children drugs and forcing them to commit violent acts on their families and communities) have been documented (Human Rights Watch, 2003, in Schmitz, Traver, & Larson, 2004; War Child, n.d.).

It is evident in public discourse, including legislation, that children's engagement in work is accorded a special status. Where work is permissible for children (as set out in national and international legislation), it is usually seen as an activity that takes place outside the home for which the child worker gets paid and that does not interfere with the 'real' work of childhood – attending school and socialising with peers. The ILO (2011) stated that acceptable work for children "includes activities such as helping their parents around the home, assisting in a family business or earning pocket money *outside school hours*" (cited in Wyness, 2015, p. 80, italics added).

Legislation in many countries includes a transitional stage of life where young people are permitted to work for a limited period of time per day. For example, UK legislation from the early twentieth century onwards has created a framework for seeing some work as acceptable for older children, with the view that children working a small number of hours under adult supervision for 'pocket money' combined with full-time education was an acceptable practice (Crafter et al., 2009; McKechnie & Hobbs, 2001). From this perspective, certain types of work may be considered to be appropriate activities if they are undertaken with adult supervision and are seen to be enhancing rather than interfering with the child's education.

However, many activities are not covered by legislation and take place outside the boundaries of the definition of work as given by the ILO. For example, in the United Kingdom, babysitting is not part of employment legislation and so does not officially 'count' as children's work. The view that work takes place outside the home in return for money has been challenged by feminists who view work as a broader set of activities, which can include caring responsibilities and domestic work (Burman, 2008; Punch & Sugden, 2013). Research that has documented the kinds of work children around the world participate in note that a considerable amount of children's work takes place within the home or family business. The most common form of work that children engage in is not in the 'commercial' or business sector, but in unpaid labour in the context of family or community life (Mizen & Ofosu-Kusi, 2012; Punch & Sugden, 2013).

A distinction is often made between children's engagement in 'work' and 'labour', in which child 'labour' is seen as harmful, or, at the very least, not in a child's best interests, whereas children's 'work' is perceived as benign or neutral (Weston, 2005). Wyness (2015) suggests that distinctive features of child labour are activities that involve children working as adults, that is, the focus is on the present rather than work activities that have a future orientation. In other words, there is an educational element and support for the child to engage in what are seen as 'age appropriate' activities.

A common assumption in the global north is that child labour is not part of our/their society. For example Liebel (2007, p. 5), writing from Germany, argued that, "In our latitudes, the work of children is generally seen as a phenomenon from distant parts of the world or from our own distant past". However, it is clear that children across the world are involved in hazardous work that equates with 'child labour'. It is also evident that the distinction between child work and child labour is not clear-cut and terms are often used interchangeably (Bourdillon, 2006) and politically (Liebel, 2007; Morrow, 2010). The notion that work for children in the global south is hazardous child labour, whereas work for children in the global north is positive and safe is simplistic and inaccurate.

There are many reasons to account for children working. Some children have no choice about whether they work. Slavery and debt bondage/bonded labour (where a child's work is linked to an adult's work contract or the child is exchanged for money) are evident in many countries, including the United Kingdom (Craig et al., 2007). There is international trade in the trafficking of women and children for sex work and domestic work (Forasteri, 1997, UNICEF, n.d.). Morrow (2010) and others have argued that the underlying causes of child labour are poverty, unbalanced economic growth and problems in the education system. Children are often key to the survival of the family in difficult circumstances. It is easy to make the assumption that the world's children work because of the economic conditions in which they live. However, many commentators have argued that whilst the overriding reason for many children is economic, reasons are complex and it is not as simple as poor children *have* to work. According to Mizen et al. (1999, p. 429), "Very little is known about the characteristics of working children or their motivations to enter work".

Globalisation and consumerism directed towards children have increasingly made children consumers, or at least aspiring consumers, of goods or particular lifestyles (Burman, 2016, 2008; White, 1996). Consequently, children may enter the labour market with or without their parents' approval. However, Burr (2006) and others have argued against a perception of street children as abandoned by their families. For example, Invernizzi (2003) noted ways in which children were inducted into work by their parents. In the case of girls working in the Bangladesh export garment industry, work (starting around the age of 11 years) offered a secure and skilled job for the future. When legislation around child workers was tightened in Bangladesh, many of the girls lost their jobs and none of those dismissed went back to school (see White, 1996). For some children, their contributions to family income serve to protect them and their families from worse exploitation or neglect (Nieuwenhuys, 1994).

Understandings of work are influenced by the specific context of families, including social class and geopolitical context as well as the gender of the child. There are gendered differences in the kinds of work many of the world's children perform. For example, Invernizzi (2003) noted that the work performed by the street children of Lima was different for boys and girls; boys tended to work independently earlier than girls. In a longitudinal study based in Kerala, India, Nieuwenhuys (1994) noted that it was common for sons to join fathers in long-established fishing businesses whereas girls most often remained in the home.

Children, school and work

Definitions of 'appropriate' work for children and legislation and public discourse about child workers draw on a view of childhood as a time for education and schooling. School is a central aspect of normative childhood, a time to develop skills to prepare for, rather than necessarily engage in, work (Burman, 2016). From this perspective, work is defined as part of the adult world and often in contrast to schooling and education. The construction of childhood as a time for play, school and friends (Jans, 2004; Wyness, 2015) feeds into national and international legislation, such as the United Nations Convention on the Rights of the Child (UNCRC, 1989). For example, article 28 of the UNCRC requires governments to "recognize the right of the child to education, and with a view to achieving this right progressively and on the basis of equal opportunity" and article 32 requires that "children's work should not jeopardize any of their other rights, including the right to education, or the right to relaxation and play" (www.unicef.org). The expectation is that children have the right to go to school and that school will benefit the child in the long term (Woodhead, 1999). Play is seen to be an essential and universal aspect of childhood, and opportunities for education and play are often assumed to be lost when children work (Burman, 2016).

Seeing work and education as incompatible is, McKechnie and Hobbs (2001) argue, a "false dichotomy" (p. 9). Indeed, these authors (and others) have argued that the cost of schooling is often part of the reason many children work. Furthermore, Lieten and White (2001, p. 6) suggest that the 'blind spot' for campaigners who want to abolish child labour is that they "consistently ignore the fact that most of the world's working children attend school". The view that most working children attend school is supported by ILO surveys (Forasteri, 1997). The World Bank (n.d., cited in Schmitz et al., 2004) estimated that 50 to 70 per cent of working children attend school, and it is likely that this figure is now much higher. For example, Liebel (2004) noted that many of the working children he met in his research had created small syndicates, cooperatives or unions; for example, shoeshine children in Paraguay allocate work places in the morning or afternoon so their peers can attend school during the other half of the day, a strategy that also helps protect their sites of work. He noted that working children in the global south "see in their work not merely a burden or a necessity, but also a chance to learn things that school does not offer them" (Liebel, 2004, p. 2).

For some children and their families, education does not have the status of paid labour/work (Jans, 2004), and many parents fail to see the value of education which takes children away from actively contributing to family income (Punch & Sugden, 2013; Schlemmer, 2000). Many children live in families and communities where children work as apprentices in a family business (Schmitz et al., 2004). In an international study that examined children's perspectives on school and work in Bangladesh, Ethiopia, the Philippines and Central America, it was found that 77 per cent of the 300 working children studied felt that combining work and school was best for them (Woodhead, 2001). Most did not see work and school as alternatives in their present situation, and reported that they felt work was a necessity whilst schooling was felt to be desirable.

In situations of chronic poverty, such as those explored in the Young Lives project, attendance at school was seen to compound family difficulties (Pells, 2012). In one example, a 15-year-old boy from rural Andhra Pradesh described the many life skills he learnt from working with his father and his cousins, listing masonry, ploughing, bulldozing, tractor mending, building walls and plastering. School attendance was seen as the 'risky' option.

Morrow (2010, p. 437) observed that in the global north, children's engagement in work has shifted historically, as "children are effectively no longer 'earners' but have become redefined as 'learners'". However, assuming that being a 'learner' only happens at school is not an accurate reflection of how children (and adults) learn.

Indeed, it could be considered that all children work (Schlemmer, 2000) because, although it is rarely viewed in this way, attendance at school can be conceptualised as a form of work (Qvortrup, 2001; Close, 2009, cited in Morrow, 2010). Learning through working in families and local communities has been neglected because of the construction of school as the dominating place where 'education' is performed (Morelli, Rogoff & Angelillo, 2003).

Children, care work and families

As discussed earlier, 'work' is still largely assumed to refer to activities that take place outside of the home and for which the worker is paid. However, care work is "a mostly hidden and unacknowledged part of national economies" (Robson, 2004, p. 229), often because it is unpaid, takes place in a domestic arena and is viewed as 'women's work' (Burman, 2008; Punch & Sugden, 2013).

The dominant construction of childhood, drawing on a view of childhood from the global north, is that children should be cared for, rather than having the responsibility for caring for others. Caring as a form of work is not seen to be part of a normative childhood. Debates about young carers in the United Kingdom (where we live and research) and in other parts of the world often centre on the assumption that young carers have lost out on their childhood through being a carer (O'Dell et al., 2010; Robson, 2004).

Children are an active part of the care relations within families in many countries (Robson, 2004; Skovdal, 2010). In many parts of the world, particularly in sub-Saharan Africa, the HIV/AIDS epidemic has led to what has been termed as a 'lost generation' of parents leaving behind children to bring up their younger siblings. In many instances, children care for dying parents or other family members. Robson (2004, p. 233) argued that young carers in these situations are "invisible in the geographical imaginations of global northerners because they do not correspond to the stereotype of 'exploited Third World child worker' labouring in a factory producing export commodities such as sports footwear".

In Kenya, the traditional view is that children are an important resource for families. Skovdal (2010) researched in the Bondo district of Kenya, a district that has high levels of poverty, an HIV rate of 13 per cent (twice the national average) and where one in nine children have lost both of their parents (Nyambedha et al., 2003, in Skovdal, 2010). Skovdal (2010) noted in his research that orphaned children are often taken in by 'guardians' who are usually a family member and are often ill themselves. Many of the children interviewed as part of the research talked about needing to work in order to feed themselves and their family, and many have full responsibility for their guardians and for younger children. All of the children performed the daily household chores and many nursed their guardian.

During Skovdal's (2010) research, children were given cameras to take pictures of their lives and to write an explanation of the pictures. Many of the children discussed negative feelings in relation to being a carer, for example, Paddy, a fifteen-year-old boy caring for his mother said:

> I took this picture to show how I have been helping my mother since she has an unpredictable disease. It may come anytime and at these times I do not go to school. When she gets sick, I am forced to leave school to help her out. I clean the house, cook for her, feed her, wash her feet and look after the animals. It affects my education and makes me suffer.
>
> *(Skovdal, 2010, p. 99)*

Other research that has taken place in sub-Saharan Africa also documents the role of young carers and the impact it has on their lives, for example:

> During the last months of his mother's life Rindai (15 years) cared for her. His only sibling – an older brother – was away studying and could only come back home in the last two weeks before their mother's death. His father had died two years previously of HIV/AIDS. Each day Rindai carried his mother outside to sit in the sun, took her to the toilet, and brought her food and drink. His mother withdrew him from school and Rindai couldn't even go out to the shops and *do normal 15-year-old things*. [...] The experience made a big impression on him. He matured overnight.
>
> *(Interview with UNICEF worker, Robson, 2004, p. 227, italics added)*

Young carers in the United Kingdom have received much policy and practice scrutiny over the past 15 years. In our research with young carers, it was evident that being a young carer was seen to be outside of the expected activities for children. For example, Louise, who was 18 at the time we met, had cared for her disabled mother from the age of 11. As part of the research, we asked her what she thought about a fictitious character, Mary, who was caring for her dad:

> That's the same as me, that's the same as I did in high school, it's the same thing, you know, you take, if you have a disabled parent it's kind of like you're split ok, you have the side that just wants to be you. You want to be able to go out, have a kick about, you wanna be able to go to the shops and buy Nike, all the retails stuff. You wanna be able to just go over to your friends and watch movies and go 'ha, ha, ha'. But then on the other side you've got your obligations to your family because no matter how much you may want to be a normal person you also, if you tried being a normal person you'd feel guilty.
>
> *(O'Dell et al., 2010, p. 651)*

The developmental assumption that young carers should be able to "do normal 15-year-old things" (Robson, 2004, p. 227) transcends the geopolitical location of the child caring for an adult family member. Young carers across the world experience a lack of visibility and value of their care work (Becker, 2007; Robson, 2004). In the example of Louise shown previously, she also articulates a sense of normative expectations against which she is aware that she is different. Louise compares her life (and that of the character, Mary, who is a young carer in the vignette she was discussing) with a 'normal' childhood and articulates how she feels torn between being a 'normal' teenager and being a carer:

> Teachers sympathise, they do sympathise and they do try it. When it comes down to disabled parents, one thing that I found like at this college, teachers do sympathise because teachers do understand that when it comes to your family if you've got a disabled parent it is very hard on you because you have to be there for the parent but also have to get your grades. So you have the stress of school but you also have the stress of family and everything else and so teachers do understand but at the same time they don't.
>
> *(O'Dell et al., 2012, p. 710)*

In our research, and in others, it is clear that young carers have complex feelings about caring for an adult family member. Intervention in both the United Kingdom and sub-Saharan Africa focuses on the (assumed) loss of childhood when children care for adult family members. It is evident that children who are given no choice but to be a carer, who perform intimate and personal care, or administer complex health treatments, find the activity challenging and stressful. However, researchers such as Skovdal (2010) and Robson (2004) challenge the view of young carers as passive 'victims' of their circumstances. Robson (2004, p. 239) argued that caring ensures that a family stays together and can be viewed as a "creative and active choice". Skovdal (2010) noted that the view of child orphans as a burden and as tragic is a partial explanation of the lives of young carers. For example, Samuel aged 13 has cared for his sick father and now cares for a disabled friend and his sick mother:

> All that I have done makes me happy. This is because I don't do bad things in the community, and the villagers love me seriously for that and the fact that I like helping sick people.
>
> *(Skovdal, 2010, p. 99)*

Many of the young carers in our research talked about a sense of pride that they can help their family and spoke of wanting to help rather than feeling forced into it. Louise exhibits agency (although not perhaps in ways that adults, particularly her teachers, may condone):

> Like, for me, I used my, I hate to say it but I did use my mum as an excuse to get out of school because I was not having a good time and everyone thought I was dumb. But in Mary's situation she may, she may love school, she may be doing fantastic, or she may be like me and hate school and use it

as an excuse. But at the same time she's still, she's still being, in a way, robbed of high school.

(O'Dell et al., 2012, p. 711)

The lifestyles and activities of young carers in very different contexts challenge ideas about normative childhood. Paradoxically, they may miss out on the formal and informal developmental opportunities that their communities offer them at school and elsewhere, but are engaged in highly skilled and emotionally challenging work as a carer. It is perhaps their agency in this role, such as avoiding welfare 'assistance', that might threaten the integrity of the family and that most strongly challenges a simplistic linear view of child development.

Conclusion: Working children and the limits of childhood

In this chapter we have argued that children's engagement in work is an activity that takes place in particular cultural and spatial locations and is given meaning within them. We have touched on some of the structural and contextual conditions that frame children's lives and those of their families. The constructions of child workers discussed in this chapter are closely linked to the historical development of education systems in different parts of the world. Systems where a prolonged childhood in formal education, with a view to future economic reward, sit at odds with learning through work where economic gains are more immediate, and often necessary. As discussed in the Young Lives project, school might be seen as the risky option by young people when paid or unpaid work with the family provides vital skills for dealing with chronic or cumulative poverty.

Parents, teachers and friends as well as the culture in which they live have an impact on children's work, and it is not possible to account for children's experiences without understanding how work as an activity is mediated through these structures (Rogoff, 2003; Woodhead, 2004). Work for many children is part of family life (when broadly defined) and is part of everyday activity. It is evident that looking at work purely as an economic activity misses out on many forms of work and many aspects of children's experiences of work (Invernizzi, 2003). Aspirations for a better life and education feature alongside a need for children to remove themselves from physical violence, poverty, poor future prospects or arbitrary punishment (Mizen & Ofosu-Kusi, 2012). Invernizzi (2003) uses a definition by Bolle de Ball (1987) in which work is conceptualised as a series of social links between an individual and the meanings given to their working activities:

- Socio-economic (material benefits)
- Sociocultural (relationships with other workers and social belonging)
- Sociopsychological (social identity and social activity)

Similarly, Woodhead (2004, pp. 333–334) argued the importance of "recognising that cultural beliefs and expectations surrounding the value of children's work, goals for their development and indicators of well-being will strongly mediate children's perspectives on and experiences of work, and in turn its positive or negative impact on their lives".

Life course transitions to adulthood and the world of work can only be viewed within prevailing 'macrosocial' conditions (economic systems, government policy, rural/industrial/mixed trade) and 'microsystems' (changing relationships with family) (Hendry & Kloep, 2011). These same authors discuss the additional complexities of existing in what they describe as "postmodern societies", whereby global relationships across societies, and the introduction of technologies, means changing situations for women and children in the labour force. Woodhead (2004) suggests that children's work should be viewed through a set of guiding principles addressing 'development', 'context' and 'mediation'. A focus on 'development' looks at the long-term perspective of children's involvement in work through various transitions or phases. 'Context' emphasises the importance of the circumstances in which the work is taking place and 'mediation' recognises that there are varying cultural beliefs and expectations surrounding work and that this will mediate the children's own perspectives of their working lives.

The view that children who work are passive victims in poor economic circumstances (Liebel, 2004) or of inescapable family difficulties (O'Dell et al., 2010) is an inadequate view of children's activities. Liebel (2004) argued that children wish to work but under their own will and under safe and reasonable conditions. Liebel provides examples of working children's movements of Latin America and Africa, which are organisations usually run by working children aged 12–16 who work in the 'informal' work sector in cities. The organisations have typically been set up as a result of initiatives by adult humanitarian organisations but are run and administered by children themselves. Working children wish to be recognised and participate in their culture as workers; children see their organisations as the best way to protect working children (Liebel, 2004). The organisations are usually framed within a rights discourse, for example, the right to vocational training in order to learn a trade; the right to carry out activities safely; the right to access to justice; the right to express themselves; and the right to organise themselves (Cited in Liebel, 2004, p. 21).

It is accepted by many commentators that rather than attempt to stop children working, there is a need to recognise the ways in which children work within communities and, where necessary, to change the ways in which children (and adults) work where the activities are hazardous and unsafe. For example, Leonard (2004) cited the case of the Bangladesh garment industry boycott on child labour in 1993, where a follow-up by UNICEF found children were vulnerable and in exploitative occupations because of the ban on factory work. Hence, moves to prohibit children working may lead to more precarious and hazardous activities. It is evident that children often work in situations where they have lower levels of status and power. The dominant construction of childhood as a time of dependency and innocence frames the kinds of work that children can engage in and how working children are viewed:

> Work is all right so long as it is unpaid; children may also work for pay when they do not need to (for 'pocket money'), but not when they need to;

children may help their parents' income-earning efforts (and gain pride and satisfaction from it) only if their parents own a family enterprise, but not if they are property less wage-workers".

(White, 1994, p. 873)

Wyness (2015, p. 80), reflecting on the ILO definition of work as activities that take place outside of school hours, argued that "In short, these kinds of activities are not perceived to threaten childhood". Similarly, Mizen et al. (1999) character-ised children's work as mainly low-paid and unskilled and therefore argued that it is "firmly rooted in the material conditions of childhood" (p. 424). Debates about child work, particularly when it is framed as labour in the global south, construct child workers as a "globally deviant category of childhood" (Wyness, 2015, p. 61) and hence engagement in work is seen to be at the limits of what is acceptable for children. It can be argued that legislation to prohibit or restrict chil-dren's engagement in work serves to distinguish children's activities from those of adults (Leonard, 2004; Wyness, 2015) and further distinguish between the worlds of children and adults.

In this chapter we have specifically discussed work within the home and the role of young carers. The assumption that parents care for children, and that chil-dren's role in families is as recipients of care, positions young carers as transgressing expectations of normative childhood. Young carers around the world are assumed to have lost out on childhood, not just in terms of lost opportunities to socialise with friends, but also a symbolic loss of childhood. This, we have argued, is a simplified and problematic view of families, particularly of disabled parents who provide effective parenting to their children but are positioned as passive recipients of care (O'Dell et al., 2010; Prilleltensky, 2004). Developmental theorising needs to take account of diverse family structures in which the roles of adults and children are multiple and reciprocal.

References

Becker, S. (2007). Global perspectives on children's unpaid caregiving in the family: Research and policy on 'young carers' in the UK, Australia, the USA and Sub-Saharan Africa. *Global Social Policy*, 7(1), 23–50.

Bolle de Ball, M. (1987). 'Aspiration au travail et expérience du chômage: Crise, déliance et paradoxes', *Revue Suisse de Sociologie*, 1: 63–83.

Bourdillon, M. (2006). Children and work: A review of current literature and debates. *Development and Change*, 37(6), 1201–1226.

Burman, E. (2008). *Developments: Child, Image, Nation*. London: Routledge.

Burman, R. (2016). *Deconstructing Developmental Psychology* (3rd Edition). London: Routledge.

Burr, R. (2006). *Vietnam's Children in a Changing World*. New Brunswick: Rutgers University Press.

Close, P. (2009). Making Sense of Child Labour in Modern Society, in Jens Qvortrup (Ed.), *Sociological Studies of Children and Youth: Structural, Historical, and Comparative Perspectives* (pp. 167–94). Bingley: Emerald Group Publishing.

Crafter, S., O'Dell, L., Abreu, de. G. & Cline, T. (2009). Young people's representations of 'atypical' work in UK society. *Children & Society*, 23(3), 176–188.

Craig, G., Gaus, A., Wilkinson, M., Skrivankova, K. & McQuade, A. (2007). *Contemporary Slavery in the UK*. Joseph Rowntree Foundation Report. ISBN: 978 1 85935 573 2.

Dayioglu, M. (2012). How sensitive are estimates of working children and child labour to definitions? A comparative analysis. *MICS Methodological Papers, No. 1, Statistics and Monitoring Section/Division of Policy and Strategy*. UNICEF, New York.

Forastieri, V. (1997). *Children at Work: Health and Safety Risks*. Geneva: International Labour Office.

Hendry, L. B. & Kloep, M. (2011). Lifestyles in emerging adulthood: Who needs stages anyway? In J. J. Arnett, M. Kloep, L. B. Hendry & J. L. Tanner (Eds.), *Debating Emerging Adulthood: Stage or Process?* Oxford Scholarship Online ISBN: 13:9780199757176.

International Labour Organization (2011). *International Programme on the Elimination of Child Labour*. Geneva: ILO.

International Labour Organization (2013a). *Global Child Labour Trends 2008 to 2012*. International Labour Office, International Programme on the Elimination of Child Labour (IPEC) Geneva: ILO.

International Labour Organization (2013b). *A Global Estimate of Work-related Injuries among Children*. International Labour Office, International Programme on the Elimination of Child Labour (IPEC) Geneva: ILO.

Invernizzi, A. (2003). Street working children and adolescents in Lima: Work as an agent of socialization. *Childhood*, 10(3), 319–341.

Jans M. (2004). Children as citizens: Towards a contemporary notion of child participation. *Childhood*, 11(1), 27–44.

Leonard, M. (2004). Children's views on children's right to work: Reflections from Belfast. *Childhood*, 11(1), 45–61.

Liebel, M. (2004). *A Will of their Own: Cross-cultural Perspectives on Working Children*. London: Zed Books Ltd.

Liebel, M. (2007). Opinion, dialogue, review. The new ILO report on child labour: A success story, or the ILO still at a loss? *Childhood*, 14(2), 279–284.

Lieten, K. & White, B. (2001). Children, work and education: Perspectives on policy. In K. Lieten & B. White (Eds.), *Child Labour: Policy Options* (pp. 1–11). Amsterdam: Aksant Academic Publishers.

McKechnie, J. & Hobbs, S. (2001). Work and education: Are they compatible for children and adolescents? In. P. Mizen, C. Pole and A. Bolton (Eds.), *Hidden Hands: International Perspectives on Children's Work and Labour* (pp. 37–54). London: Routledge-Falmer.

McKechnie, J., Hobbs, S. & Lindsay, S. (1998). Working children: The health and safety issue. *Children & Society*, 12, 38–47.

Mizen, P., Bolton, A. & Pole, C. (1999). School age workers: The paid employment of children in Britain. *Work, Employment & Society*, 12(3), 423–438.

Mizen, P. & Ofosu-Kusi, Y. (2012). Engaging with a world outside of ourselves: Vistas of flatness, children's work and the urban informal economy. *Sociological Research Online*, 17, 1–17.

Morelli, G., Rogoff, B. & Angelillo, C. (2003). Cultural variation in children's access to work or involvement in specialized child-focused activities. *International Journal of Behavioral Development*, 27, 264–274.

Morrow, V. (2010). Should the world really be free of 'child labour'? Some reflections. *Childhood*, 17(4), 435–440.

Nieuwenhuys, O. (1994). *Children's Lifeworlds: Gender, Welfare and Labour in the Developing World*. London: Routledge.

Nyambedha, E., Wandibba, S. & Aagaard-Hansen, J. (2003). Changing patterns of orphan care due to the HIV epidemic in Western Kenya. *Social Science & Medicine*, 57(2), 301–311.

O'Dell, L., Crafter, S., de Abreu, G. & Cline, T. (2010). Constructing "normal childhoods": Young people talk about young carers, *Disability & Society*, 25(6), 643–655.

O'Dell, L., Crafter, S., Abreu, G. D. & Cline, T. (2012). The problem of interpretation in vignette methodology in research with young people. *Qualitative Research*, 12(6), 702–714.

Pells, K. (2012). 'Risky lives': Risk and protection for children growing-up in poverty. *Development in Practice*, 22(4), 562–573.

Prilleltensky, O. (2004). My child is not my carer: Mothers with physical disabilities and the well-being of children. *Disability and Society*, 19(3), 209–223.

Punch, S. & Sugden, F. (2013). Work, education and out-migration among children and youth in upland Asia: Changing patterns of labour and ecological knowledge in an era of globalisation. *Local Environment: The International Journal of Justice and Sustainability*, 18(3), 255–270.

Qvortrup, J. (2001). School-work, paid work and the changing obligations of childhood. In. P. Mizen, C. Pole and A. Bolton (Eds.). *Hidden Hands: International Perspectives on Children's Work and Labour* (pp. 37-54). London: Routledge-Falmer.

Robson, E. (2004). Hidden child workers: Young carers in Zimbabwe. *Antipode*, 36(2), 227–247.

Rogoff, B. (2003). *The Cultural Nature of Human Development*. Oxford University Press: Oxford, New York.

Schlemmer, B. (2000). *The Exploited Child*. London: Zed Books Ltd.

Schmitz, C. L., Traver, E. K. & Larson, D. (2004.) *Child Labour: A Global View*. Westport: Greenwood Publishing Group.

Skovdal, M. (2010). Children caring for their "caregivers": Exploring the caring arrangements in households affected by AIDS in Western Africa. *AIDS Care*, 22(1), 96–103.

United Nations (1989). Convention on the Rights of the Child. https://www.unicef.org.uk/what-we-do/un-convention-child-rights/ (accessed April 2017).

UNICEF (n.d.) *Reference Guide on Protecting the Rights of Child Victims of Trafficking in Europe*. Available at www.unicef.org/ceecis/UNICEF_Child_Trafficking_low.pdf.

War Child (n.d.). *Child Soldiers*. Available at www.warchild.org.uk/what-we-do/protection/child-soldiers. (accessed 24 November 2016).

Weston, B. (2005). *Child Labor and Human Rights: Making Children Matter*. Boulder, CO and London: Lynne Rienner.

White, B. (1994). Children, work and 'child labour': Changing responses to the employment of children. *Development and Change*, 25, 849–878.

White, B. (1996). Globalization and the child labour problem. *Journal of International Development*, 8(6), 829–839.

Woodhead, M. (1999). Reconstructing developmental psychology – Some first steps. *Children & Society*, 13, 1: 3–19.

Woodhead, M. (2001). The value of work and school: A study of working children's perspectives. In K. Lieten & B. White (Eds.), *Child Labour: Policy Options* (pp. 103–116). Amsterdam: Aksant Academic Publishers.

Woodhead, M. (2004). Psychosocial impacts of child work: A framework for research, monitoring and intervention, *The International Journal of Children's Rights*, 12: 321–377.

Wyness, M. (2015). *Childhood*. Cambridge: Polity Press.

10

PARRICIDES, SCHOOL SHOOTINGS AND CHILD SOLDIERS

Constructing *criminological phenomena* in the context of children who kill

Amanda Holt

There are more academic articles published in the United Kingdom about *two particular children who killed* than there are articles published more generally about *children who kill*. The murder of James Bulger in 1993 by two ten-year-old boys has produced both empirical and theoretical outputs from a range of academic disciplines across the arts and social sciences, including psychology (e.g. Levine, 1999), sociology (e.g. Hay, 1995), theatre studies (e.g. Ravenhill, 2004), law and human rights (Wolff & Smith, 2000), media studies (e.g. Franklin & Petley, 1996), history (Rowbotham et al., 2003) and criminology (e.g. Turner, 1994). Indeed, identifying research about children who kill whose names are *not* Robert Thompson or Jon Venables is a challenge. And while many of the academic outputs concerning this particular case are illuminating (as case studies often are), the "immediate and ferocious moral panic" (Cohen, 2002, p. 11) that the Bulger case triggered means that it should not speak for all. That it does is particularly troubling given the diverse range of contexts that surround children who kill. There are a number of reasons why it is important to recognise this imbalance, not least because the circumstances of the Bulger case do not represent those commonly found in most other cases of children who kill.

Analysis of the Homicide Index collated by the UK Home Office (see next section) suggests that, while it is true that most children who kill are male (as are most adults who kill), most cases (i) involve older perpetrators in their mid-teens (rather than pre-teens); (ii) involve spontaneous acts of violence that are over within seconds (rather than hours); (iii) involve older victims (rather than infants); and (iv) do not involve abductions. Indeed, it is likely that it was the very unusual characteristics of the Bulger case that garnered such widespread attention. One particularly fascinating aspect of the academic discourse surrounding the Bulger case is that it has focused almost exclusively on its symbolic properties: what it *means* for how we construct children, what it *means* for our juvenile justice system, and what it *means* for newspaper reporting and media campaigns for 'justice'. Many researchers have pointed out that the Bulger case was a 'watershed' in changing how we conceptualise children who harm others (Muncie, 1999). The potency of collectivised media, and police and court 'narratives of wickedness' served to produce two modern day 'folk devils' (Cohen, 2002, p. 38) who were set adrift from the multiple structural and cultural inequities – including their own victimisation – that anchored Thompson's and Venables' violence (Scraton, 1997).

While the obliteration of context and the foregrounding of the individual are most keenly felt in the Bulger case, it appears to be a feature of our understandings of children who kill across a range of settings. To explore this issue further, this chapter examines the nuanced ways in which discourses of childhood development frame our understandings of *children who kill*. Children who kill arguably operate at the limits of what we understand 'childhood' to be because they challenge our normative understandings of the moral, cognitive and physical competencies of children. Thus, while such cases are relatively rare, they can be instructive in helping us to question dominant ideas about childhood that configure particular subjectivities and set up assumptions about 'norms' against which 'the other' is judged. The chapter begins by drawing on original Home Office data to examine what 'children who kill' look like in terms of gender, age and circumstances of the incident. With this in mind, the chapter then explores how three particular contexts in which children kill have preoccupied academics and researchers to such an extent that they have become 'criminological phenomena' and have consequently shaped our thinking about *all* children who kill. This has troubling implications for both the groups of children they speak of, and for our understandings of childhood more generally.

Children who kill

In England and Wales, the only way we can identify 'children who kill' is through the Homicide Index, a database collated by the Home Office that is compiled from 'homicide returns' that are completed for offences initially recorded as 'homicide'[1] by all 44 police services across England and Wales (including the British Transport Police). An offender-based analysis tells us that, in the 11 years between April 2003 and April 2014, there were 530 offenders involved in homicide who were aged 17 years or younger, whether as a 'principal offender' (58 per cent) or as an accomplice (42 per cent). This constitutes almost 9 per cent of all recorded homicide offenders where his/her age is known. The majority of child offenders (72 per cent) were aged 16 and 17 years at the time of the killing, and the youngest was 12 years old. In terms of gender, 91 per cent of child offenders were male and 66 per cent were involved in the offence with others (whether as 'principal offenders' or as accomplices). In total, 41 per cent of child offenders killed a stranger, 29 per cent killed a friend/acquaintance and 7 per cent killed a family member.[2] Most victims (86 per cent) were male with an age range of 0–93 years (median age = 24 years). The most common methods of killing amongst child offenders were the use of a sharp instrument (e.g. a knife) (41 per cent); hitting or kicking (25 per cent); and the use of a blunt instrument (11 per cent). Only 3 per cent of child offenders used a firearm, and only 2 per cent of offenders killed in a location that could be described as a public institution (such as a school, hospital or church) – the most common-place location where children killed was outdoors on a street or footpath (30 per cent). The most commonly recorded 'circumstances of offence' (as identified by the police) were 'pub fight, argument over girlfriend' (32 per cent), 'neighbour, feud' (16 per cent) and 'robbery' (13 per cent). The circumstances of the offence were recorded as 'unknown' for 15 per cent of child offenders. In terms of court outcomes, 53 per cent of child offenders were found guilty of murder, 45 per cent were found guilty of manslaughter (common law) and 2 per cent were found guilty of manslaughter (diminished responsibility). It is worth noting here that the minimum age of criminal responsibility in England and Wales is currently 10 years. While no homicide suspect was identified in the Homicide Index as being under that age between 2003 and 2014, there have been historical cases where children younger than 10 years have been suspected of killing another: for example, the case of George Burgess, killed in Stockport by two eight-year-old boys in 1861 (see Rowbotham et al., 2003).[3]

As useful as these data and analyses are, they give little indication of the par-ticular dimensions of *children who kill* that researchers and academics have focused on. Attention has certainly not focused on the most commonplace contexts in which children kill, which – as the previous analysis suggests – are rather mun-dane and appear to be the product of arguments or through the engagement of other offences. Aside from the disproportionate focus on the Bulger case, atten-tion has instead been organised into clusters of particular – and fairly spectacular – criminological phenomena: *parricides*, *school shootings* and *child soldiers*. This is trou-bling because once a broad range of behaviours becomes organised into discrete categories of specific phenomena, they tend to become dominated by particular disciplinary frameworks and much of the potential for multidisciplinarity is lost. Furthermore, such academic constructions inevitably foreground the defining set-ting of the offence (such as 'the family, 'the school', 'the warzone') and the devel-opmental status of the offender is reduced to the single homogeneous variable of 'child'. This is problematic because each of these so-called 'phenomena' represents a rather unusual context for children who kill, yet the theoretical models that are used to explain them dominate our understandings of *all* children who kill. Fur-thermore, they serve to exclude other frameworks that might more usefully explain the majority of cases of children who kill and which may tell us something more illuminating about children and childhood more generally. A review of these afore-mentioned categories of crime will illustrate.

Parricide

The killing of one's parents, known as parricide, is incredibly rare. It constitutes only 4 per cent of all known homicides in England and Wales. It is particularly rare for a person under the age of 18 years to engage in parricidal acts: only 9 per cent of all parricide offenders are aged 17 years or younger (Holt, 2017). Of child-aged perpetrators of parricide, 90 per cent are male, 68 per cent of their victims are fathers and most killings are particularly violent, using sharp or blunt instruments (Holt, 2017). Despite the rarity of parricides committed by children, such cases have received a disproportionate amount of academic attention, with significantly more research published on parricides perpetrated by children compared with parricides perpetrated by adults, resulting in the terms *parricide* and *child-perpetrated parricide* becoming virtually synonymous (Evans et al., 2005). As Holt and Shon (2016) suggest, one possible explanation for this academic focus on child perpetrators may be that high-profile cases of parricide have tended to feature child offenders. In the United States, the first parricide to grab media attention featured the case of 16-year-old Richard Jahnke and his 17-year-old sister Deborah Jahnke in Cheyenne, Wyoming, in 1982, who shot and killed their father in an alleged pre-planned attack after years of experiencing physical and sexual victimisation. Furthermore, the first seminal academic publications on parricide[4] focused exclusively on child-aged perpetrators, and these texts have subsequently served to frame the terms of the academic debate. In particular, these early texts established the dominant discourse of *the abused perpetrator*. Based on analysis of their own legal and clinical case notes, both Mones (1991) (a defence attorney) and Heide (1992) (a forensic psychotherapist) claimed that parricide was the result of early abuse and maltreatment suffered by the child at the hands of their parent(s). Drawing on Wertham's (1937) early theoretical work on parricide, psychoanalytic notions of *catathymic violence* have been drawn on by many researchers in this field in an attempt to explain parricide as a release of frustration that protects one's self-identity from psychic and physical disintegration (e.g. Galatzer-Levy, 1993; Strong, 1988). Furthermore, claims of extreme emotional disturbance due to past experiences of childhood abuse have been used successfully as a defence in cases of child-perpetrated parricide in the United States and elsewhere, achieved through the operationalisation of 'battered child syndrome' and its assumed link to post-traumatic stress disorder (PTSD) (Hart and Helms, 2003; Malmquist, 2010). This emphasis on victim precipitation has served to position the perpetrators of parricide as *victims*, and the victims of parricide as *aggressors*. Such reverse positioning is made all the more credible because of the role of parental responsibility in accounting for crimes perpetrated by children. Predicated on the notion of 'parental determinism' (Vincent & Ball, 2007), there is an assumption derived from developmental psychology that the life chances of children are determined entirely by the choices made and practices exercised by their parents. This assumption has found its way into many youth justice systems across westernised jurisdictions through the codification of 'parental responsibility laws' (see Holt, 2008 for discussion).

This discourse on child parricide, which is circulated in popular media and can be found in lay understandings of parricide[5], is shaped by a strong developmental determinism that is predicated on an assumed developmental vulnerability that removes any sense of childhood agency (after all, *adult-perpetrated* parricide is not assumed to be the result of childhood abuse: see Heide, 2013). Furthermore, the dominance of this discourse functions to obscure other important dimensions of such incidents. For example, like other forms of homicide, parricide is deeply gendered: across the international literature, male perpetrators account for approximately 90 per cent of cases, and this includes those cases that involve child-aged perpetrators (Holt, 2017). While this gender disparity is often acknowledged, few researchers have attempted to include it within their theorisation, and its bracketing off in explanations of parricide also works to bracket off gender in the models of child abuse which are embedded within these explanations. Second, the dominance of forensic psychiatry within this field of enquiry serves to obscure the complex and diverse ways in which children actively negotiate and manage experiences of abuse, which in the vast majority of cases, *do not* produce homicidal acts of violence, whether against their tormentors or anyone else. Child abuse is much more commonplace and mundane than this, and the continuing dominance of such discourses within the parricide literature has profound implications for all children, not least through its stigmatisation of childhood abuse through notions of disrupted childhoods and pathological/homicidal outcomes. Third, this model is almost entirely rooted in research from the United States in the late twentieth and early twenty-first centuries. Yet, like all categories of crime, our understandings of parricide are both historically and culturally produced: indeed, the term 'parricide' was once used to define the killing of *any* elderly family member, such as a grandparent, aunt or uncle, and the term is still used in this way in some countries such as South Korea (see Keum, 2000; Kim, 2012). The reconfiguration of family structures over the past century, and the ensuing dominance of the nuclear family, may well have instigated the more narrow term we use in westernised cultures today. In turn, this has likely narrowed our theoretical possibilities as children who kill other family members are eliminated from any analysis due to their absence as a recognised 'field of enquiry'. Furthermore, we need to recognise that the dominance of the psychoanalytic discourse that is used to theoretically ground our understandings of child-perpetrated parricide is also a recent product of the West: analysis of historical cases of parricide that took place prior to the emergence of *developmentalism* (Morss, 1996, p. 28) highlight the historical specificity of such explanatory models. For example, an analysis of newspaper reports from the United States in the nineteenth century found that most cases of parricide were explained in terms of trivial family arguments that, in a minority of cases, escalated into lethal violence (Shon, 2009). In a different time, and with no dominant psychoanalytic discourse to draw on, other more mundane explanations were found which, in the context of what we know about the circumstances of more common kinds of child-perpetrated homicide (see earlier sections), may perhaps be more fitting.

School shootings

Broadly speaking, 'school shootings' constitute a criminological phenomenon that refers to gun violence against persons within a school setting. It can take a number of forms: the most common are *targeted attacks* against specific victim(s) while the least common form (but which receives most publicity) are *rampage attacks* that involve multiple victims who are seemingly selected at random (Muschert, 2007).[6] School shootings can be perpetrated by adult offenders but, as with parricide, the term has become almost synonymous with child-perpetrated offences. School shootings are very rare: in the United States, less than 1 per cent of all child-perpetrated homicides take place in school, and those which take the form of rampage-type school shootings constitute a very small proportion of this figure (Modzeleski et al., 2008). In the rest of the world, this figure is even smaller.[7] In their analysis of all recorded rampage-style school shootings from around the world up to the end of 2011 (n=120), 63 per cent of all cases took place in the United States (Böckler et al., 2013). Böckler et al. (2013) also found that most cases (76 per cent) involved perpetrators of adolescent age (i.e. between 12–21 years), 97 per cent of perpetrators were male, most perpetrators (97 per cent) acted alone and just over a quarter (27 per cent) took their own lives following the attack. An analysis of 37 incidents of rampage-style school shootings between 1974 and 2000 in the United States found that most incidents were planned and 44 per cent of offenders had identified at least one target against whom, in the majority of cases (77 per cent), the perpetrator held a grievance. Most perpetrators (78 per cent) had a history of suicidal ideation and/or had made previous suicide attempts, and 68 per cent of perpetrators had a documented history of "feeling extremely depressed or desperate" (Vossekuil et al., 2002, p. 25).

As with parricide, the criminological phenomenon of rampage-style school shootings emerged during the 1990s when seemingly isolated and sporadic incidents reached a "provisional peak" by the end of that decade (Böckler et al., 2013, p. 9). These incidents culminated in the case of Columbine High School in 1999 (Littleton, Colorado, US) when 17-year-old Dylan Klebold and 18-year-old Eric Harris killed 12 students and 1 teacher, and injured a further 21. Following the attack, they both took their own lives. The case was seminal because CCTV images of the attacks were taken from inside the school and were made available for public consumption across media outlets, enabling the incident to become the most covered news story of that year in the United States. However, unlike cases of child-perpetrated parricide, school shootings present little ambiguity about who are the victims and who are the perpetrators. Furthermore, unlike cases of parricide, which are very much constructed as extreme responses to intrafamilial problems, school shootings have instigated the development of explanatory frameworks that go beyond the individual. School shootings have been linked to wider social discourses about 'the youth problem' through a range of sociological concepts, including *hegemonic masculinity* (Kimmel & Mahler, 2003), *the spectacle of violence* (Frymer, 2009) and *the performative script* (Muschert & Ragnedda, 2010).

While parricides tend to be considered as impacting only those directly affected by the violence (i.e. the victims and their immediate family), school shootings are frequently constructed as having a much wider social impact. Indeed, dominant cultural discourses about their wider symbolism often eclipse any recognition of the more immediate harm it causes to those directly affected. Empirical work has highlighted how school shootings shape children's and parents' perceptions about the likelihood of being a victim of such a crime, and about perceptions of children's safety in schools more generally (Jones, 2013; Madfis, 2016). Furthermore, school shootings have instigated wider academic debates and policy changes about school security, student profiling and gun control (Borum et al., 2010) and, in the case of Columbine, have been linked to broader academic concerns about increased surveillance, security measures, public fear and terrorism in a new *discourse of control* for the twenty-first century (Altheide, 2009). This is not to suggest that more individualistic explanations are not also put forward to explain school shootings in academic discourse, but the deep symbolism imbued by school shootings has meant that such explanations do not dominate the debate. Thus, when factors such as 'mental illness' or 'family dysfunction' are identified as important contributory factors, they are used in combination with other levels of understanding to produce *multi-level* theories (e.g. see Harding et al., 2002; Heitmeyer et al., 2013; Levin & Madfis, 2009; Madfis & Levin, 2013). However, this is not an altogether positive shift, since the theoretical process is an 'additive' one. That is, while the preoccupation with the cultural symbolism of school shootings may provide us with *additional* explanatory frameworks to help us make sense of them, their reliance on the traditional Western dualism between 'individual' and 'society' ensures that they are never *transformative*. As Burman found in her analysis of conventional writings on child development, the "optional overlay" (1997, p. 136) that constitutes the sociocultural milieu occasionally surrounds the individualised domain of the psychological, but it never fundamentally constructs it. As Burman explains, individuals are constructed as existing "prior to sociality, and relationships are only formed by exchanges between these already-enclosed individuals. There is no scope here for an account that tries to address our culturally defined construction of forms of experience" (1997, p. 136).

In the case of school shootings, the academic research merely adds together psychological characteristics of a particular 'sociocultural milieu' (gun culture, masculine culture, American culture™, etc.) to explain something that is extremely rare, in apparent decline and is not representative of the majority of contexts in which children kill. Neither do children represent the perpetrators of 'mass shootings', which, as Squires (2014) points out, mostly involve adults and mostly take place in other public arenas. Yet, as with parricides, it is a criminological phenomenon that has become associated with child perpetrators, again serving to obscure the wider violence and harms that impact children every day.

Child soldiers

Child soldiers refer to boys and girls who are under the age of 18 and who are engaged in armed conflict, whether recruited through state forces (such as the military or police) or through non-state armed groups that have political goals. The term is broad and refers to a range of roles, which include fighting but also encompass cooking, portering, spying, minesweeping, guarding and/or performing sexual roles (Child Soldiers International, 2012). To reflect this complex range of roles, and the archetypal masculinity evoked by the term 'soldier', *children associated with fighting forces* is sometimes used in the academic literature, although this term is not without its problems in its connotations of passivity and peripherality. Furthermore, in non-westernised countries (e.g. in sub-Saharan Africa), where the demarcation between 'child' and 'adult' is less legally defined and more socially defined (determined by the completion of culturally scripted initiation ceremonies), community members may instead refer to 'underage soldiers' or 'minor soldiers' (Wessells, 2006).

It is therefore evident that the term 'child soldiers' is not synonymous with 'children who kill', though it nevertheless includes such children. Thus, we do not know how many children kill within this context, although it is estimated that approximately 300,000–500,000 children from around the world are engaged in armed conflict (Song & de Jong, 2015). Despite the almost universal principle that children should not be engaged in armed conflict (reflected in the ratification of the Optional Protocol to the *Convention on the Rights of the Child* by almost two-thirds of UN states), children are engaged in armed conflict in many parts of the world, including the Democratic Republic of Congo, Afghanistan, Myanmar and Syria (Child Soldiers International, 2012). Children's entry into soldiering inevitably varies: while some children are recruited voluntarily, others are recruited compulsorily, whereas others are recruited through force or abduction, in some cases from as young as 10 years (Child Soldiers International, 2016). However, as with school shootings, child soldiering should not be constructed as a 'cultural problem' that is 'over there': the UK government allows children aged 16 and 17 to engage in hostilities, despite protocols apparently set up to prevent under-18s being deployed in such ways (UNICEF, 2007; Principle 6.4.1).

Denov's (2012) analysis of representations of child soldiers in newspaper print in the United States, Canada and the United Kingdom identifies three categorical themes. The first theme identified is *dangerous and disorderly*, which signifies child soldiers as threatening, uncivilised and permanently damaged (having perverted from the natural course of 'childhood innocence'). This theme serves to pathologise and dehumanise the child and represent warfare in non-westernised countries as inexplicable and savage. The second theme identified is *the hapless victim*, which signifies child soldiers as victims of powerful warlords: helpless, dependent and non-agentic. Such representations highlight what Burman (1994, p. 246) refers to as "the iconography of emergencies": that is, media imagery that is used strategically to capture attention but which is ultimately disempowering and degrading for those rendered as 'other' by the Western gaze.[8] The third theme identified is *the hero*, which signifies child soldiers as having overcome extreme violence and adversity to achieve redemption, and who may acquire celebrity status having undergone a transformative westernisation, such as in the case of Ishmael Beah[9] (Denov, 2012).

However, when examining academic texts of child soldiers, it is the second theme – the hapless victim – that is dominant. Academic research examining child soldiers is dominated by a biopsychomedical framework and a focus on the post-war impact of trauma on former child soldiers (e.g. Amone-P'Olak et al., 2014; Hermaneu et al., 2013). Trauma is found to be particularly associated with 'toxic' soldiering experiences such as surviving rape and perpetrating violence (Betancourt et al., 2013). Randomised controlled trials for treating PTSD in former child soldiers are common in the literature, with a focus on measuring post-treatment reductions in quantitative measurements of 'psychosocial distress' (e.g. Bayer et al., 2007; McMullen et al., 2013). Summerfield (1999) locates the emergence of the trauma discourse as an international humanitarian issue to the 1990s, when a number of 'trauma projects' headed by a range of intergovernmental organisations (e.g. UNICEF, World Health Organisation) began to proliferate in war-affected settings. However, Summerfield (1999) and others (e.g. Both & Reis, 2014; Harlacher et al., 2006) are highly critical of the assumptions that underpin this framework, notably how they objectify suffering and relocate it within the biopsychomedical realm that demands technical solutions (e.g. psychological counselling) to a technical problem (i.e. 'trauma'). There are also concerns about the assumption that westernised psychological frameworks capture a universal human response to such suffering (Summerfield, 1999), or that specific 'vulnerable' groups (such as child soldiers) need to be targeted for psychological intervention, an assumption based on westernised conceptions of healthy and pathological child development (Boyden, 1994). Summerfield (1999) cites evidence that child soldiers who have been forced to kill require not psychological intervention, but attention to their families, their education and their communities to repair the harms caused (in effect, to *return* them to childhood). Thus, such frameworks and associated practices risk eroding traditional values and practices, familial networks, civic services and social cohesion "…and [which] therefore destabilizes the entire social ecology of affected communities" (Vindevogel et al., 2012, p. 2). Yet again, we see the construction of a criminological phenomenon that overemphasises the psychologised individual child and which serves to obscure both the wider social contexts of war that impact on children every day (including UK contexts), and the more commonplace contexts in which children kill others.

Such complexities are illuminated in the recent case of Dominic Ongwen, a former member of the Lord's Resistance Army (LRA) in northern Uganda who is to be tried at the International Criminal Court (ICC) for a series of war crimes, including murder, pillage and enslavement (Burke, 2016). His legal team plans to raise the defence that he was abducted by the LRA when he was nine years old and should therefore be considered a victim as much as a perpetrator. In her research with child soldiers following post-war reintegration in Sierra Leone, Shepler identified "discourses of abdicated responsibility" (2005, p. 199) within their narrative accounts, whereby agency was practiced paradoxically through claims of wartime *non-agency* by drawing on appeals to their victimhood and innocence. Such discursive practices enabled their reintegration into their communities and facilitated forgiveness and acceptance. Similar examples of agentic claims of non-agency are evident in the defence claims made during parricide trials through appeals to 'battered child syndrome' and PTSD, and in school shooting trials through appeals to psychotic disorders and childhood trauma (see Langman, 2009). Thus, the status of childhood, and its implicit assumptions of non-agency, can be usefully mobilised in cases of children who kill, such that while children who kill question our understandings about the limits of childhood, they never transform them.

Conclusion

While there is much to distinguish prevailing discourses about these three dominant categories of 'children who kill', they also have much in common. All three criminological phenomena emerged during the 1990s and all construct the problem as exclusive to children. Furthermore, they all serve to decontextualise and dehumanise the children of which they speak. The complexity of the children's lives – before, during and after the critical 'incident' that defines them – is lost, and the dichotomous discourses that construct them both as *victims* and as *threats* represent westernised constructions of childhood more generally: at once, they are both innocent and passive, and deviant and duplicitous. The relative rarity of children who kill contributes to their exoticisation, and the academic fetishisation of these three particular criminological phenomena – at the expense of exploring the more mundane and more commonplace contexts in which children kill – exacerbates this. And despite academics' continual calls for the media to avoid focusing only on 'sensational' crimes that fuel moral panics and skew public discourse, we may be guilty of such practices ourselves.

Furthermore, the even greater rarity of female children who kill renders gender invisible from the analysis: 'children' and 'boys' become synonymous, and rather than being foregrounded as a clearly important analytic dimension to all three phenomena, gender remains on the sidelines. Other important contextual dimensions are also lost: in their detailed longitudinal analysis of child-perpetrated homicide, Loeber and Farrington (2011) identified a series of 'risk factors' that differentiated children who kill from other child offenders and child non-offenders. They found that neighbourhood, low socio-economic status, and being born into unemployment were key factors, and were far more predictive of child-perpetrated homicide than any individual factor. Factors that were of no significance were parental factors, peer relationships and psychopathic characteristics. The 'exceptional' status of children who kill and claims of their aberration has the potential to open up space for alternative understandings of childhood to emerge and allow us to challenge the status quo. Unfortunately, current dominant discourses of children who kill merely serve to perpetuate entrenched westernised conceptions of child development.

Final word: Transgressing the final frontier of childhood

This chapter is oriented to the idea of 'the limits of childhood'. Children who kill – in any context – raise uncomfortable questions about the extent to which we can apply a critical framework that celebrates *difference* and questions so-called normative trajectories. In the context of children who kill, we cannot suggest that their 'transgressions' have equal moral weight to some of those other 'transgressions' identified in this collection. However, as this collection has emphasised, children are *not only* their difference, they are so much more than that, and one concern is that, once children transgress the final frontier of childhood and kill another, then that is *all* they are. In some cases, an option is available for such children to find their way 'back' to childhood (whatever that means). In other cases (such as the case of Thompson and Venables), even that option is unavailable.

Notes

1   In initial police reports, 'homicide' refers to the suspected killing of another. In England and Wales, possible offences that might constitute unlawful 'homicide' at the stage of charge, indictment and/or conviction are *murder, manslaughter, infanticide* and *corporate manslaughter*.
2   *Family member* constitutes *parent* in 2.6 per cent of cases, *other relative* in 1.5 per cent of cases, *son/daughter* in 1.3 per cent of cases, *brother/sister* in 0.9 per cent of cases and *step-parent* in 0.4 per cent of cases.
3   Back in 1861, the age of criminal responsibility in England and Wales was seven years, and one example of the way in which the 'limits of childhood' (and thus childhood transgressions) vary across context is found in the varying age of criminal responsibility, both historically and currently around the world, where it varies from 7 years (in North Carolina, US) to 18 years (e.g. in Uruguay, though children younger than 18 who 'offend' can be subject to 'socio-educative measures'). The median age of criminal responsibility around the world is 12 years, which is the minimum age recommended by the Committee on the Rights of the Child (UNCRC, 2007: para. 32).
4   See *When a Child Kills* by Mones (1991) and *Why Kids Kill their Parents* by Heide (1992).
5   For example, see headline: "Son charged with fatally stabbing dad 'definitely pushed' to commit act after years of abuse, neighbour says" (New York Daily News, 20 July 2015).
6   It is this second, rarer form of school shooting that is the subject of the analysis presented here, since this is the form that has attracted most empirical and theoretical attention and is the form that is generally understood to represent the *criminological phenomenon* known as 'school shootings'. However, this is not an unambiguous category: for further discussion of definitional problems, see Harding et al. (2002).
7   School shootings are often constructed as an 'American problem', and there are certainly a number of macro-level factors that make the United States a more likely context (such as gun availability, exposure to 'cultural scripts' that suggest that school shootings provide resolution, and the failure of support systems for young people – see Harding et al., 2002). However, as Böckler et al. (2013) identify, school shootings have taken place around the world in a surprisingly diverse range of countries, including China, Saudi Arabia and Sweden.
8   For example, consider the title of the recent report by Child Soldiers International, *Lost Childhood: Caught in Armed Violence in Jharkhand* (April 2016) which, as Burman (1994) identified over 20 years earlier, represents "an idealised representation of Northern models of childhood, [that] achieves globalized status through its inscription within international development policies and legislation" (Burman, 1994, p. 242).
9   Ishmael Beah was forced to become a child solder at the age of 13 during the Sierra Leone civil war (1991–2002). After three years he was rescued by UNICEF and moved to New York, where he was fostered and eventually graduated with a degree. His highly acclaimed memoir *A Long Way Gone: Memoirs of a Boy Soldier* was published in 2007.

References

Altheide, D. L. (2009). The Columbine shootings and the discourse of fear. *American Behavioral Scientist*, 52 (10), 1354–70.

Amone-P'Olak, K., Jones, P., Meiser-Stedman, R., Abbott, R., Ayella-Ataro, P. S., Amone, J. & Ovuga, E. (2014). War experiences, general functioning and barriers to care among former child soldiers in Northern Uganda: The WAYS study. *Journal of Public Health*, 36(4), 568–576.

Bayer, C. P., Klasen, F. & Adam, H. (2007). Association of trauma and PTSD symptoms with openness to reconciliation and feelings of revenge among former Ugandan and Congolese child soldiers. *Jama*, 298(5), 555–559.

Betancourt, T. S., Newnham, E. A., McBain, R. & Brennan, R. T. (2013). Post-traumatic stress symptoms among former child soldiers in Sierra Leone: Follow-up study. *The British Journal of Psychiatry*, 203(3), 196–202.

Böckler, N., Seeger, T., Sitzer, P. & Heitmeyer, W. (2013). *School Shootings: Conceptual Framework and International Empirical Trends* (pp. 1–24). New York: Springer.

Borum, R., Cornell, D. G., Modzeleski, W. & Jimerson, S. R. (2010). What can be done about school shootings? A review of the evidence. *Educational Researcher*, 39(1), 27–37.

Both, J. & Reis, R. (2014). Unfulfilled promises, unsettled youth: The aftermath of conflict for former child soldiers in Yumbe District, north western Uganda. *Intervention*, 12(3), 344–355.

Boyden, J. (1994). Children's experience of conflict related emergencies: Some implications for relief policy and practice. *Disasters*, 18, 254–267.

Burke, J. (2016). Child soldier to war criminal: The trial of Dominic Ongwen. *The Guardian* (27 March 2016). Available at www.theguardian.com/law/2016/mar/27/dominic-ongwen-war-crimes-trial-former-child-soldier-icc-uganda.

Burman, E. (1994). Innocents abroad: Western fantasies of childhood and the iconography of emergencies. *Disasters*, 18, 238–253.

Burman, E. (1997). Developmental psychology and its discontents. In D. Fox and I. Prilleltensky (Eds.) *Critical Psychology: An Introduction* (pp. 134–149). London: Sage.

Child Soldiers International (2012). *Louder than words: An agenda for action to end state use of child soldiers* [online]. Available at file:///C:/Users/Amanda/Downloads/louderthanwordsseptember20124903558%20(2).pdf (accessed 18 April 2016).

Child Soldiers International (2016). *Who are child soldiers?* [online]. Available at www.childsoldiers.org/about_the_issues.php (Accessed 18 April 2016).

Cohen, S. (2002). *Folk devils and Moral Panics: The Creation of the Mods and Rockers*. (3rd Edition). London: Routledge.

Denov, M. (2012). Child soldiers and iconography: Portrayals and (mis) representations. *Children & Society*, 26(4), 280–292.

Evans, T. M., McGovern-Kondik, M. & Peric, F. (2005). Juvenile parricide: A predictable offense? *Journal of Forensic Psychology Practice*, 5(2), 31–50.

Franklin, B. & Petley, J. (1996). Killing the age of innocence: Newspaper reporting of the death of James Bulger. In J. Pilcher and S. Waag (Eds.) *Thatcher's Children? Politics, Childhood and Society in the 1980s and 1990s* (pp. 134–154.). FalmerPress: London.

Frymer, B. (2009). The media spectacle of Columbine: Alienated youth as an object of fear. *American Behavioral Scientist*, 52(10), 1387–404.

Galatzer-Levy, R. (1993). Adolescent violence and the adolescent self. *Adolescent Psychiatry*, 19, 418–441.

Harding, D. J., Fox, C. & Mehta, J. D. (2002). Studying rare events through qualitative case studies lessons from a study of rampage school shootings. *Sociological Methods & Research*, 31(2), 174–217.

Harlacher, T., Okot, F. X., Obonyo, C. A., Balthazard, M. & Atkinson, R. (2006). *Traditional Ways of Coping in Acholi*. Gulu, Northern Uganda: Caritas.

Hart, J. L. and Helms, J. L. (2003). Factors of parricide: Allowance of the use of battered child syndrome as a defense. *Aggression and Violent Behavior*, 8(6), 671–683.

Hay, C. (1995). Mobilization through interpellation: James Bulger, juvenile crime and the construction of a moral panic. Social & Legal Studies, 4(2), 197–223.

Heide, K. (1992). *Why Kids Kill Parents*. New York: Sage.

Heide, K. M. (2013). Understanding Parricide: When Sons and Daughters Kill Parents. New York: Oxford University Press.

Heitmeyer, W., Böckler, N. & Seeger, T. (2013). Social disintegration, loss of control, and school shootings. In W. Heitmeyer, H. Haupt, A. Kirschner & S. Malthane, *School Shootings* (pp. 27–54). Springer: New York.

Holt, A. (2008). Room for resistance? Parenting orders, disciplinary power and the construction of the 'bad parent' in P. Squires (Ed.), *ASBO Nation: The Criminalisation of Nuisance* (pp. 103–122). Bristol: Policy Press.

Holt, A. (2017). Parricide in England and Wales (1977–2012): An exploration of offenders, victims, incidents and outcomes. *Criminology and Criminal Justice*, doi 1748895816688332.

Holt, A. & Shon, P. C. (2016). Exploring fatal and non-fatal violence against parents: Challenging the orthodoxy of abused adolescent perpetrators. *Journal of Offender Therapy and Comparative Criminology*, doi: : 0306624X16672444.

Jones, J. M. (2013). Parents' school safety fears haven't receded since Newtown, *Gallup* [online], August 29 2013. Available at www.gallup.com/poll/164168/parents-school-safety-fears-haven-receded-newtown.aspx (accessed 29 February 2016).

Keum, J. T. (2000). *Confucianism and Korean Thoughts*. Seoul, Korea: Jimoondang Publishing Company.

Kim, C. S. (2012). *Hyoungbeop Hyoungsahsoseongbeop Jisik Sajeon*. Seoul, Korea: Beopmoon Books.

Kimmel, M. S. & Mahler, M. (2003). Adolescent masculinity, homophobia, and violence: Random school shootings, 1982–2001. *American Behavioral Scientist*, 46(10), 1439–1458.

Langman, P. (2009). Rampage school shooters: A typology. *Aggression and Violent Behavior*, 14(1), 79–86.

Levin, J. and Madfis, E. (2009). Mass murder at school and cumulative Strain: A sequential model. *American Behavioral Scientist*, 52(9), 1227–1245.

Levine, M. (1999). Rethinking bystander nonintervention: Social categorization and the evidence of witnesses at the James Bulger murder trial. *Human Relations*, 52(9), 1133–55.

Loeber, R. and Farrington, D. P. (2011). *Young Homicide Offenders and Victims: Risk Factors, Prediction, and Prevention from Childhood*. New York, NY: Springer.

Madfis, E. (2016). "It's Better to Overreact": School officials' fear and perceived risk of rampage attacks and the criminalization of American public schools. *Critical Criminology*, 24(3), 1–17.

Madfis, E. & Levin, J. (2013). School rampage in international perspective: The salience of cumulative strain theory. In N. Böckler, T. Seeger & W. Heitmeyer (Eds.), *School Shootings: International Research, Case Studies, and Concepts for Prevention* (pp. 79–104). New York: Springer.

Malmquist, C. P. (2010). Adolescent parricide as a clinical and legal problem. *Journal of the American Academy of Psychiatry and the Law Online*, 38(1), 73–79.

McMullen, J., O'Callaghan, P., Shannon, C., Black, A. & Eakin, J. (2013). Group trauma-focused cognitive-behavioural therapy with former child soldiers and other war-affected boys in the DR Congo: A randomised controlled trial. *Journal of Child Psychology and Psychiatry*, 54: 1231–1241.

Modzeleski, W., Feucht, T., Rand, M., Hall, J., Simon, T., & Butler, L., Taylor, A., Hunter, M., Anderson, M., Barrios, L., and Hertz, M. (2008). School-associated student homicides–United States, 1992–2006. Morbidity and Mortality Weekly Report, 57(2), 33–6.

Mones, P. (1991). *When a Child Kills*. New York: Pocket Books.

Morss, J. R. (1996). *Growing Critical: Alternatives to Developmental Psychology*. London: Routledge.

Muncie, J. (1999). Exorcising demons: Media, politics and criminal justice. In. B. Franklin (Ed.), *Social Policy, the Media and Misrepresentation* (pp. 174–190). London: Routledge.

Muschert, G. W. (2007). Research in school shootings. *Sociology Compass*, 1(1), 60–80.

Muschert, G. W., & Ragnedda, M. (2010). Media and violence control: The framing of school shootings. *The control of violence in modern society: Multidisciplinary perspectives, from school shootings to ethnic violence*, 245–61.

New York Daily News (2015). Son charged with fatally stabbing dad 'definitely pushed' to commit act after years of abuse, neighbour says, *New York Daily News* [online]. Available at www.nydailynews.com/new-york/nyc-crime/bklyn-man-stabbed-dad-pushed-years-abuse-article-1.2297021 (accessed 6 April 2016).

Ravenhill, M. (2004). A tear in the fabric: The James Bulger murder and new theatre writing in the nineties. New Theatre Quarterly, 20(4), 305–314.

Rowbotham, J., Stevenson, K. & Pegg, S. (2003). Children of misfortune: The parallels in the cases of child murderers Thompson and Venables, Barratt and Bradley. *Howard Journal of Criminal Justice*, 42(2), 107–22.

Scraton, P. (1997). *'Childhood' in 'Crisis'?* (Ed.). London: Routledge.

Shepler, S. (2005). The rites of the child: Global discourses of youth and reintegrating child soldiers in Sierra Leone. *Journal of Human Rights*, 4(2), 197–211.

Shon, P. C. H. (2009). Sources of conflict between parents and their offspring in nineteenth-century American parricides: An archival exploration. *Journal of forensic psychology practice*, 9(4), 249–79.

Song, S. J. & de Jong, J. (2015). Child soldiers: Children associated with fighting forces. *Child and Adolescent Psychiatric Clinics of North America*, 24(4), 765–775.

Squires, P. (2014). *Gun Crime in Global Contexts*. London: Routledge.

Strong, R. A. (1988). *Parricide: Children who kill their parents*. Master's Thesis. Criminal Justice: California State University.

Summerfield, D. (1999). A critique of seven assumptions behind psychological trauma programmes in war-affected areas. *Social Science & Medicine*, 48(10), 1449–1462.

Turner, J. N. (1994). The James Bulger case: A challenge to juvenile justice theories. *Law Institute Journal: Melbourne, 68(8)*, 734–7.

United Nations Committee on the Rights of the Child (UNCRC) (2007). *Children's Rights in Juvenile Justice*, 44th Session General Comment No. 10. CRC/C/GC/10, United Nations, Geneva.

UNICEF. (2007). *The Paris Principles: Principles and Guidelines on Children Associated with Armed Forces or Armed Groups*. New York, NY: UNICEF.

Vincent, C. and Ball, S. (2007). 'Making up' the middle-class child: Families, activities and class dispositions. *Sociology*, 41(6), 1061–1077.

Vindevogel, S., Wessells, M., De Schryver, M., Broekaert, E. & Derluyn, I. (2012). Informal and formal supports for former child soldiers in Northern Uganda. *The Scientific World Journal*, Article ID 825028.

Vossekuil, B., Fein, R. A., Reddy, M., Borum, R. & Modzeleski, W. (2002). *The final report and findings of the Safe School Initiative: Implications for the prevention of school attacks in the United States*. Washington, DC: U.S. Secret Service and U.S. Department of Education.

Wertham, F. (1937). The catathymic crisis. *Archives of Neurology and Psychiatry*, 37, 974–978.

Wessells, M. G. (2006). *Child Soldiers: From Violence to Protection*. London: Harvard University Press.

Wolff, S., & Smith, R. A. A. M. (2000). Child homicide and the law: Implications of the judgements of the European Court of Human Rights in the case of the children who killed James Bulger. Child Psychology and Psychiatry Review, 5(03), 133–8.

11

CONCLUSION

Theorising transgressive developmental trajectories and understanding children seen as 'different'

Lindsay O'Dell, Charlotte Brownlow and Hanna Bertilsdotter-Rosqvist

In this final chapter we revisit the three interrelated themes that have structured the book to explore how they offer possibilities with which to refine and extend knowledge about non/normative development and 'different' childhoods. Burman (2008b) asks: "How can we move from being subjects of development's collusions to becoming agents of its change?" (p. 230), and calls for new ways of viewing development that cease to perpetuate 'deviations' from the norm as pathological, but rather challenge hegemonic cultural norms. Through the book, authors have discussed ways of showing (and imagining) how development can be done and experienced differently, producing different kinds of possible child subjects. In the discussion below we consider possibilities of understanding, theorising and researching development differently.

Themes of 'deconstructing developmental tasks', the 'location of development' and the 'limits of childhood'

This collection has been structured around three core themes that speak to critiques (both within and outside) of developmental psychology. It is clear that the themes are interrelated and that the topics covered by individual chapters move across themes. The chapters bring together a number of issues that are relevant to understanding and developing theory about non-normative or different childhoods. In the first theme, *deconstructing 'developmental tasks'*, the authors explored the ways in which normative development is concerned with the successful mastery of (appropriate, normative) skills and abilities. The specific tasks discussed were the assumed need to develop appropriate (but not excessive) engagement with hobbies and interests; the need to develop a gendered identity (rather than a fluid gendered identity or a non-binary identification) and the development of (assumed to be) appropriate styles of friendship and ways of being social.

The second theme focused on *locating development* and explored how development takes place in particular geopolitical and classed spaces and within particular understandings of gender, ethnicity and other intersections of social identity. The chapters discussed geographical location as it intersects with understandings of nation, childhood and gender for child migrants in a host country; gender and role models within families and other care settings; the location of the child as a vulnerable subject; and development as located within particular understandings of mothers' work, food and social class.

The third theme of this collection explored *the limits of childhood* and the ways in which children who are seen to stand outside the category of 'child' are represented and understood. The two examples offered in the book were child workers and children who have committed murder. In both chapters the construction of a child was seen in relation to the duties of adults to provide for and protect children and to ensure that they develop appropriately.

Contributors to the book have explored a number of ways through which 'normality' and hence difference is brought into being. The first is through technologies to measure development and normative functioning. These include Ryder and Brownlow's discussion (in Chapter 2) of using the Diagnostic and Statistical Manual (DSM) to understand and make sense of children's hobbies and interests as either normative or in need of control and correction. Psy disciplinary knowledge more generally is brought into play in understanding the lives of many children, for example, in Robb et al.'s discussion (in Chapter 6) of the assumed need for male role models for boys. Johnson's chapter discusses the ways in which 'gender' as a binary category is brought into being through psy disciplinary knowledge of gender development. Other technologies are also invoked to measure development in particular ways and are used to hold parents (particularly mothers) to account if their child is not developing 'appropriately'. For example, Woolhouse (in Chapter 5) discusses the use of body mass index (BMI) as a technology to measure children's weight as a way to frame and problematise working class women's food practices.

It is evident from contributing chapters, and from our previous work (O'Dell & Brownlow, 2015) and that of others (for example, Goodley et al, 2016; Walkderine, 1993), that developmental discourse has constructed a notion of a 'normal' child against which particular children are measured against and seen to be different. This is addressed by Ryder and Brownlow in Chapter 2, where they discussed how mothers compare their child (all of whom had a diagnostic label of autism) to an idealised 'normal' child in order to understand and locate their child's hobbies and interests as either acceptable or in need of modification. Ideas about normative childhoods are also played out in the media, as shown, for example, by Bertilsdotter-Rosqvist and Brownlow in Chapter 4 who discussed how girls' magazines serve as a site of management and articulation of normative friendship and sociality for girls.

Comparisons of 'different' childhoods with assumed normative activities and tasks of childhood position children who transgress these as either culpable or as in need of protection. For example, in Chapter 9, O'Dell et al. discussed how the dominant construction of childhood as a time for play and school position child workers as unable to be 'real' children. Intervention is thus required to enable child workers to 'have a childhood' (i.e. to attend school) and participate in work but only if it fits with engagement under the direction and protection of adults.

Commentators such as Mayall (2012) have noted that International Non-Governmental Organisations (INGOs) that have traditionally aimed campaigning at a model of childhood as one in need of protection have moved to a focus on children's rights. This is evident most clearly in the human rights perspective on childhood articulated in the United Nations Convention on the Rights of the Child, (UNCRC, 1989). However, universal ideas about childhood as a time for play and school continue to dominate, with the assumption that development is unquestionably good (Burman, 2008b).

Although INGOs may have shifted to an understanding of children's rights rather than a focus on protection, dominant understandings of childhood still draw on a view of children as in need of protection, adult supervision and dependency. Contributors to the book have critiqued the dominant discourse of childhood being inherently in need of protection. For example, in Chapter 7, Callaghan, Alexander and Fellin detail ways in which children who live with domestic violence utilise creative strategies for keeping themselves and their siblings safe and to find spaces of safety and comfort. Discussions on unaccompanied child migrants and child workers also point to the complex interplay in seeking to protect (particular kinds of) children and the conditions in which children live. The authors argue for children to be seen as active agents in their development, but note that they are often operating within systems and institutions that, in acting on their behalf, often constrain and limit, or fail to see their resilience or agency.

The construction of the child as in need of protection positions children, who for many reasons act independently of adult supervision, as culpable. For example, Mahati and Palmary (in Chapter 8) discuss how the role of aid workers to protect independent child migrants is conflicted with judgements about the children and whether they 'deserve' help. Transgressions, particularly for girls working outside the camp to earn money, move them from the category of child and thus position them as undeserving, contributing to the high level of incidents of sexual assault/rape for these girls.

Authors in the book have powerfully demonstrated the dangers of 'difference' for children, adults and cultures/nations. Callaghan, Alexander and Fellin (in Chapter 7) discussed how mothers who have been subjected to domestic abuse are blamed (or at the least held accountable) for the well-being and potential harm arising from their children witnessing violence in the home. Blame and accountability is a common thread throughout the book. For example, working class mothers are held accountable for the health of their families (as discussed by Woolhouse in Chapter 5), whereas in discussions, particularly within the media but also enacted in policy, the need for boys to have male role models renders invisible the role (and contribution) of women present in the lives of children and normalises the absence of fathers (see Phoenix, 2009).

Accountability and moral judgements are starkly in evidence in Holt's discussion in Chapter 10 about children who kill. Holt discusses ways in which previous experiences of abuse or 'damage' in childhood can shift blame to construct children who have killed others as concurrently a victim as well as an aggressor. Holt is careful to argue that not all difference is of equal moral weight and that children who kill may be thought of as at 'the final frontier' of childhood. She argues that it is important to view children as "not only their difference", rather that children move in and out of normativity and difference.

Possibilities for understanding and theorising normality and difference

The idea that children's development is not universal, but rather contextual and socially/historically constructed, has been advocated by both those within and outside of developmental psychology as a discipline (for example, Burman, 2008a, b; 2015; James & Prout, 2015; Morss, 1996; Walkderine, 1993). In the following section, we discuss how the collection of chapters as a whole can inform critique and theory about development and the move through time. The discussion moves between and through developmental psychology as a discipline, reflecting our alliances and affiliations as a set of authors and reflects a broader tension in considering how to theorise the move through time and ideas about deconstructing development. Morss (1996) argued that "Human development is too important to be left to psychology". Responses have variously been described as 'deconstruction', 'anti-development', 'post-development' and 'non-development' (see Burman, 2008b; Morss, 1996). Burman's work illustrates, particularly through her two 'sister' books *Deconstructing Developmental Psychology* and *Developments: Child, Image, Nation*, the need to be both within and outwith the discipline to critique the notion of development and knowledge about different childhoods. As Callaghan et al. (2015, p. 256) suggest:

> Burman encourages us to see our scholarly activities as always contextual, as produced within and for specific contexts and moments, and as fulfilling particular purposes.

Our aim is to open up spaces for discussion rather than close down or fracture debate into disciplinary boundaries. In this respect our endeavour is similar to Burman's and is also informed by the approach taken by Goodley et al. (2016) in their theorisation of being human. Goodley et al. argue, in their discussions about disability and being human (which at times is difficult for disabled people to claim or be accorded by others), that they want to "remain *critical* of the category of the human, at the same time as we *claim* the human" (p.772, italics in original). Similarly, we want to remain *critical* of the notion of development (as a progressive unitary cumulative acquisition of skills through time) but at the same time *claim* development (in its diverse forms) as a powerful discourse for articulating children's move through time in ways that are strategic, political and provisional. Further, Goodley et al. argue that "We find ourselves disavowing the human (we desire it but also resist its narrow confines) whilst re-centering disability as the space through which to rethink what it means to be human" (p. 772). Similarly, we find ourselves wanting to recognise development (but also resist its narrow confines) to use developmental claims where required, and also acknowledge that the need to be legitimated and seen as 'normal' is powerful for many who struggle with difference.

In the following section, we sketch out issues that we view as tasks for engaging in thinking differently about development. The themes we have identified as useful in this endeavour (and discussed hereafter) are: the need for technologies of measuring development; rethinking the move through time; challenging representations of different and normative childhoods and prioritising a relational focus.

Developmental psychology and technologies of measuring development

Considering developmental psychology as a discipline, Burman (2015, p. 412) noted that "We are far from knowing or being able to deliver on models, theories, and practices concerning what developmental psychology could be." If we view developmental psychology as a discipline producing knowledge and technologies with which to measure normative development, one task would be to think critically and creatively to produce different technologies with which to understand and document development in its diverse forms. For example, in considering friendship (a core topic in developmental psychology curricula, texts and research), developmental psychologists have traditionally focused on particular tasks, such as reciprocity and sociality. Traditional developmental research operationalises ideas about being social, making friends and playing in particular ways (Brownlow et al., 2015). As an illustration, parallel play is where children engage in activity by themselves but in proximity to or 'parallel' with another child. It is assumed to be common in young children but gives way to more social forms of play involving others as the child grows older. Children (and adults) with autism who do not progress from parallel to social play are seen to be developing inappropriately (Brownlow et al., 2015). Failure to play 'properly', in this instance engaging in social kinds of play, pushes the child into a category of not developing appropriately (Goodley & Runswick-Cole, 2010).

In the example of children with autism, mainstream understandings of the development of sociality and friendship construct the normal child against which autistic development is seen as in need of concern and correction. Work is required to broaden, enrich and extend ideas about what it means to be social, including the need to recognise diversity, enable autistic socialising and recognise alternative ways of being social. Developmental descriptions need to take account of the diversity of children's experiences, capabilities and capacities. Continuing with this example, the task is then to produce technologies, measures and ways of viewing friendship that attend to the abilities and location of the child rather than an assumed universal norm.

Rethinking the move through time

The assumption of a universal developmental trajectory brings into being particular kinds of children, developmental activities and normative development. Within this assumption there are two interrelated issues in need of critique. The first is the proposition of a developmental trajectory, that is, the assumed link between past, present and future, and the second is the need to question the assumed inevitability and naturalness of particular outcomes of development.

Viewing development as an uncomplicated link between past, present and future is unhelpful to many. There is a body of literature that has critiqued the notion of inevitable harm arising from childhood trauma (including Callaghan & Fellin's chapter in this volume; O'Dell, 1997, Warner, 2008). It is clear that the rehabilitated subject is constructed in normative ways; particular kinds of long-term outcomes are seen as demonstrating 'recovery' from abusive experiences (such as being sexually active within largely heteronormative, monogamous limits) whereas other kinds of outcomes are seen as directly linked to past trauma (such as being celibate or choosing not to become a parent) (O'Dell, 1997, 2015). Linked to the themes in this book, we argue that there is a need to trouble the assumed outcomes of development and to query the notion of successful transitions into adulthood, where success is narrowly measured in terms of independent living, a regular paid job at the regular labour market and forming a long-lasting partnership and family in a social and chronologically age-appropriate time.

The construction of development as progression is naturalised in everyday practice and discourse. For example, in the introductory chapter to this book we discussed the 'red book' (Personal Child Health Record, Royal College of Paediatricians, 2009, cited in Goodley et al., 2016), a small book with a red cover given to all parents/carers of newborn children in England. The book is a way for practitioners and parents/carers to record measurements of a child's health and development from birth until they are at least school age. Goodley et al. (2016) argued that mechanisms such as the 'red book' structure ideas about normative development within normative trajectories. They give the example of children with Down's Syndrome whose parents/carers are given a special insert for their red book which charts the development of a typically developing Down's child, although Goodley et al. note that development is conceptualised in this insert as very similar to 'normative' development, just at a slower pace. Goodley et al. highlighted the experiences of parents whose child had Down's Syndrome and how their child's development does not accord with the trajectory outlined in the special insert. Children with Down's Syndrome are constructed concurrently as needing to follow a similar developmental path to 'normal' children but at the same time as deficient and different to them. The opportunity to articulate the development of disabled children in a different way is lost within attempts to maintain development as a singular, progressive and cumulative move through time (Goodley et al., 2016).

There is an established body of work (within and outside of developmental psychology as a discipline) that has sought to deconstruct developmental psychology and offer an alternative approach to understanding the move through time that is not conceptualised as a coherent, cumulative process. Theorists, particularly those informed by critical disability, queer and crip approaches, have interrogated assumptions of development and ability in imagining the future (Slater, 2015). In the book *Growing 'Sideways'*, Bond Stockton (2009) discusses the notion of 'sideways growth' to interrogate the assumptions of a normative trajectory through time. Stockton talks about ways of growing that sidestep normative expectations of development as a progressive move through time, suggesting that, "One could explore the elegant, unruly contours of growing that doesn't bespeak continuance" (Bond Stockton, 2009, p. 13).

Similarly, a queer theoretical perspective of normative development and time, or what Halberstam (2005) refers to as 'queer temporality', enables an alternative to heteronormative time (in which time and developmental trajectories are not based on the generation of families, with development and life course revolving around heterosexual reproduction) and resists definitions of non-normativity (such as voluntary childlessness) as an expression of immaturity or a lack of development (see also Hemmings, 2002, among others' critiques of a linear model of sexual development from the perspective of bisexuality).

If the move through time is conceptualised as "elegant and unruly" (as suggested by Bond Stockton, 2009) rather than progressive and cumulative, theorising development takes on a different focus. The move through time may be best understood as a process of flux and fluidity, in which links between past, present and future are partial and subject to renegotiation rather than being pre-determined.

Challenging representations of different/normative childhoods

Through this collection, the authors have discussed ways in which the image of a normative child is invoked to exemplify particular concerns, such as symbols of a nation (Mahati & Palmery, Chapter 8), as well as an overarching concern about the state of childhood. Earlier in this chapter, we discussed how representations of childhood are drawn on in campaigns by INGOs, which have largely shifted from a focus on protection to that of child rights, whilst retaining a normative construction of childhood and assumptions about appropriate tasks and activities for children. However, the appeal to protect (particular kinds of) children is still powerfully felt and represented in media images of children.

Where children transgress assumptions about normative childhood, they are generally positioned as having lost out on childhood, or seen as outside of the realm of being a child. This is particularly evident in Holt's chapter (Chapter 10) in this volume. The discourse of loss of childhood is strongly articulated in public discourse, policy and media; the need to protect (particular kinds of) children and permit them to 'be children' is strongly articulated, however, other kinds of children (such as unaccompanied child migrants) demonstrate the limits of adult concern and the intersection of protection with constructions of childhood innocence.

Knowledge about the developing child and processes of development is picked up in particular ways within public discussion and the representation of normative/different childhoods. Developmental psychology and ideas about children's development are invoked and used in uncomfortable and unhelpful ways in policy and practice concerning children and families, for example, the use of developmental knowledge in parenting programmes, which "entrench normative assumptions about childhood in the production of 'good outcomes' for children" (Callaghan et al., 2015, p. 263; see also Holt, 2010). Critical work is necessary to highlight the ways in which knowledge about children's development is being selectively (and politically) drawn on to inform policy and intervention.

Burman (2015, p. 413) notes the "disjuncture between the imagined child and the everyday lives of children". Work is required to broaden, enrich and extend the scope of investigation into the everyday lives of children, and to see them in a unidimensional way – as the young carer, the child with autism, and so on, but also as inhabiting a number of positions and identities, at times normative and at others non-normative or transgressive. We are not arguing that all difference is good, there are examples provided in this volume where difference is contested, uncomfortable and problematic. However, in discussing children who kill, Holt (this volume) argues that 'children are not only their difference'. It is evident that children move in and out of difference and normativity as "commonality and diversity are, simultaneously, at work in all children's everyday experiences of childhood" (James, A. & James, A. L., 2001, p. 30).

A relational focus

Throughout the book, the authors have discussed examples of childhoods and families that transgress normative assumptions of care as provided by adults and given to children. Rather than simplifying care as unidirectional, a more helpful frame is to view childhood as a time in which responsibility and the ability to care for others is not dependent on categorisations such as age, but rather on participation in society, community and family. A critically informed relational focus is required to examine the many forms of family structure and children's varied roles within them with a focus on interdependencies rather than the assumed dependency of a child on adults (Riggs & Peel, 2016; Mayall, 2012).

The construction of children and childhood as different to adults and adulthood is both self-evidently 'real' (age definitions permeate legislation and conventional understandings of, for example, being a citizen with the right to remain in host countries; Bhabha, 2003) and also illusory (the move between childhood and adulthood is self-evidently blurred and fluid). Holding 'childhood' and 'adulthood' as binary concepts simplifies experiences and creates the conditions for some forms of non-normativity. Drawing on the educational theorist Dewey who was writing at the beginning of the twentieth century, Quennerstedt, A. and Quennerstedt,

M. (2014, p. 125) suggest that "Neither adulthood or childhood is to be regarded as a finished 'product' – rather, *change* is the constant". Hence, work both within and outwith developmental psychology is needed to broaden, enrich and extend knowledge about childhood in diverse family structures, including other institutions/spaces that children are located within, rather than the traditional focus on school and home (Mayall, 2012).

Different childhoods, transgressive trajectories: Considering childhood differently

We have used the notion of transgression as an analytical tool to destabilise the assumption of a normative trajectory, to explore how 'deviations' from assumed normative development need not be considered as pathological or in need of correction, but as locations/sites of renegotiation, transforming how we understand children's spaces, tasks and abilities. We have argued that work within and outside of developmental psychology as a discipline is needed.

Lee and Motzkau (2011) argue for childhood to be understood as multiplicities, with the generation of what they call 'navigational aids' rather than grand theory. Such navigational aids can come from many sources: critical kinship studies (Riggs & Peel, 2016) to locate children in diverse families; postcolonial theory (Balagopalan, 2014) and cultural psychology (Crafter, 2015) to locate children in cultural contexts; critical developmental feminist work (Burman, 2008b, 2016) to locate children's development in an intersectional analyses of gender, class and ethnicity; and queer, crip and critical disability theories to deconstruct notions of time, ability and normativity (Slater, 2015).

Callaghan et al. (2015) point to the tension of challenging and dismantling developmental psychology while also using it as a platform to speak and to practice. Whilst recognising the tension, we argue that moving between and within developmental psychology as a discipline offers an effective critique for the use of developmental research/knowledge to naturalise normativity in interventions and policies for/about children, as well as tools to deconstruct development as a singular, cumulative progression through time.

References

Balagopalan, S. (2014). *Inhabiting 'Childhood': Children, Labour and Schooling in Postcolonial India*. London: Palgrave Macmillan.

Bhabha, J. (2003). The Citizenship Deficit: On being a citizen child. *Society for International Development*, 46(3), 53–59.

Bond Stockton, K. (2009). *The Queer Child or Growing Sideways in the Twentieth Century*. Durham: Duke University Press.

Brownlow, C., Bertilsdotter-Rosqvist, H. & O'Dell, L. (2015). Exploring the potential for social networking among people with autism: Challenging dominant ideas of 'friendship'. *Scandinavian Journal of Disability Research*, 17(2), 188–193.

Burman, E. (2008a). *Developments: Child, Image, Nation*. London, New York: Routledge.

Burman, E. (2008b). *Deconstructing Developmental Psychology* (2nd Edition). London: Routledge.

Burman, E. (2015). Limits of deconstruction, deconstructing limits. *Feminism & Psychology*, 25(3), 408–422.

Burman, E. (2016). *Deconstructing Developmental Psychology* (3rd Edition). London: Routledge.

Callaghan, J., Andenaes, A. & Macleod, C. (2015). Deconstructing Developmental Psychology 20 years on: Reflections, implications and empirical work. *Feminism & Psychology*, 25(3), 255–265.

Crafter, S. (2015). Cultural psychology and Deconstructing Developmental Psychology. *Feminism & Psychology*, 25(3), 388–401.

Goodley, D., Runswick-Cole, K. and Liddiard, K. (2016). The DisHuman child. *Discourse: Studies in the Cultural Politics of Education*, 37(5), 770–784.

Goodley, D. & Runswick-Cole, K. (2010). Emancipatory play: Dis/abled children, development and deconstruction. *Disability & Society*, 25(4), 499–512.

Halberstam, J. (2005). In a Queer Time and Place: Transgender Bodies, Subcultural Lives. New York: New York University Press.

Hemmings, C. (2002). Bisexual Spaces: A Geography of Sexuality and Gender. New York: Routledge.

Holt, A. (2010). Managing 'spoiled identities': Parents' experiences of compulsory parenting support programmes. *Children & Society*, 24(5), 413–423.

James, A. & James, A. L. (2001). Childhood: Toward a theory of continuity and change. *Annals of American Academy of Political and Social Science*, 575(1), 25-37.

James, A. & Prout, A. (Eds.) (2015). *Constructing and Reconstructing Childhood: Contemporary Issues in the Sociological Study of Childhood*. London: RoutledgeFalmer.

Lee, N. & Motzkau, J. (2011). Navigating the bio-politics of childhood. *Childhood: An International Journal for Childhood Studies*, 18(1), 7–19.

Mayall, B. (2012). An afterword: Some reflections on a seminar series. *Children's Geographies*, 10(3), 47–355.

Morss, J. R. (1996). *Growing Critical: Alternatives to Developmental Psychology*. London: Taylor & Francis.

O'Dell, L. (1997). Child sexual abuse and the construction of academic symptomologies. *Feminism & Psychology*, 7(3), 334–339.

O'Dell, L. (2015). Observation and commentary: Whose development are we talking about? *Feminism & Psychology*, 25(3), 402–407.

O'Dell, L. and Brownlow, C. (2015). Normative development and the autistic child. In M. O'Reilly & J. Lester (Eds.) *The Palgrave Handbook of Child Mental Health* (pp. 296–309). Hampshire, UK: Palgrave Macmillan.

Personal Child Health Record, Royal College of Paediatricians, 2009, cited in Goodley, D., Runswick-Cole, K. and Liddiard, K. (2016). The DisHuman child. *Discourse: Studies in the Cultural Politics of Education*, 37(5), 770–784. http://www.rcpch.ac.uk/PCHR (accessed April 2017).

Phoenix, A. (2009). De-colonising practices: Negotiating narratives from racialized and gendered experiences of education. *Race, Ethnicity and Education*, 12(1), 101–114.

Quennerstedt, A. & Quennerstedt, M. (2014). Researching rights in education: Sociology of childhood encountering educational theory. *British Journal of Education*, 35(1), 115–132.

Riggs, D. & Peel, E. (2016). *Critical Kinship Studies: An Introduction to the Field*. London: Palgrave Macmillan.

Slater, J. (2015). Youth and Disability: A Challenge to Mr Reasonable. London: Routledge.

Robb, M., Featherstone, B., Ruxton, S., & Ward, M. (2015). Beyond male role models: Gender identities and work with young men. An Open University Research Project Working with Action for Children. Walton, UK.

United Nations Convention on the Rights of the Child (UNHRC) (1989). https://www.unicef.org.uk/what-we-do/un-convention-child-rights/ (accessed April 2017).

Walkerdine, V. (1993). Beyond developmentalism? *Theory & Psychology*, 3(4), 451–469.

Warner, S. (2008). *Understanding the Effects of Child Sexual Abuse: Feminist Revolutions in Theory, Research and Practice*. Routledge: East Sussex, UK.

INDEX